I0795019

IMAGES
of America

GARDINER AND LAKE MINNEWASKA

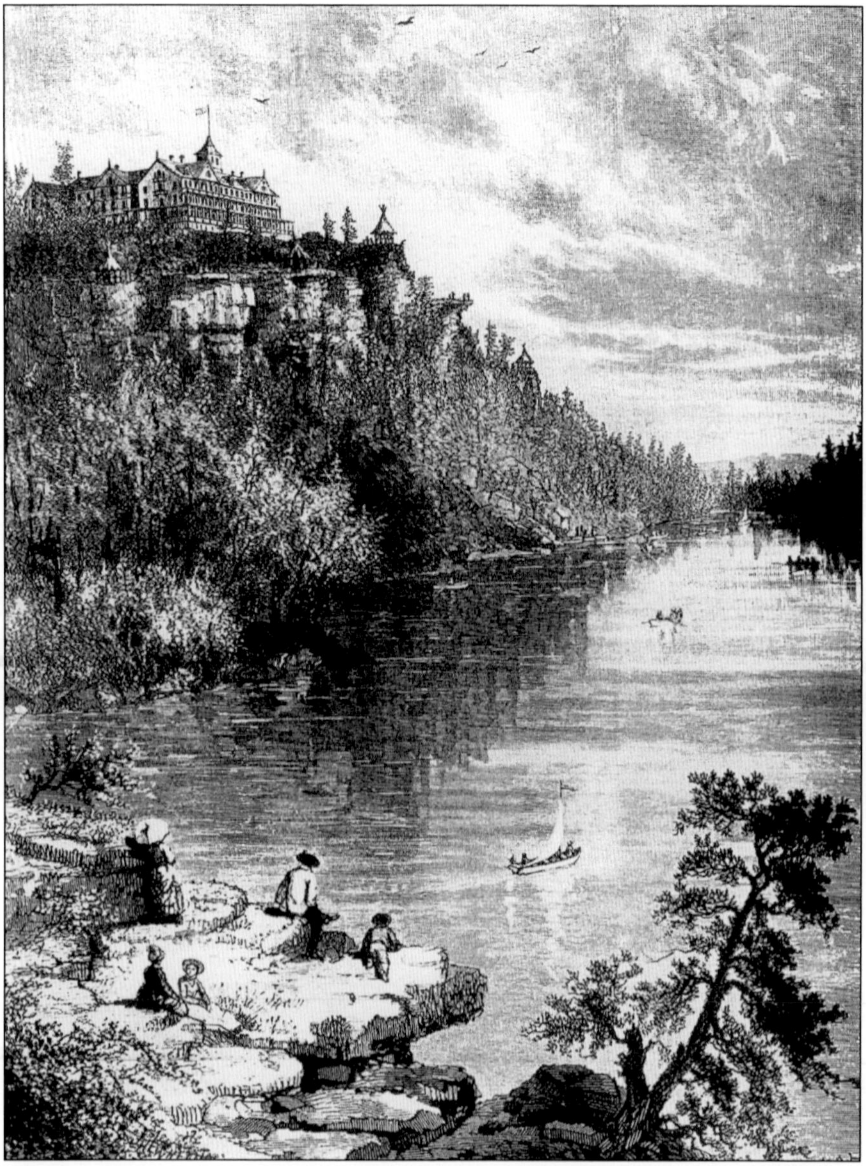

Cliff House was built by the Smiley family on the east side of Lake Minnewaska, on cliffs overlooking the lake. The first hotel on this mountain lake, it accommodated more than 200 guests. It offered swimming and boating on the lake below. It also offered rugged cliffs to scramble on, as well as awesome views of the Catskill Mountains and Gardiner's valleys. (Engraving by E.J. Whitney, 1887 Minnewaska brochure, courtesy of Mohonk Archives.)

On the cover: To grind grain in his Tuthilltown Mill, George Smith used millstones, as those who worked the mill long had before him, sometimes using millstones cut in the mountains near Minnewaska. Smith cleaned his millstones by hand, scraping grain out of each groove with a wire pick, as shown here *c.* 1950. The cleaning had to be done thoroughly when the stones ground kosher grain. It was especially the production of kosher flour that enabled the Smiths over two generations to continue to operate their mill. (Courtesy of Dan Smith.)

IMAGES
of America

GARDINER AND LAKE MINNEWASKA

Carleton Mabee

ARCADIA
PUBLISHING

ISBN 978-0-7385-1185-6

Published by Arcadia Publishing
Charleston, South Carolina

Printed in the United States of America

Library of Congress Catalog Card Number: 2003101270

For all general information, contact Arcadia Publishing:
Telephone 843-853-2070
Fax 843-853-0044
E-mail sales@arcadiapublishing.com
For customer service and orders:
Toll-free 1-888-313-2665

Visit us on the Internet at www.arcadiapublishing.com.

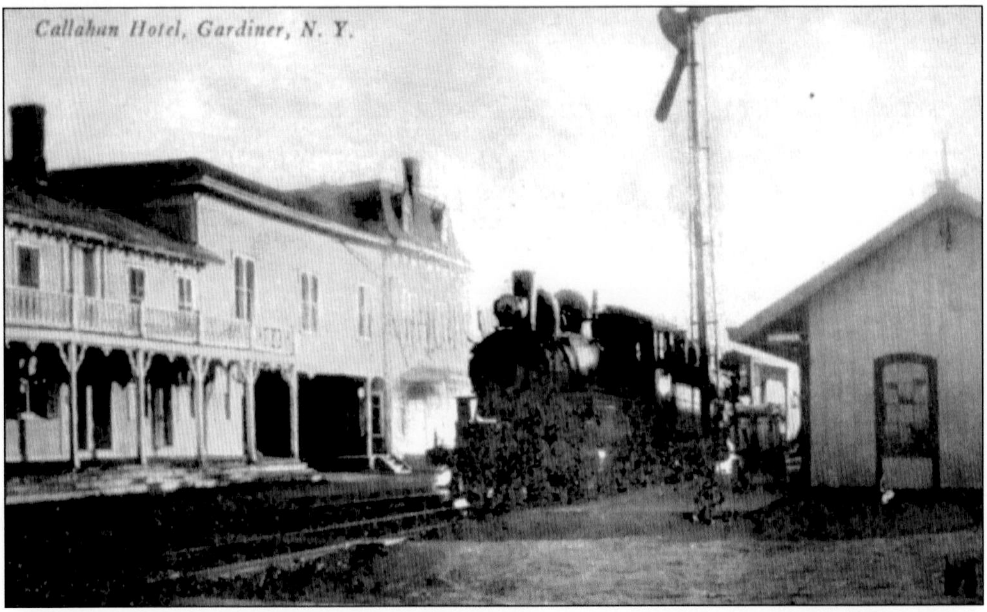

A Wallkill Valley Railroad train stops at the Gardiner station (right), opposite Callahan Hotel. This station, shown *c.* 1900, was built in 1869 when the rail line first reached Gardiner. Built on what had been open farm land, the station created the hamlet of Gardiner. Because train service was available, the hamlet grew, making it instead of Tuthilltown the commercial center of the town of Gardiner. (Courtesy of William and Carol Majestic Lohrman.)

Contents

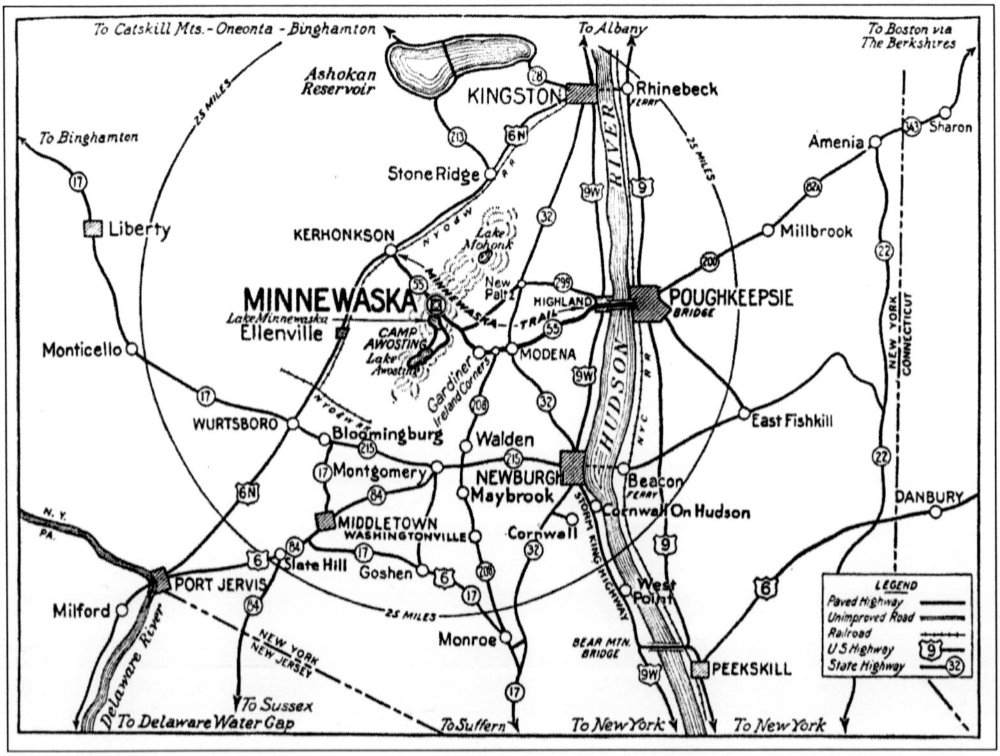

This 1932 map of Minnewaska and vicinity, published in a Minnewaska Mountain Houses brochure, shows Minnewaska Trail (also marked Route 55 on the map) as beginning at the Mid-Hudson Bridge, which crossed the Hudson River at Poughkeepsie. Both the bridge and Minnewaska Trail had just opened in 1930. At the time, the new bridge was the only highway bridge over the Hudson in the mid-Hudson region. The highway bridge at Kingston was not built until 1957, and the one at Newburgh was not built until 1963. From the new bridge, the new Minnewaska Trail, a macadam-paved road, extended westward through Modena, Ireland Corners, and the Gardiner hamlet on to the Minnewaska resort and Kerhonkson. (Courtesy of Dan Smith.)

INTRODUCTION

Europeans may first have visited what is now Gardiner in 1663, when the Hudson Valley was under Dutch rule. At that time Dutch soldiers from Wiltwyck (Kingston) were engaged in chasing Native Americans who had kidnapped a group of European women and children. The soldiers did so by following Native American paths along Gardiner's future rivers. By 1687, after the English had replaced the Dutch as rulers of the region, a European had settled in what is now Gardiner, apparently becoming its first documented settler. She was the widow Gertrude Bruyn and came from a Norwegian family. She settled near where the Klyne Kill flows into the Shawangunk Kill, on the edge of what came to be called Bruynswick, after her family name.

By the 1700s and early 1800s, settlers in considerable numbers had arrived in the Gardiner region, especially the Dutch, French Huguenot, and English, assisted by a few African slaves. They developed the region's lowlands into a predominantly farming community. They grew diversified crops for self-support and also produced grain to ship out by the Hudson River. Somewhat later, a few settlers developed the nearby Shawangunk Mountain region into small farms, supplemented by the production of lumber, barrel hoops, and millstones. In the 1800s, most of the nation's millstones were said to have come from the Shawangunk Mountains. The town of Gardiner, founded on April 2, 1853, was predominantly a lowlands farming community, with a small mountain community attached. It was carved largely out of the towns of New Paltz and Shawangunk and slightly out of the town of Rochester. Its original population was about 1,900, similar to that of neighboring towns.

About the time when the town of Gardiner was created, farming in the region began a long decline. Not having significant manufacturing, when Gardiner's farming declined, its population also declined. It declined from 1,923 in 1855 to 1,289 in 1950. Only recently, as the town has became more suburban, has its population begun to grow rapidly. Still, although Gardiner's acreage is similar to that of the towns around it, the town's population in 2000 was only 5,238, lower than any of the adjoining towns.

Gardiner's population, mixed from the beginning, received additional waves of immigrants, such as Irish in the mid-1800s and Italians by the late 1800s. In the 1900s, many escapees arrived from the New York metropolis looking for space, rural charm, and unspoiled mountains. The population became mixed in ethnicity, race, religion, style, education, and economic status—each family learning to live with more or less tolerance for others.

In the 1860s, Gardiner led the way in building the Wallkill Valley Railroad, Ulster County's first railroad. The railroad opened the region to summer visitors. It enabled farmers to ship their produce to market quickly while it was still fresh, encouraging them to specialize more in producing fruit and milk. Although the railroad ceased running in 1977, its memory is preserved by its rail line having been transformed in a rail trail open for walking and bicycling. Other historic landmarks in Gardiner or along its borders include the old school building, which is preserved as the Gardiner Town Hall; the Tuthilltown Grist Mill, which has been used continuously for more than 200 years; churches such as those in Bruynswick and New Hurley; farmhouses, some built of stone; New York City's Catskill Aqueduct line, visible at many points and still in use; and the remains of the great mountain hotels at Lake Minnewaska.

From the 1870s, much of the Shawangunk Mountains region near Gardiner was bought up by the Smileys, a Quaker family, who built hotels at Lake Minnewaska and Lake Mohonk. For a century Gardiner was a major entry point into the Minnewaska mountain resort area, and from the 1970s on, as the resort was gradually transformed into a state park, Gardiner has been a major entry point into the park. Today, Gardiner is blessed to have along its western edge, in a stretch of the Shawangunk Mountains reaching 20 miles from Rosendale on the north to Cragsmoor on the southwest, more than 23,000 acres of magnificent protected land, the largest portion of it being Minnewaska State Park and the second largest portion being Mohonk Preserve, both partly in Gardiner.

In recent years the Gardiner region has become increasingly concerned over its rapid growth. This concern is focused on such issues as preserving the region's remaining farms and preserving the nearby mountains unspoiled. Whether this concern has become strong enough to guide the region's growth remains a question. In the meantime Gardiner has become a mecca for daring adventurers: for sky divers dropping out of the sky and for rock climbers dangling from the awesome Shawangunk cliffs.

In 2003, the town of Gardiner is celebrating the 150th anniversary of its founding, and this book is part of that celebration. It is being published for the benefit of the Gardiner Library. It has been put together in large part as a community enterprise. Its images and background information have been acquired with generous help from individuals, families, Minnewaska State Park, Mohonk Preserve, town officials, historical societies, and libraries. While it is impossible to specify all of this help, some of it is mentioned in the image captions and on the Acknowledgments pages.

Special thanks go to my parents for tying me to Minnewaska forever by honeymooning there; Marion Ryan, Carol Johnson, and Laura Walls for encouraging me to undertake this book when I considered it impossible; Marybeth Majestic, the Gardiner Historical Society, the Gardiner Library, and the Gardiner Town Hall for opening a flow of pictures and recollections; Hatti Langsford, Bob Larsen, and Joan Lachance for access to their archives and their wisdom; Kenneth Hasbrouck for his indispensable early historical work; John Jamiolkowski for technological interpretation; Karen Vassell for computer crisis management; and veteran hiker Bob Fisher for persistent, informed support.

One

FARMING AND LANDSCAPE

The town of Gardiner drains primarily into the Wallkill River. The Minnewaska mountain region, which is only partially located in the town of Gardiner, mostly within the town of Rochester, drains into Rondout Creek. Eventually, the Wallkill and the Rondout flow into each other and on into the Hudson River.

Into the early 1800s, what is now the Gardiner region was gradually cleared for farming—farming that was somewhat self-sufficient and considerably diversified. When the town of Gardiner was formed in 1853, it was primarily a farming community. Since then, farming in the region has declined. It also has become increasingly specialized. This has improved efficiency but also increased the use of chemical fertilizers and insecticides, threatening air and water quality.

An early form of specialized farming, dairying, once flourished in Gardiner, supplying local creameries, a condensery in Wallkill, the Minnewaska resort hotels, and the New York metropolis. Dairying contributed much to the charm of the landscape, but it has died out. Another early form of specialization, fruit farming, has outlived dairying, but competing as it now must with imports from the West Coast and abroad, it is under siege, alarming those who value open farmland. More recent forms of farm specialization in Gardiner include wineries, horse farms, beef farms, and tree nurseries. A new kind of farm arrived in Gardiner in the 1990s, the Community Supported Agricultural (CSA) farm, which is in part a throwback to earlier, more diversified farming. CSA farmers argue that diversification is environmentally healthier than specialization.

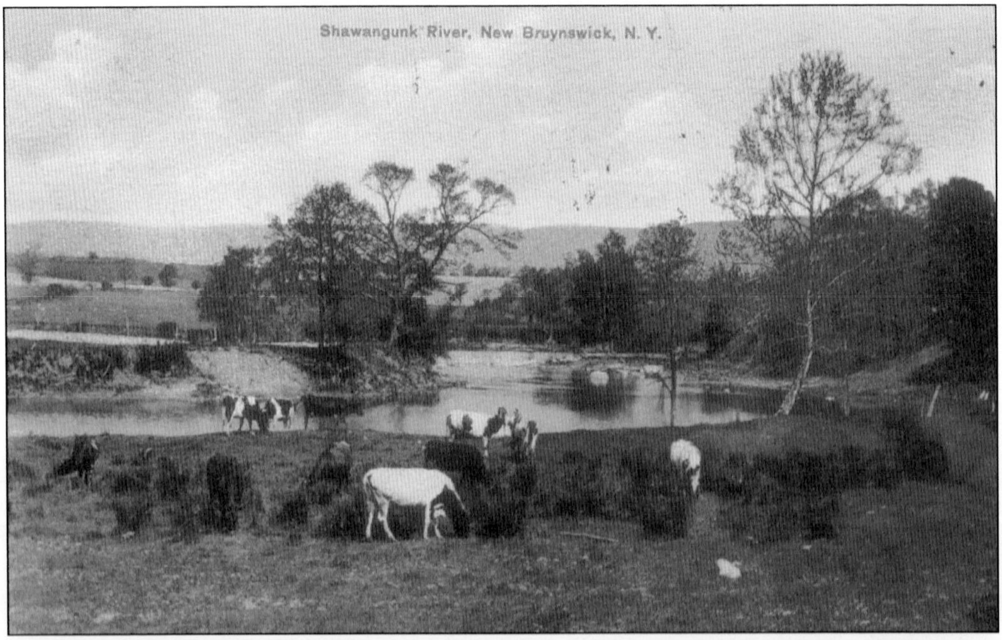

Cows graze along the Shawangunk River in the Bruynswick neighborhood on the southwestern boundary of Gardiner. At the time portrayed in this view postmarked 1911, dairying was common in the region, contributing to a gentle, peaceful landscape. The ridge of the Shawangunk Mountains rises in the background. (Courtesy of Daryl P. Carr.)

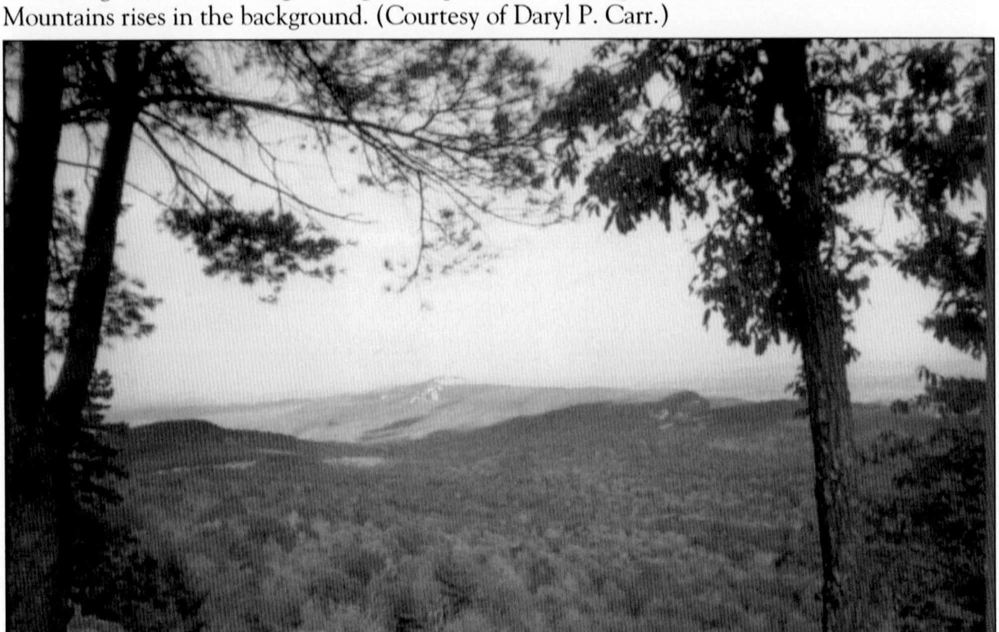

This 1999 view is from a picnic site on Minnewaska Mountain, looking northeast. Dickie Barre Mountain is to the left of center. The valley of the Coxing Kill, the heart of the Trapps neighborhood of Gardiner, is in the center. Trapps Mountain, also part of Gardiner, is in the shadow to the right of center. The main part of Gardiner is to the right in the distance behind the tree. (Photograph by Bob Fisher.)

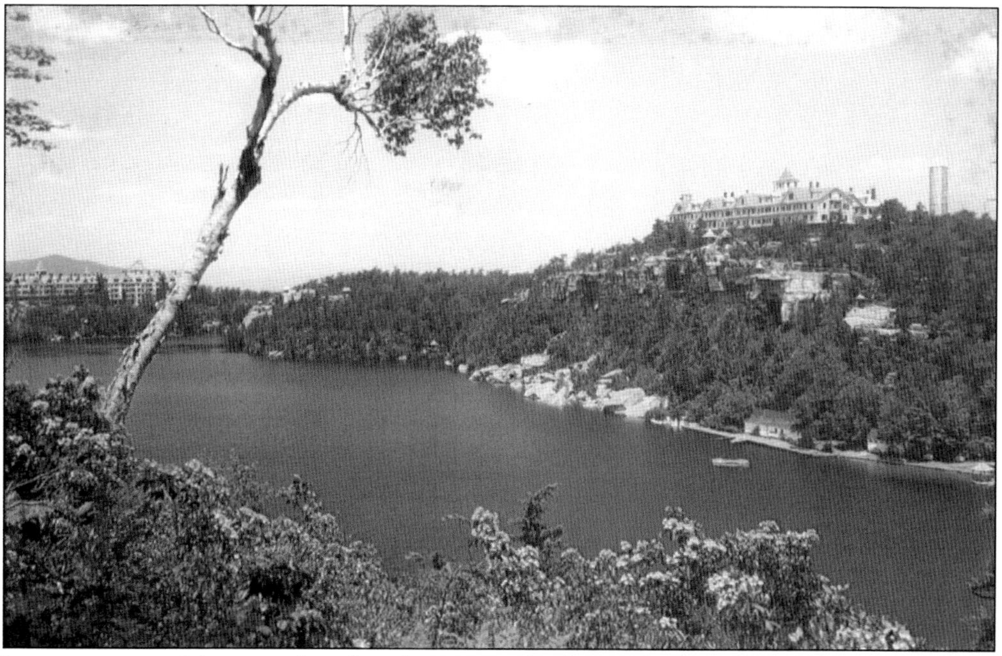

It is springtime. Mountain laurel and evergreen bushes with glossy leaves display their lush blossoms. In the 1940s and 1950s, the Minnewaska resort widely circulated this view of its two hotels, Wildmere House (left) and Cliff House (right). The tall water tower to the right of Cliff House could be seen from a distance, pointing out to much of Gardiner, where among the mountains Minnewaska was. (Courtesy of Haviland-Heidgard Historical Collection.)

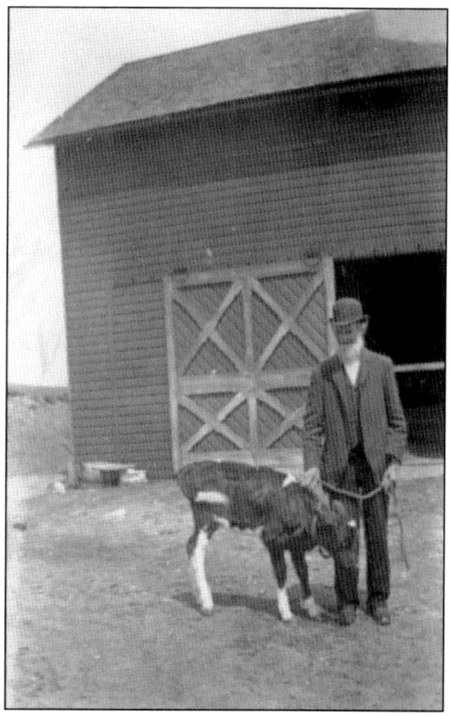

Titus C. White holds a calf at Orchard Hill farm in New Hurley, along the southeast border of Gardiner. While the precise location of the farm is uncertain, at the time the picture was taken, c. 1910, its mailing address was Gardiner. White, who was born in 1834, volunteered for the Union in the Civil War. (Courtesy of Richard Tuman.)

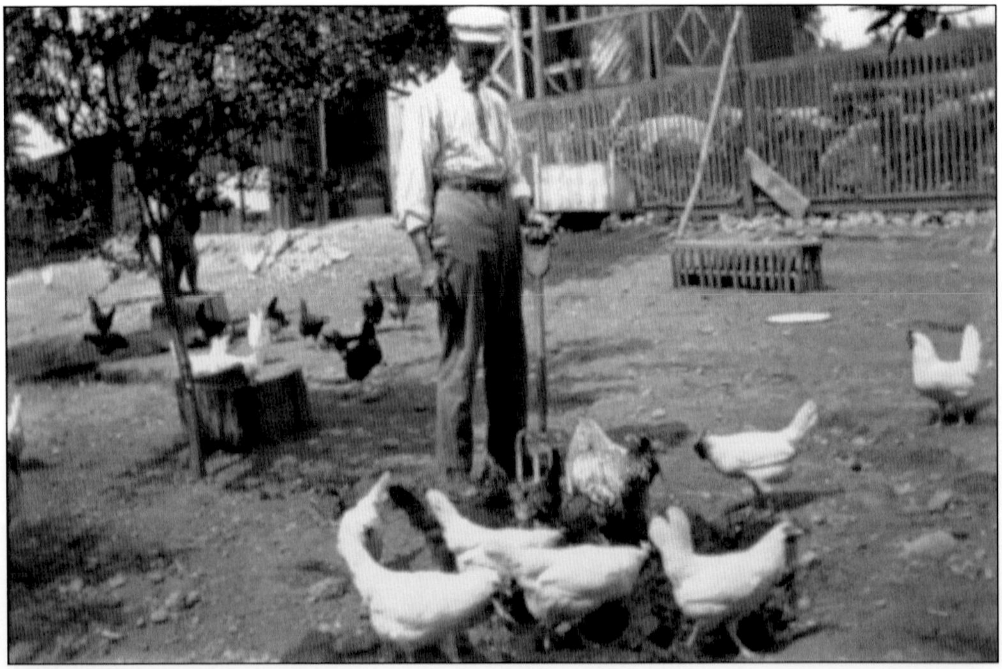

William Hemingway, son-in-law of Titus C. White, raised chickens on Orchard Hill farm c. 1910. Influenced by custom as he was, White evidently considered it appropriate to sport a cap, necktie, and pipe while caring for his chickens. As for the chickens, programmed as they were, they had pecked their yard bare of grass. (Courtesy of Richard Tuman.)

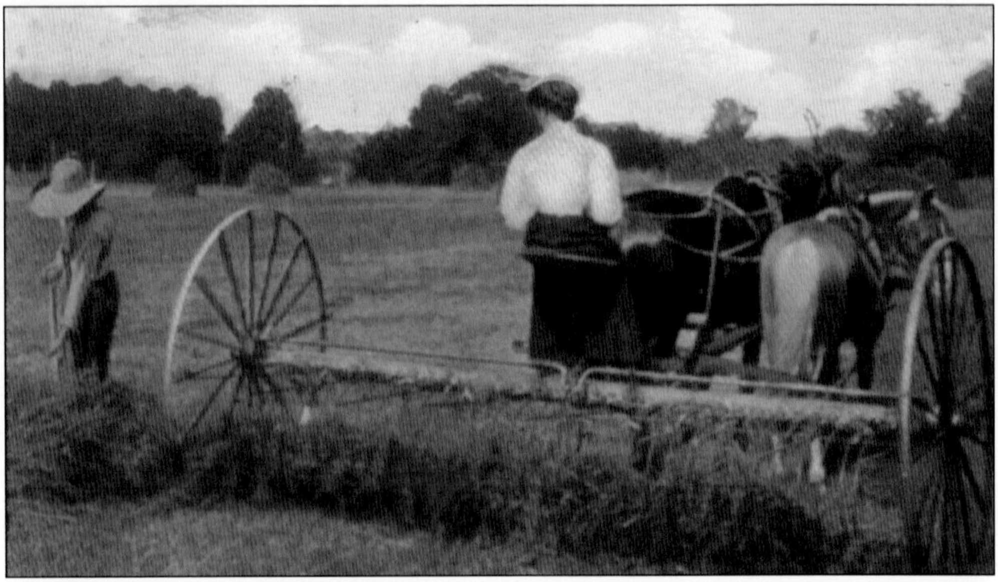

A woman wearing a long skirt drives a hay rake in Plattekill on Gardiner's eastern border, shown here on a view postmarked 1915. At about this time in the Gardiner region, farm women were customarily limited to such work as feeding farm crews, growing vegetables, picking small fruit such as berries, picking up dropped apples, and raising chickens. Although they often drove the wagons that delivered milk to creameries, it is unclear how often they drove farm machinery. (Courtesy of Daryl P. Carr.)

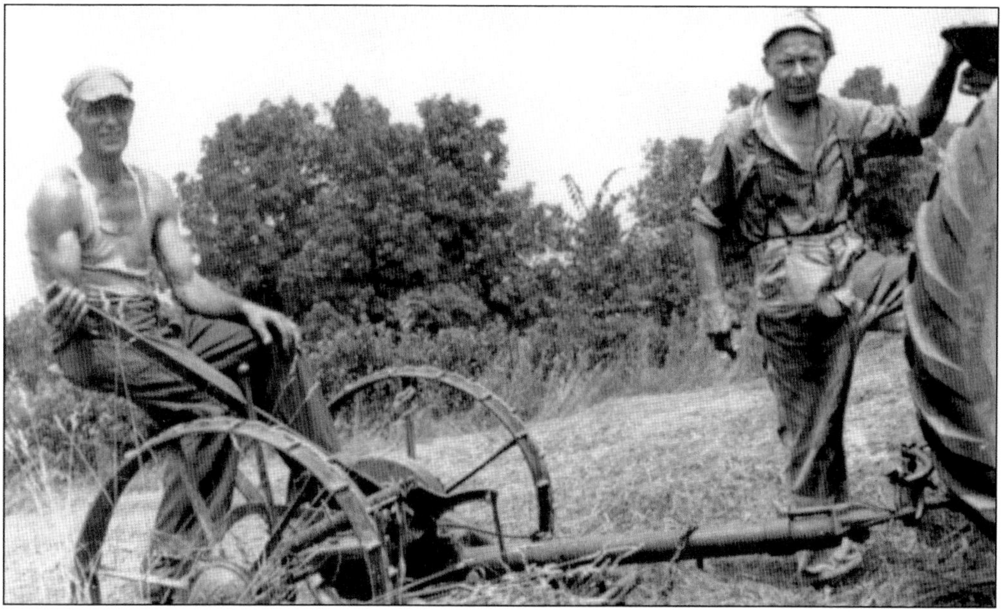

Horse-drawn farm machinery only gradually gave way to tractor-drawn machinery, and the transition was often awkward, as this 1948 photograph illustrates. Although the farmer, Mr. Huebeck (right) of Gardiner's Burnt Meadow Road, could afford a tractor, he could not also afford a mower designed to be pulled by a tractor. He set up his tractor to pull a mower designed to be pulled by a horse. The misfit meant that two men, rather than the usual one man, were required to operate the mower, and that farm laborer Tony Togna, an Italian immigrant, was in danger of being tipped over as he rode the mower. (Courtesy of Enrico Togna.)

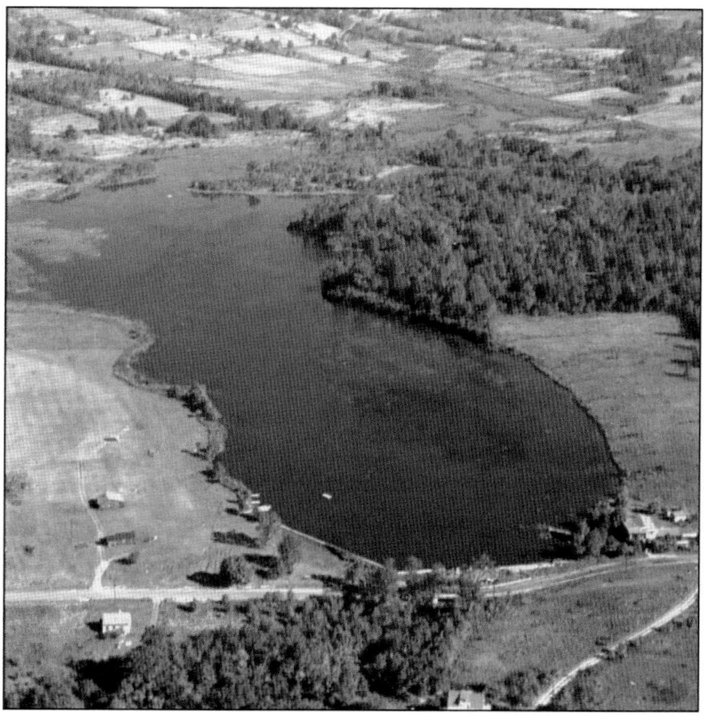

Oscar Hedden, the owner of Benton's Corners hotel who is rumored to have grown rich from bootlegging, created this 40-acre lake by damming the Mara Kill *c.* 1930. The lake, often called Hedden's Lake, stretches from the dam that created it, close to Bruynswick Road (crossing the foreground), north and northeast to Route 44–55 (upper right). Although this 1941 aerial photograph portrays a lot of land cleared for farming, today, much of it has grown up again to woods. (Courtesy of Joseph L. Katz.)

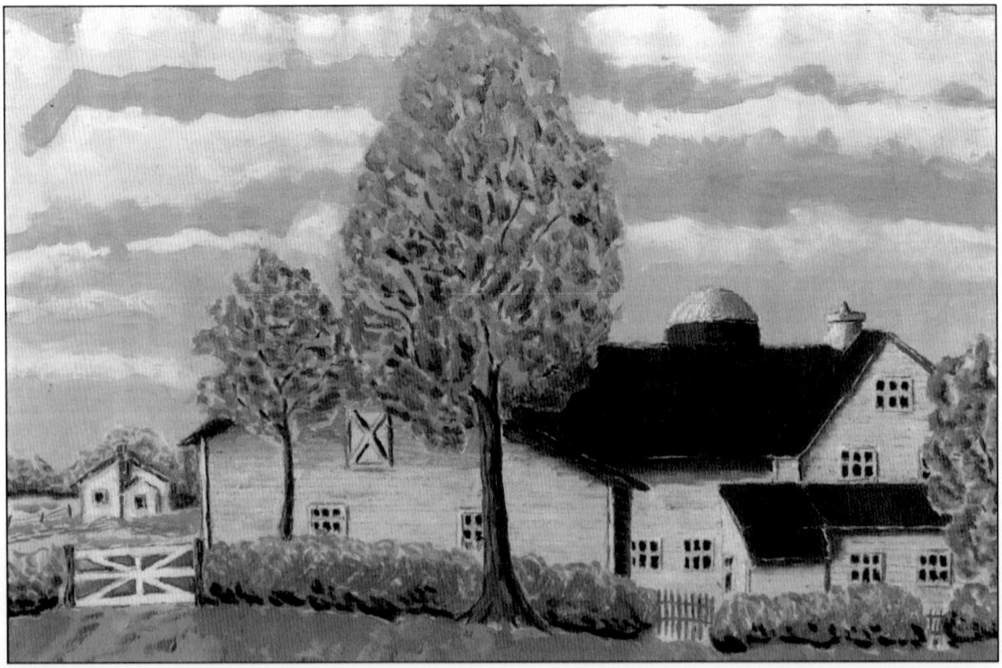

The barn depicted here, belonging to what was originally the James Hasbrouck farm, was located on a lane leading south off Guilford School House Road. This oil painting was done in the 1950s by Werner Kaelin, a Swiss-born manufacturer of neckwear in Jersey City, who had bought the farm in the 1930s as a summer retreat and rented its land to the Keeping family. Kit LeFevre, the present owner of the farm, raises horses on it. Having built a new barn, he uses the old barn as a workshop. (Courtesy of Haviland-Heidgard Historical Collection.)

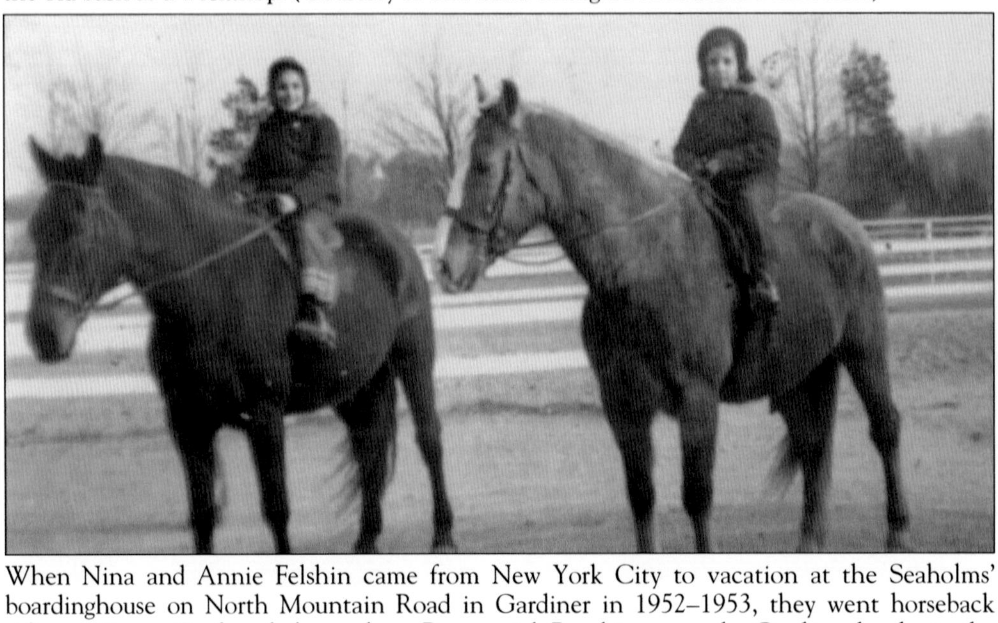

When Nina and Annie Felshin came from New York City to vacation at the Seaholms' boardinghouse on North Mountain Road in Gardiner in 1952–1953, they went horseback riding at Sunny Croft, a dude ranch on Bruynswick Road just over the Gardiner border in the town of Shawangunk. Today the ranch is gone. A Jehovah's Witness church occupies the site. (Courtesy of Annie Felshin O'Neill.)

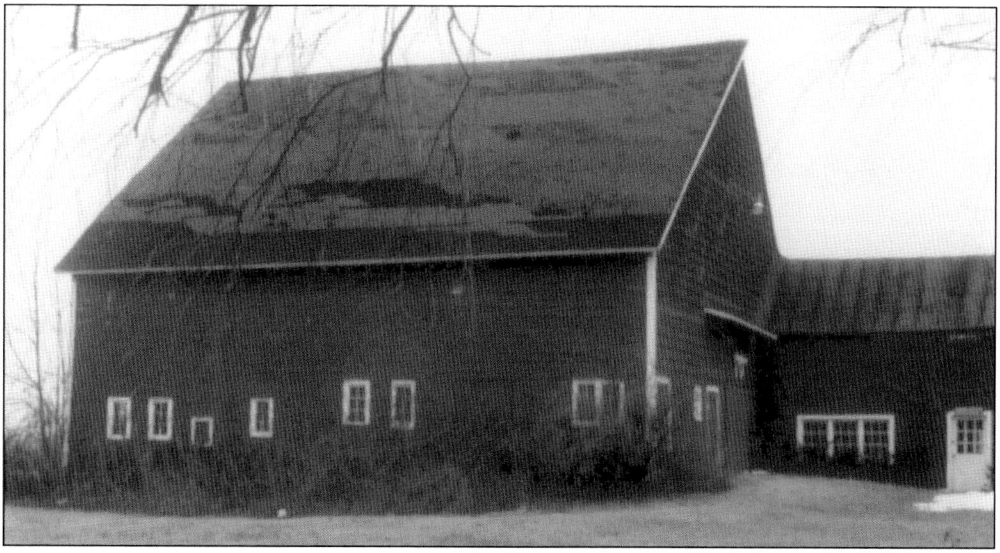

This Dutch barn, about a mile south of Ireland Corners on the west side of Route 208, was photographed in March 1983. At that time, it was painted traditional barn red and looked probably much the same as when originally built more than a century before. By 1990, however, it had been renovated for use by Cathgro Industries, a linen distributor, which retained the barn's essential shape but painted it white. This renovation exemplifies the decline of farming in Gardiner and the frequent recycling of farm buildings for other purposes. (Courtesy of William B. Rhoads.)

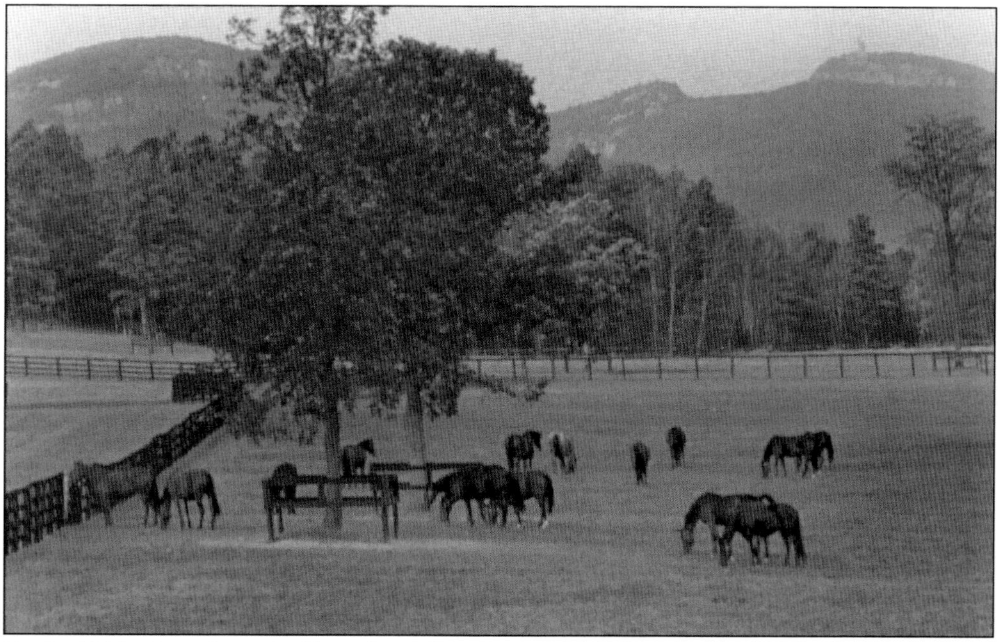

By the 1980s, dairy farms had long been disappearing in Gardiner, sometimes being replaced by horse farms. As photographed in 1984, this horse breeding farm, Blue Chip Farms, was at the junction of Bruynswick and Shaft Roads, below the Shawangunk Ridge. It is still a horse farm, but it is now operated by Majestic View Farms International. (Photograph by Jon Margolis, courtesy of the *Huguenot Herald*.)

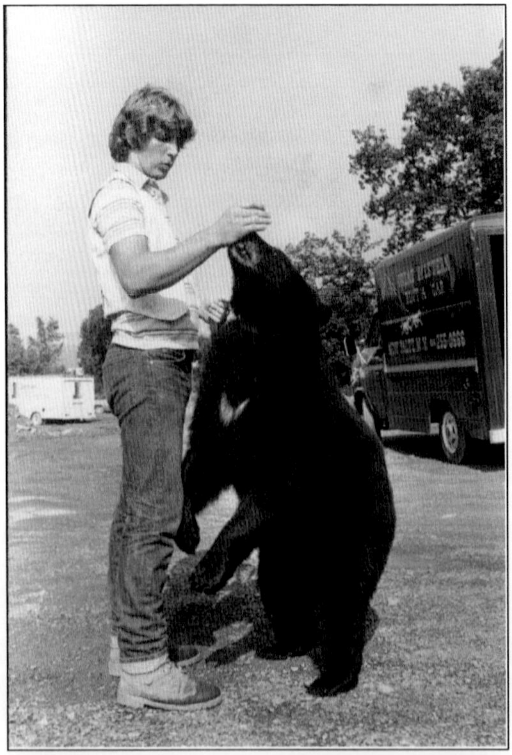

Scott Widmark is shown in 1984 with a black bear he trained at his family's farm. The Widmark farm, on Route 44–55 near Benton's Corners, has survived for decades on raising not only bees, whose honey it sells, but also black bears, sheep, and other animals which are a year-round family attraction. (Photograph by Jon Margolis, courtesy of the *Huguenot Herald.*)

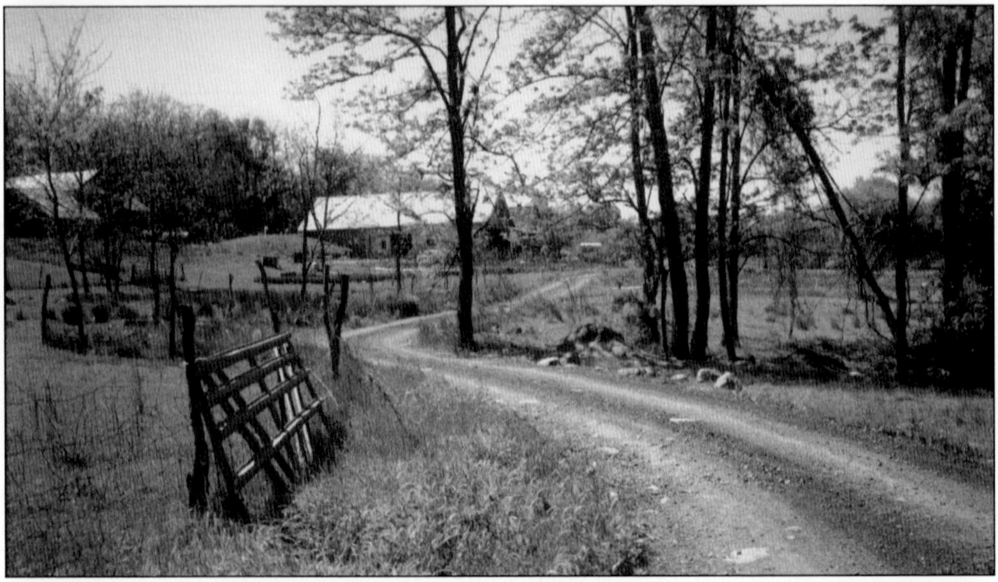

Four Winds Farm on Marabac Road is part of what was a large farm owned by Dr. Abraham Deyo c. 1900. Since 1988, it has been a 24-acre farm owned by Polly and Jay Armour. Pictured in 2002, it grows organic produce. Organized as a Community Supported Agriculture (CSA) farm, it is one of two such farms in Gardiner. Families can purchase shares in the farm, contribute labor to it, and receive produce in return. One of the aims of the CSA initiative is to keep farming alive in the area at a time when farmers are likely to be pressed to sell out to housing development. (Photograph by Carleton Mabee.)

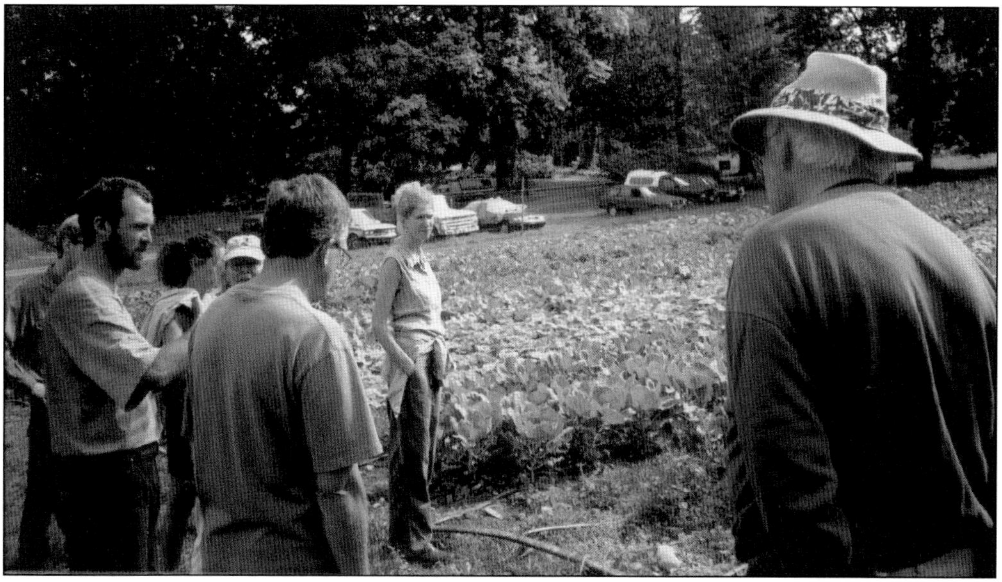

Peter Brady (left) of Phillies Bridge Farm, and Lee Gartrell (right), the farm's treasurer, explain to visitors the farm's use of organic rather than chemical pest controls. Shown in 2002, this farm on Phillies Bridge Road, like Four Winds Farm, has since 1995 been a Community Supported Agriculture farm, a nonprofit enterprise with participating members. Jim Ottaway, of Ottaway newspapers, who formerly occupied the farm, made it available for this purpose. (Photograph by Carleton Mabee.)

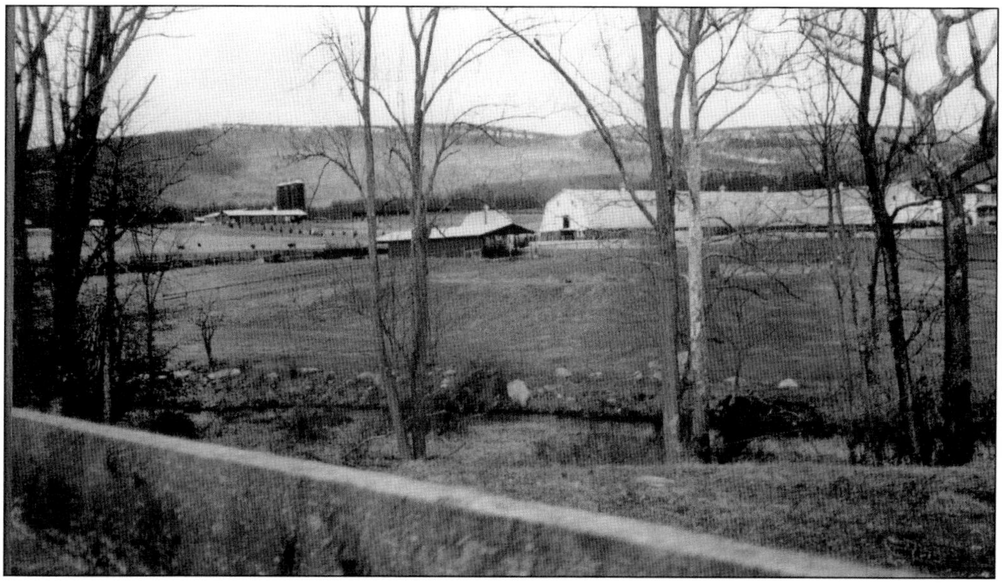

Cattle graze on a farm in the Bruynswick section of Gardiner. In the background of this 2002 photograph is the Shawangunk Ridge, with Millbrook Mountain (center) and Trapps Mountain(right). On this farm, acquired by Jehovah's Witnesses from the Costa family in 1966, as well as on other farms they have been acquired in the region, the religious group has raised dairy cattle, beef cattle, hogs, vegetables, and small fruit to supply its own membership. In recent years, however, the group has found it more economical to concentrate on beef cattle. (Photograph by Bob Fisher.)

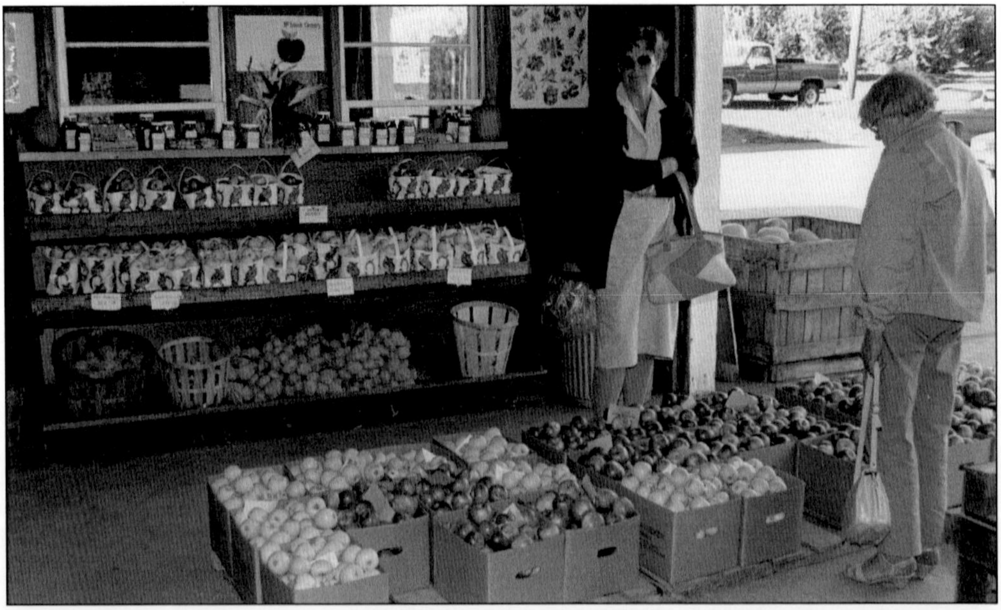

The market of Jenkins-Lueken Orchards, located where Yankee Folly Road meets Route 299, displays a variety of apples. Pictured in 1984, the market is still open today. Several Gardiner area orchards, including the Dressel, Tantillo, and Wright orchards, have found that selling their fruit directly to consumers at their own roadside markets has helped them survive. (Photograph by Jon Margolis, courtesy of the *Huguenot Herald*.)

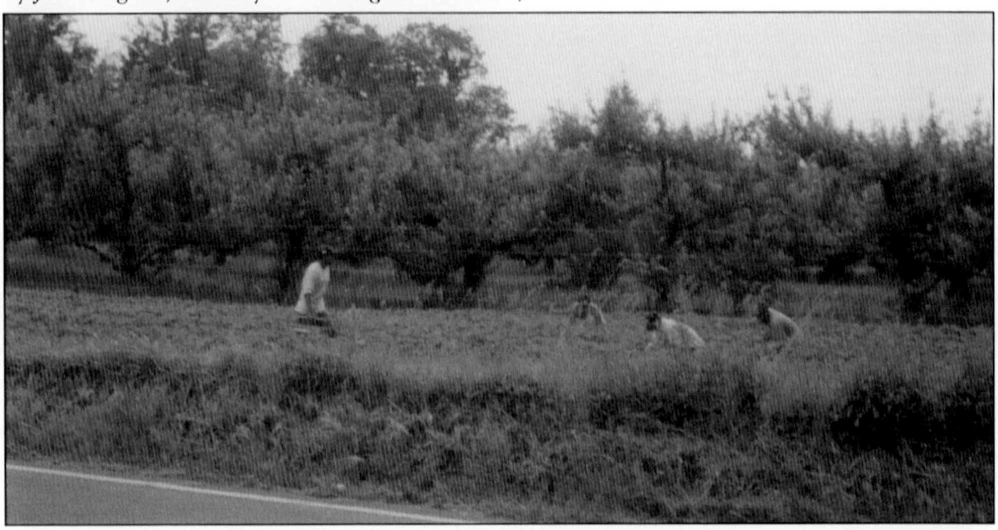

With apple trees in the background, Mexican workers pick strawberries on Route 208 in Kettleborough for Dressel's farm. As far back as the mid-1800s, farmers in the Gardiner area recruited recent immigrants, just off the boat in New York City, to provide farm labor. At first they were predominantly Irish, but by the 1880s, most were Italian. By the 1950s, they were often West Indian blacks, who usually came to the United States only temporarily without their families. Since the 1980s, they have increasingly been Latin Americans. This picture was taken in June 2002. Pressure to improve the lot of these migrant laborers conflicts with pressure to support hard-pressed farmers who need to keep their labor costs down. (Photograph by Carleton Mabee.)

Two

TRANSPORTATION

In the age of horses, at least five significant wooden bridges existed in Gardiner, perhaps all of them covered. Two crossed the Shawangunk River and three crossed the Wallkill River. All have disappeared. The highways, unpaved, were often maintained by the required labor of those who lived near them, and they were often impassable in heavy snow or spring mud. A major south–north highway through Gardiner ran via Albany Post Road through Tuthilltown and Libertyville. Milton Turnpike, a major east–west highway, ran from Milton on the Hudson River through Modena and Tuthilltown into the Trapps mountain gap. Some of the turnpike's Gardiner portion was known as Farmer's Turnpike.

When the Wallkill Valley Railroad was built through Gardiner in 1869, it created the Gardiner hamlet. It helped farmers market their produce. It also helped summer visitors reach boardinghouses, and once Minnewaska's first hotel was built in 1879, it helped them reach that destination as well.

It was for automobiles that in 1929–1930 the state first built a paved highway across Gardiner, creating great excitement. Called Minnewaska Trail, or State Route 55, it reached from the new mid-Hudson Bridge at Poughkeepsie through Modena and the Gardiner hamlet, using part of the old Farmer's Turnpike route, and on into the Shawangunk Mountains, serving the Minnewaska hotels. Meanwhile, from 1926 to about 1936, the road that came to be called Route 208, passing from Walden through Ireland Corners to New Paltz, was gradually cemented, making it Gardiner's major south–north artery.

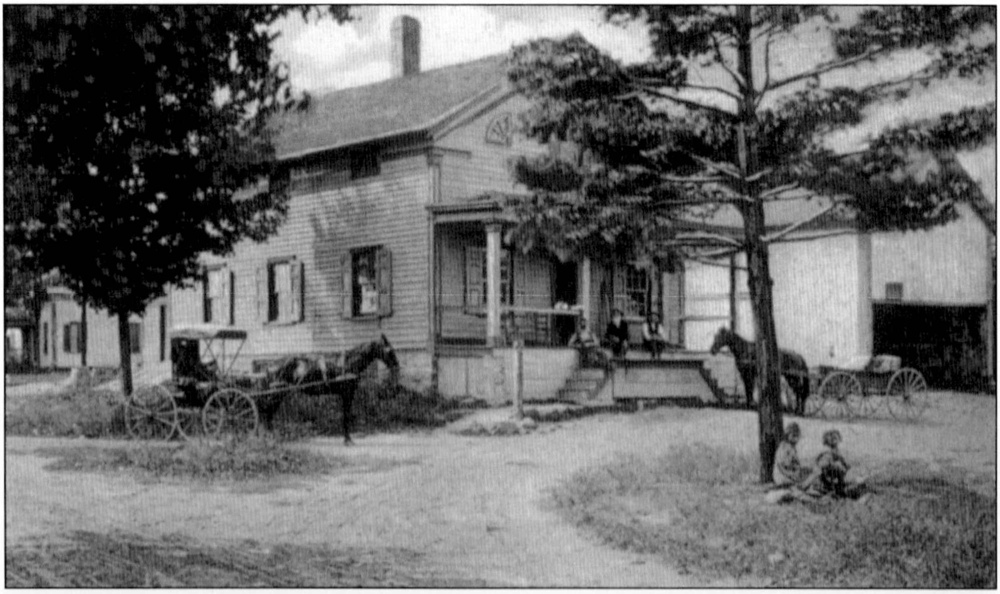

This rural store was in the Bruynswick neighborhood, on the southern edge of Gardiner bordering the town of Shawangunk. As portrayed here the horses and people, all waiting, suggest a slow pace of life. They seem little related to the frenzy that prevailed only 80 miles away in the New York metropolitan region. (Courtesy of Daryl P. Carr.)

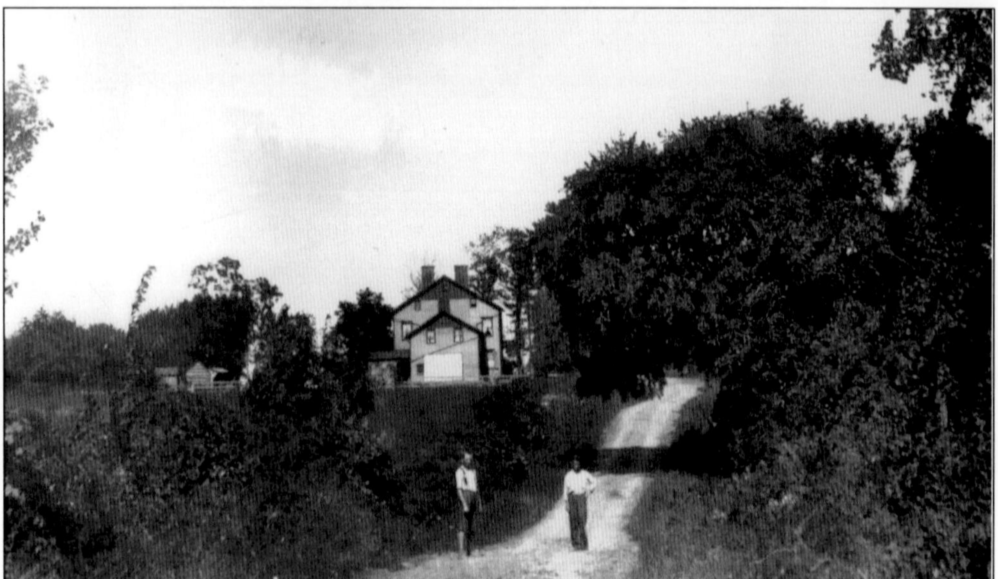

Kettleborough Road, the road from Ireland Corners to New Paltz, is unpaved and little more than a cow path in this late-1890s photograph. The road passes the John H. Wurts farm (now the McCord farm). By *c.* 1926, the state was building a concrete road from Walden north to Ireland Corners, but the work abruptly stopped there. Because the road from Ireland Corners to New Paltz continued to be in poor condition, Gardinerites tended to shop in Walden, even though it was farther than New Paltz. It was only in the mid-1930s that the state extended the concrete road, by this time called Route 208, from Ireland Corners north to New Paltz. (Courtesy of Carol B. LeFevre.)

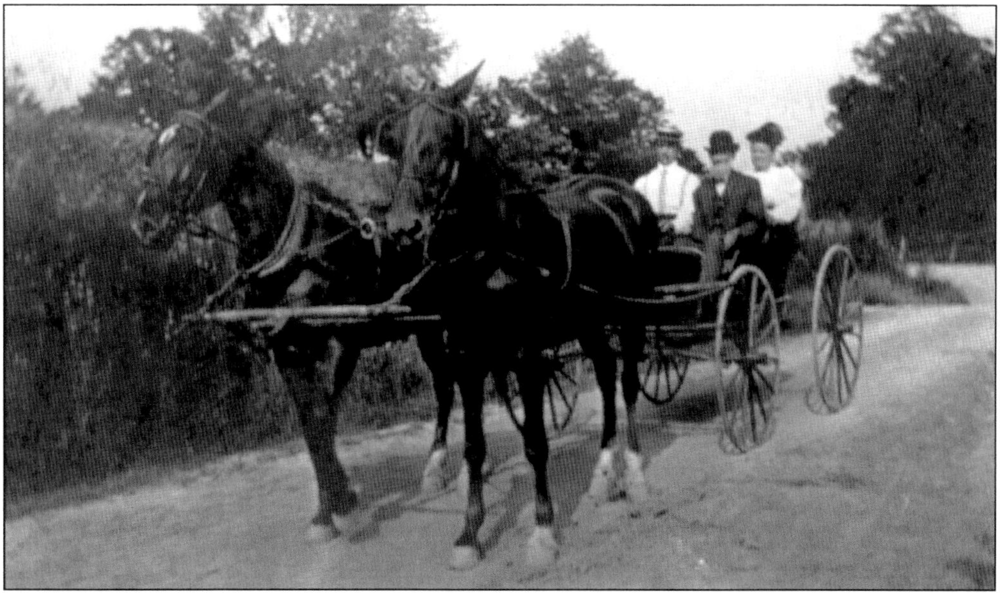

This c. 1909 view shows Titus C. White of New Hurley (center) in an open carriage with his wife, Emma K. White (right), and his son-in-law, William E. Hemingway. The people and horses all seem well groomed. (Courtesy of Richard Tuman.)

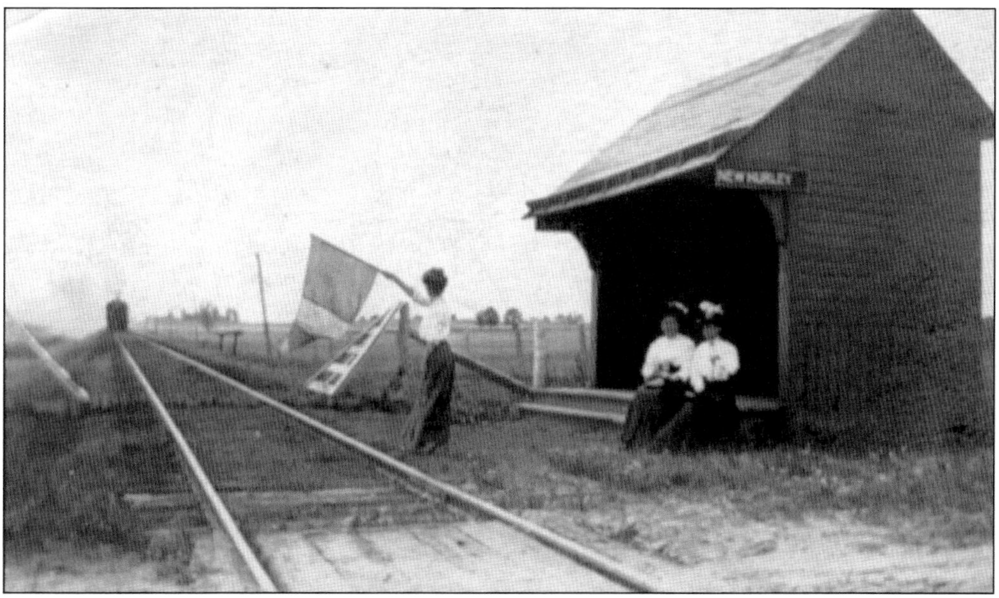

In 1909, a Wallkill Valley Railroad train approached the New Hurley station at Gardiner's border with the town of Shawangunk, on what came to be called Denniston Road. The station was only a flag stop; it never had an enclosed building or a station agent. The woman shown signaling the train to stop may have been Marie White Hemingway of New Hurley, because it was her family who preserved the photograph. The slanted boards on each side of the tracks may have been culvert protection. (Courtesy of Richard Tuman.)

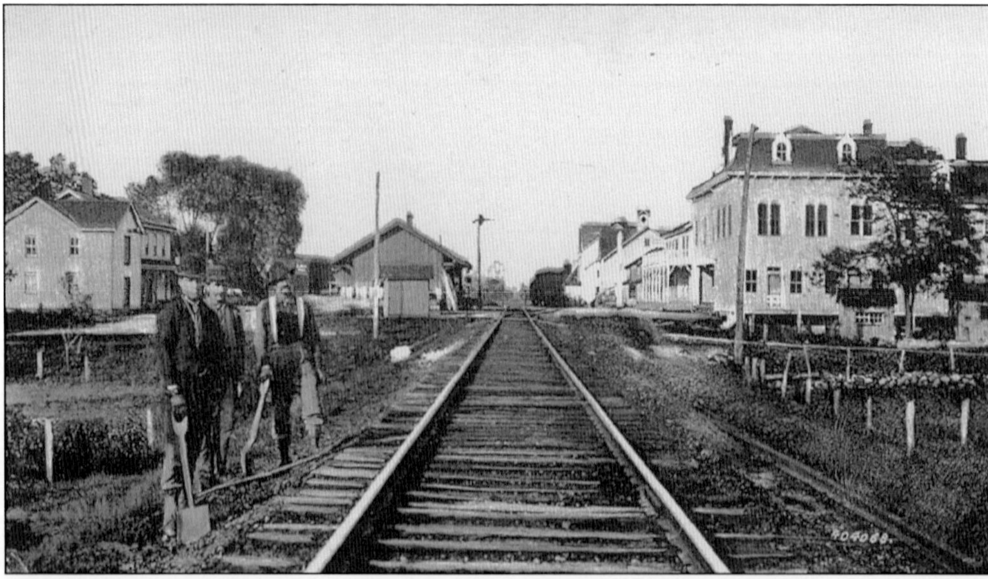

Trackmen were maintaining the Wallkill Valley Railroad's tracks in this view, postmarked 1919. It shows the Gardiner firehouse (far left) and the Gardiner station (left of center). What looks like three separate buildings (right), one of them with pillars in front, are all part of the Gardiner Hotel (also called Callahan's). In the right background along the tracks, are structures that were destroyed by a 1925 fire. (Courtesy of William and Carol Majestic Lohrman.)

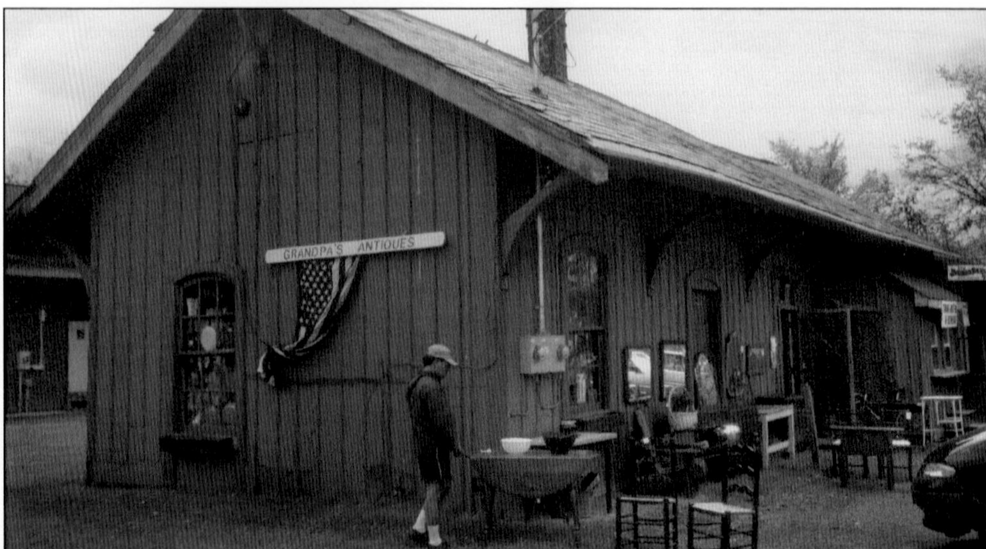

The Gardiner Station became obsolete as a rail station in 1977 when trains ceased to run by it. In the early 1990s, it was used as a video store. At the time of this photograph, May 2002, Grandpa's Antiques occupied its north end, with antiques spilling out into the yard. A barber shop occupied its south end (right). A bicycle shop occupied an eastern section that faced the railroad bed, remade into a rail trail open for walking and bicycling. On October 10, 2002, the 123-year-old building, which had been central in Gardiner's history, burned, leaving only a shell. (Photograph by Carleton Mabee.)

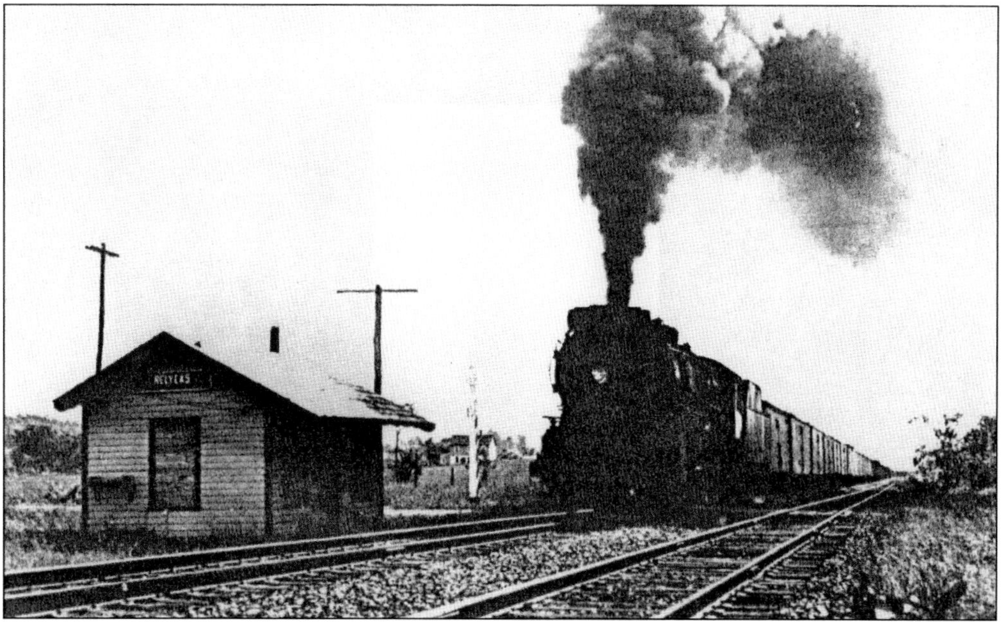

This freight train passes the Relyea(s) station, near New Hurley on the Poughkeepsie Bridge Route. It was a railroad line that opened in 1889 as single tracked and was later double-tracked. The train pictured here had come from the Maybrook rail yard in Orange County in 1936 and was heading through Modena and Clintondale to the Poughkeepsie Railroad Bridge over the Hudson River. Gardiner area farmers often used both Bridge Route and Wallkill line trains to ship out their milk and fruit. (Courtesy of Ken Shuker.)

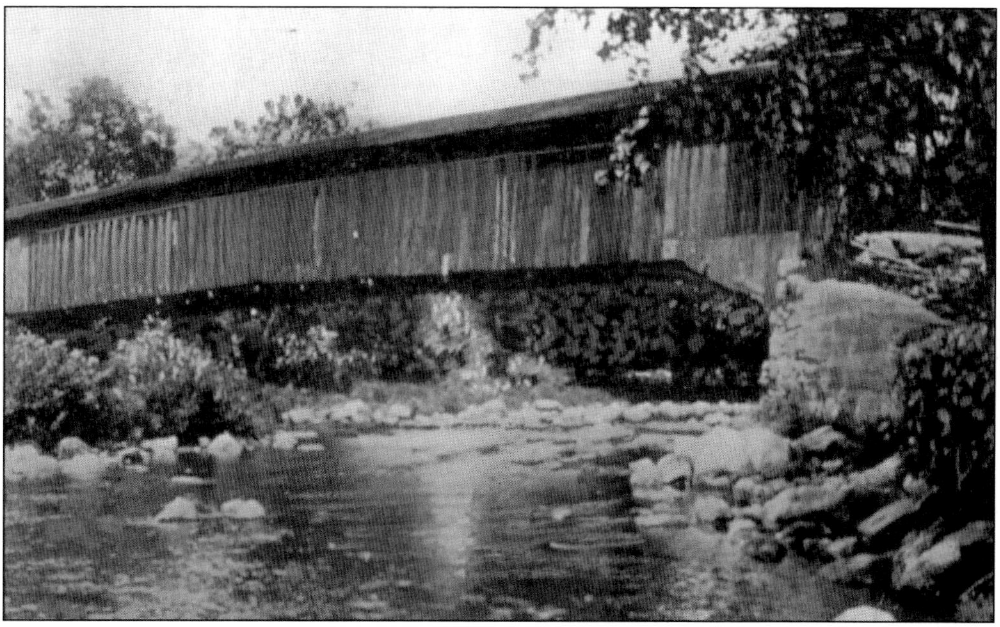

This wooden bridge crossed the Shawangunk Kill at Tuthilltown, shown looking downstream. The Tuthilltown mill, not shown, was at the bridge's left. In the 1800s, such wooden bridges were commonly covered to protect their timbers and planking from the weather, with the hope of slowing their deterioration. (Courtesy of William and Carol Majestic Lohrman.)

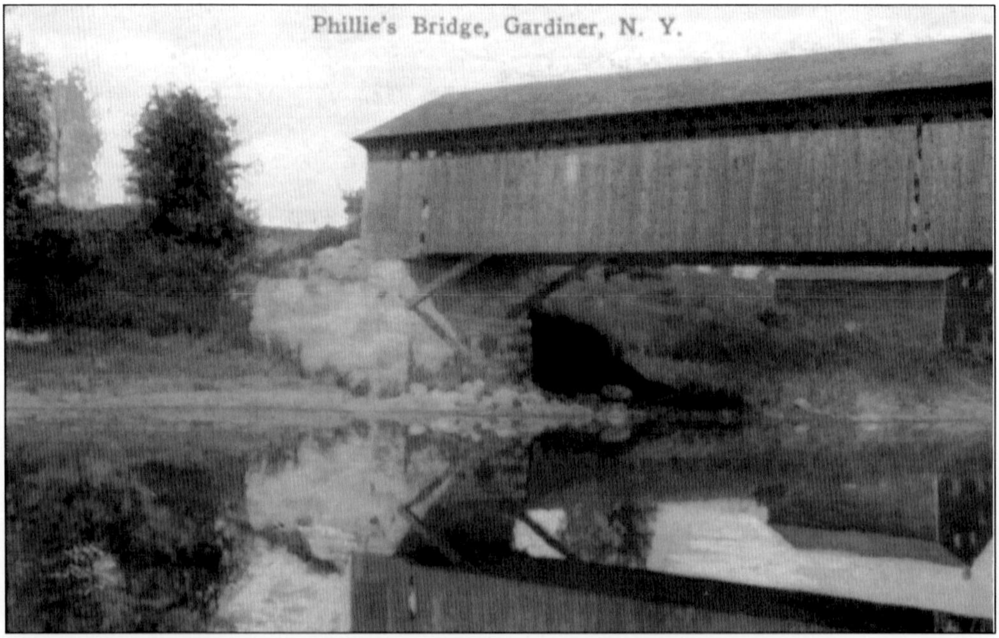

Both Phillies Bridge and Phillies Bridge Road are said to have received their names from Philip Hasbrouck, who lived in an old farmhouse near the Wallkill River by the east end of the bridge. In this postcard, a well-kept barn is visible under the bridge. (Postcard courtesy of William and Carol Majestic Lohrman.)

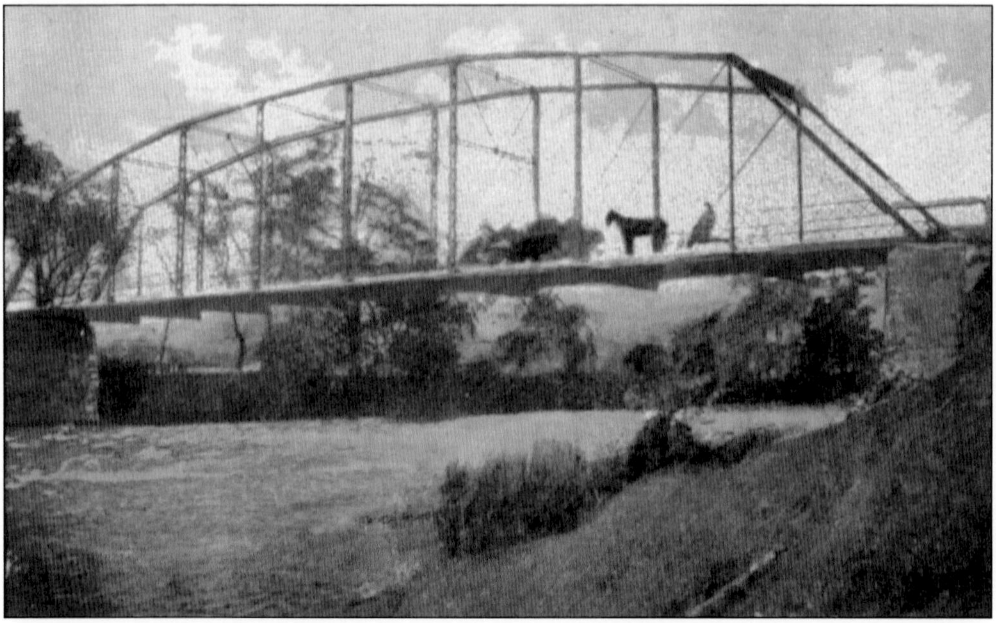

This view of the Wallkill River bridge is on a postcard marked in ink "1911." A metal truss bridge, a type commonly built at about that time, it connected Farmer's Turnpike on the east side of the river to Tuthilltown Road on the west. Although this bridge was replaced by the present bridge serving Route 44–55, slightly to the north, its stone buttresses remain visible today. (Courtesy of Daryl P. Carr).

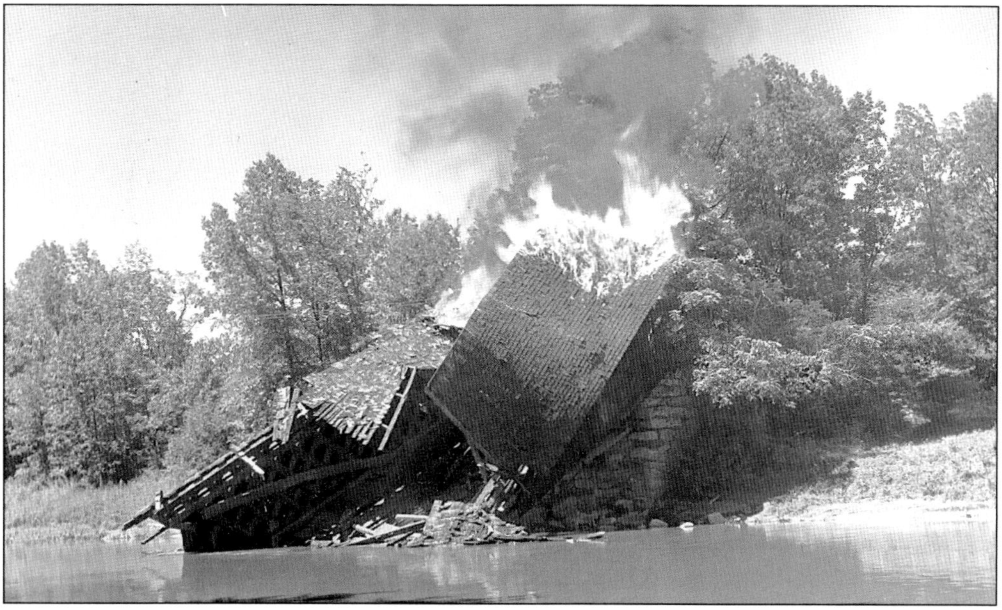

By 1948, Phillies Bridge had deteriorated to such a point that the town closed it. Its friends talked of rehabilitating it, but town officials, taking a short view, did not do so. On August 16, 1952, the bridge collapsed. Because it was considered to be blocking the river dangerously, the town arranged to have it burned, and never replaced it. This photograph, taken four days later by Gardiner photographer Erma De Witt, shows the burning of the bridge's west end. (Courtesy of Haviland-Heidgard Historical Collection.)

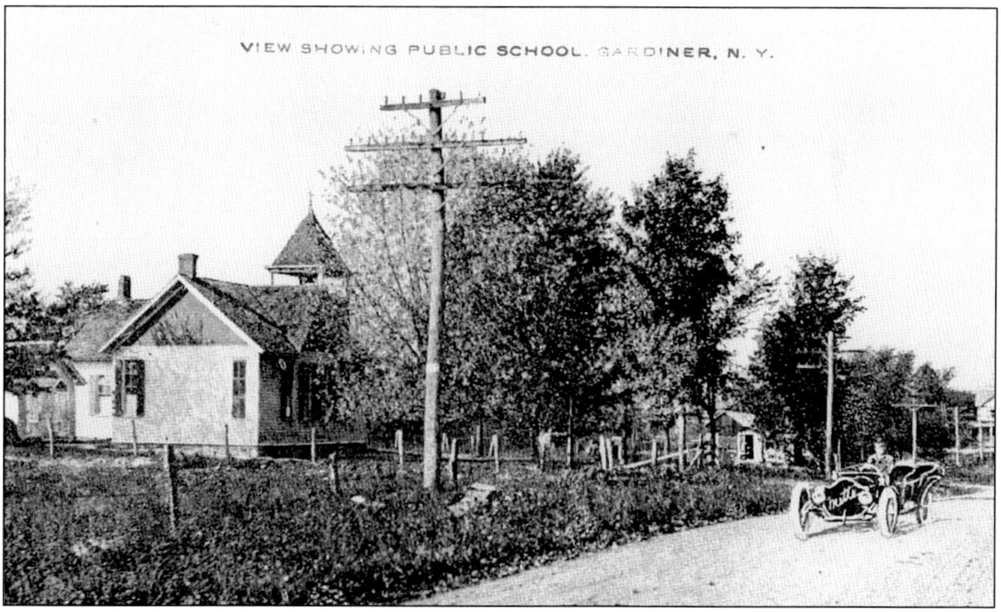

A touring car passes the Gardiner School, heading east toward Ireland Corners. The car's radiator is labeled "Nutte," perhaps in whimsy. The design of the car, as well as the size of the trees by the school, suggests this postcard was published between 1907 and 1912. The road, which was later to be called Route 44–55, appears to be unpaved. (Courtesy of William and Carol Majestic Lohrman.)

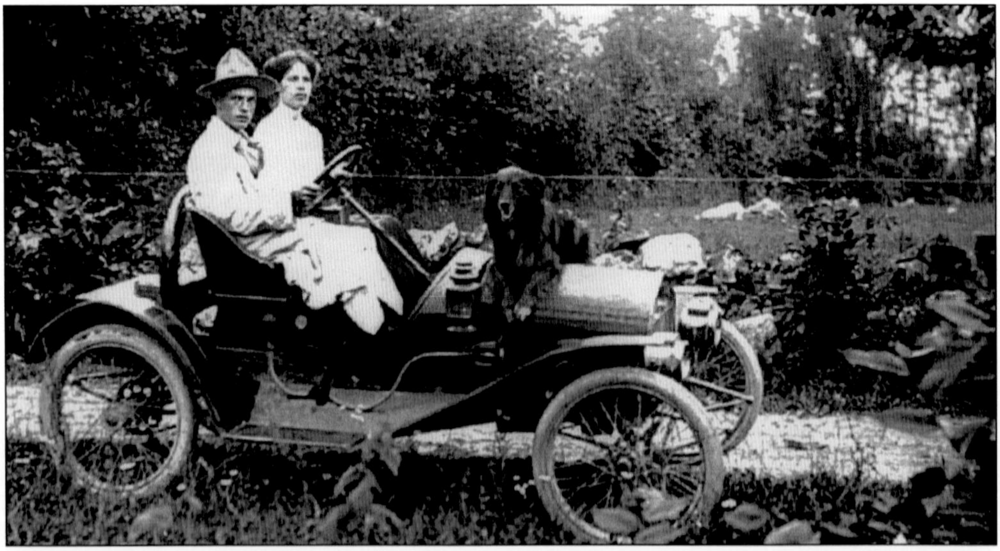

Frank and Mildred Terwilliger show off their car in this *c.* 1910 view. Both were from families long settled in the region. The daughter of George Enderly who operated the Enderly Saw Mill at Split Rock, Mildred grew up in the Trapps. Her husband worked at the Minnewaska hotels. They lived on the eastern slope of Trapps Mountain on the unpaved road, later to be called Minnewaska Trail, between its present junction with Route 299 and the present Gardiner Auxiliary Fire Station. Mildred died in the devastating flu epidemic of 1918, along with others of her family. (Courtesy of Joan Wustrau.)

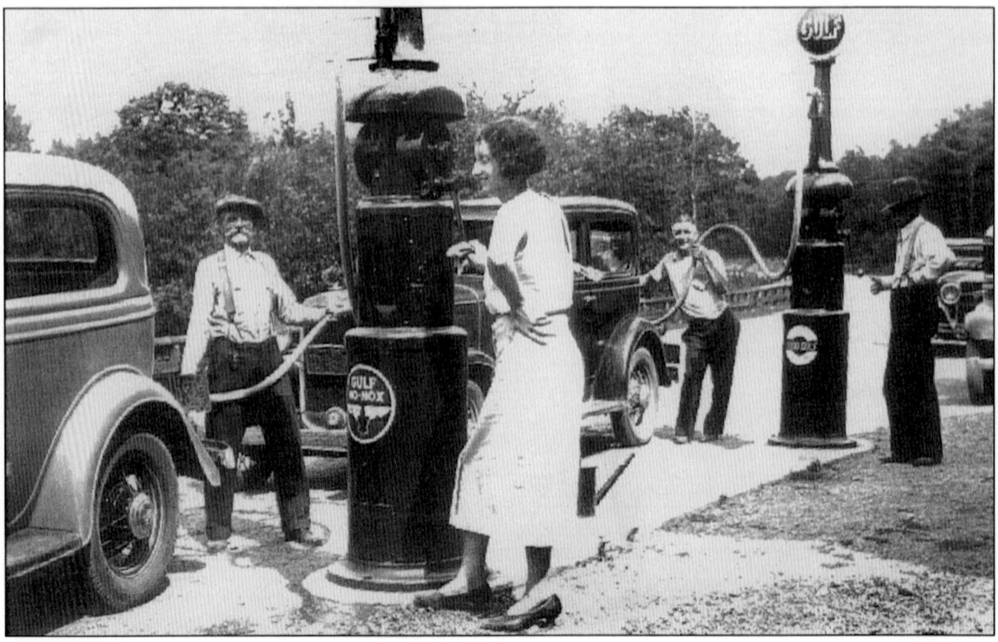

The Burger brothers, Sheridan and Ambrose, ham it up for this photograph, as they and friends pump gas at their new gas station. The station was at the edge of the Trapps neighborhood near Minnewaska Mountain on Minnewaska Trail. The station was opened soon after the Minnewaska Trail was completed as a paved road in 1930, and the photograph was probably taken soon after that. (Courtesy of Joan Wustrau.)

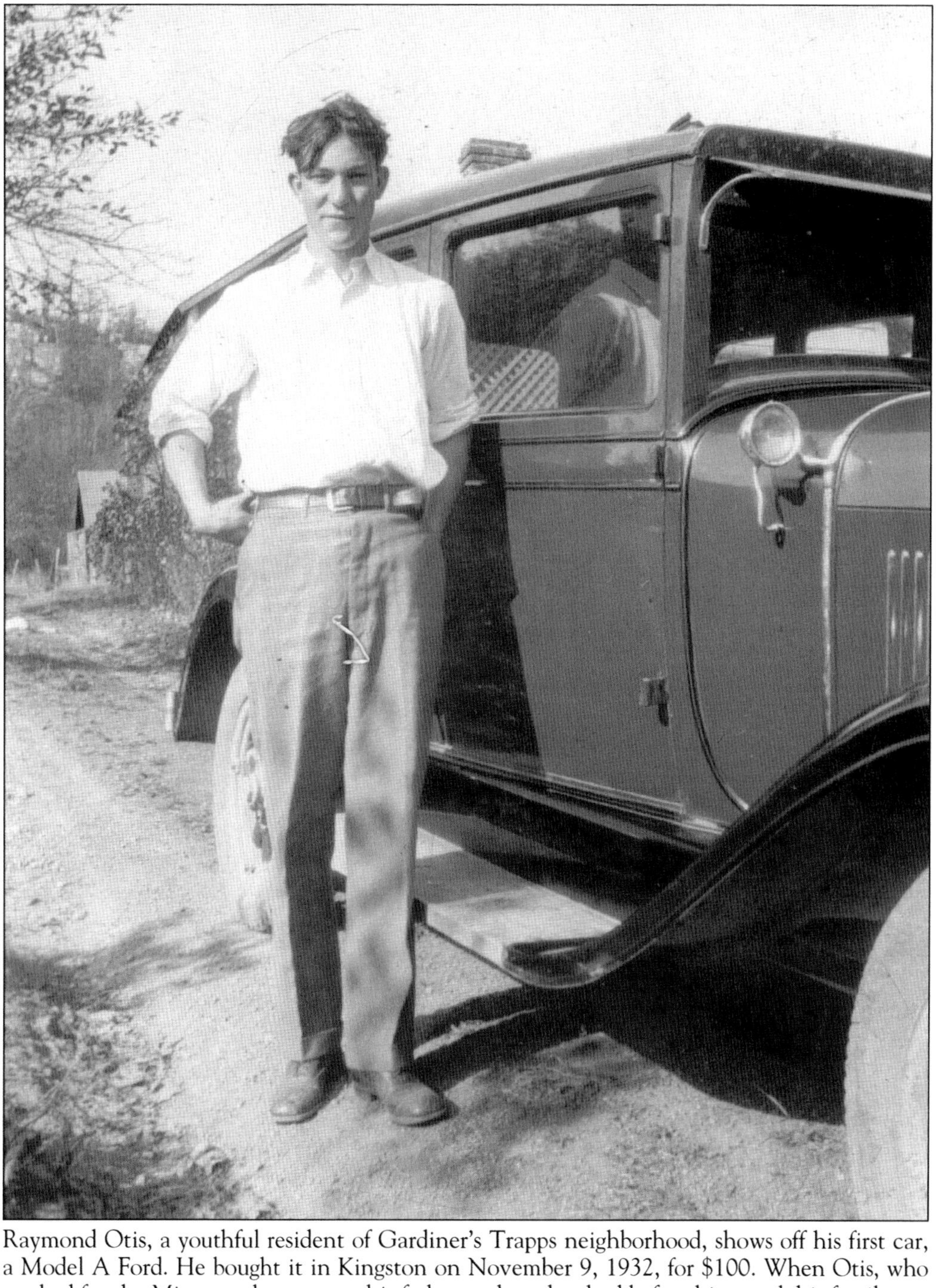

Raymond Otis, a youthful resident of Gardiner's Trapps neighborhood, shows off his first car, a Model A Ford. He bought it in Kingston on November 9, 1932, for $100. When Otis, who worked for the Minnewaska resort as his father and mother had before him, took his family out in his new car, they might drive eastward on the new Minnewaska Trail up through the Trapps Mountain gap, under the new steel bridge there, and down around the hairpin turn. If they were in a hurry, they might shop at the Benton's Corners general store. If they had more time, they might drive on to Kingston. Grandfather liked a fish market there—he might buy a whole barrel of mackerel at a time. (Courtesy of Don Otis.)

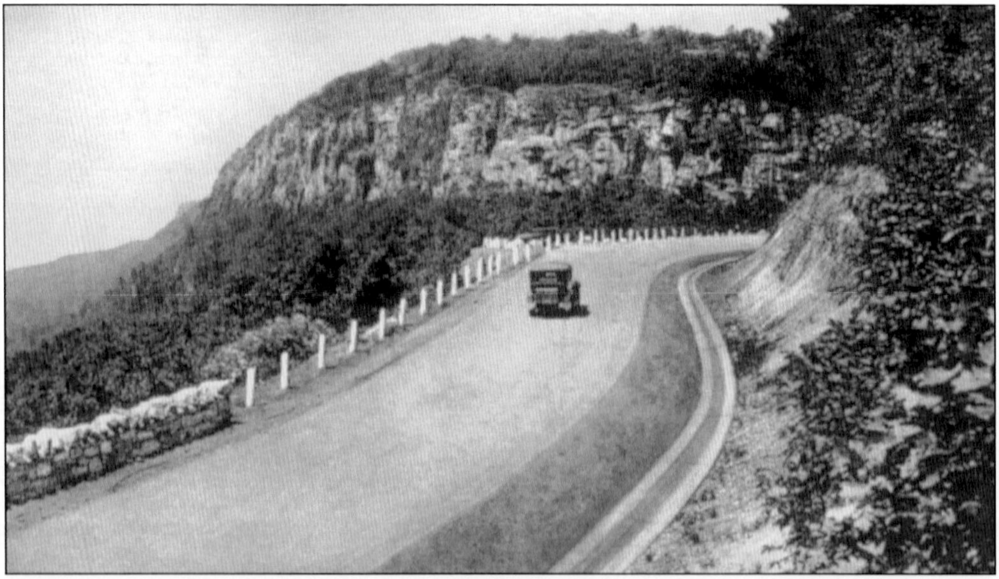

This car was on the Minnewaska Trail, climbing up from Gardiner's Wallkill Valley on its way to cross the Shawangunk Ridge. The car had just come around the hairpin turn. As it approached the curve leading up to the Trapps gap, the driver did not seem to expect much traffic, as he was not keeping to the right. The year must be at least 1930, as it was only then that the Minnewaska Trail in this section was paved. In preparation for the paving, the state had somewhat realigned the road in this section, taking into account the Smiley family's concern for preserving the area's natural beauty. (Courtesy of Shirley Anson.)

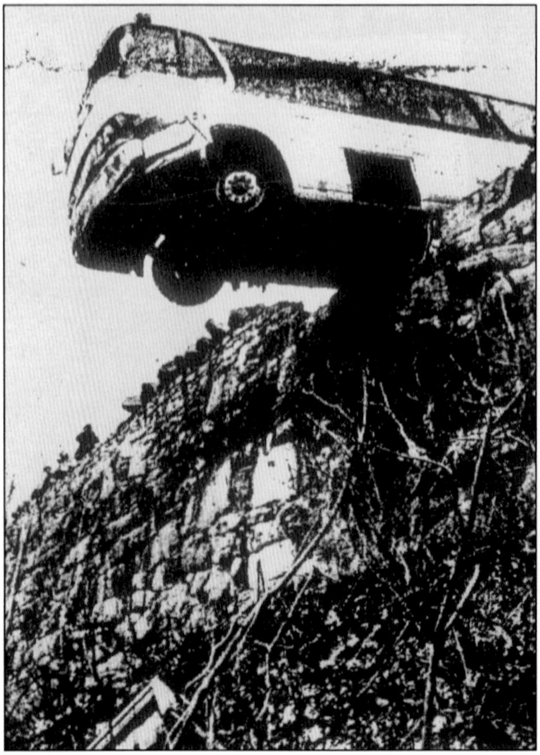

A bus coming fast down Trapps Mountain on the Minnewaska Trail was unable to make the famous hairpin turn on February 25, 1981. The bus tore through a stone wall. Its nose moved out into space. Mary Widmark, who was at the hairpin turn selling honey from her family's farm in Gardiner, heard passengers scream; however, they were able to escape from the rear of the bus. The bus was pulled back from the cliff by five wreckers, three from Bill's Garage in Gardiner and two from Sonny's Garage in Modena. (Photograph, courtesy of the *Huguenot Herald*.)

Three

Neighborhoods

When the town of Gardiner was founded in 1853, its commercial center was Tuthilltown, a waterpower site on the Shawangunk River. By 1869, however, the new Wallkill Valley Railroad had placed a station east of Tuthilltown, on what had been open farmland. Soon, the railroad had developed the station neighborhood into the Gardiner hamlet, the town's new commercial center.

According to an 1875 map of Gardiner, the most prominent neighborhoods in the town, beside Tuthilltown and the Gardiner hamlet, were Jenkinstown (waterpower was available on the Plattekill), Libertyville (with waterpower on the Wallkill), and Ireland Corners (a crossroads). Tuthilltown, Libertyville, and Jenkinstown, not being located on either a railway or what became a main automobile route, long ago lost most of their commercial character, while Ireland Corners, benefiting from an increase in automobile traffic, grew.

Modena was a neighborhood entirely over Gardiner's eastern town line, but it was closely related to Gardiner. Located in the town of Plattekill, Modena was a lively crossroads. It had its own church and school and, after 1889, its own railroad station on the Poughkeepsie Bridge line. Bruynswick was a neighborhood partly over Gardiner's southern town line. It had its own school and church, both of which were in the town of Shawangunk. Gardiner's mountain neighborhood, the Trapps, where waterpower was available, had its own school and church. A neighborhood next to the Trapps and much related to it was the Minnewaska resort, located mostly in the town of Rochester. For more than a century, the resort provided employment to Gardiner residents and a market for Gardiner farmers.

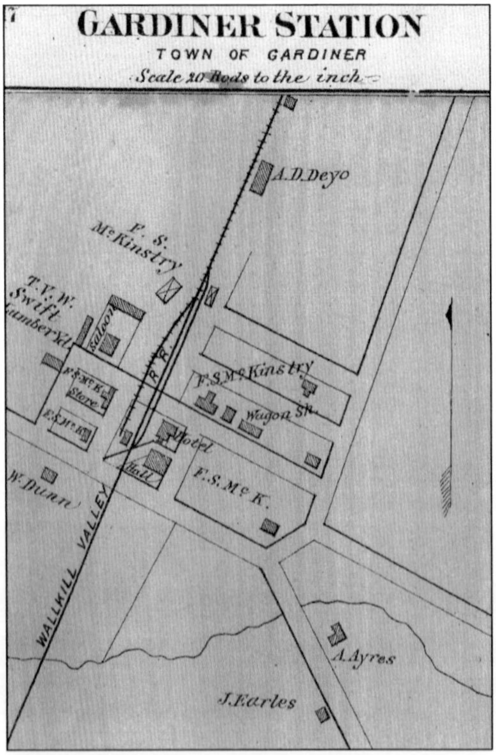

This map names as "Gardiner Station" what later came to be known as the Gardiner hamlet. The map was published in 1875, only six years after the Wallkill rail line that created the hamlet had reached there. As the map indicates, Main Street ran only one block west of the railroad tracks. The principal east–west thoroughfare was not Main Street but Farmer's Turnpike, which ran south of Main Street and parallel to it. Much of the hamlet's property shown here was owned by Floyd S. McKinstry, president of the Wallkill Railroad. (From F.W. Beers *Atlas*, 1875.)

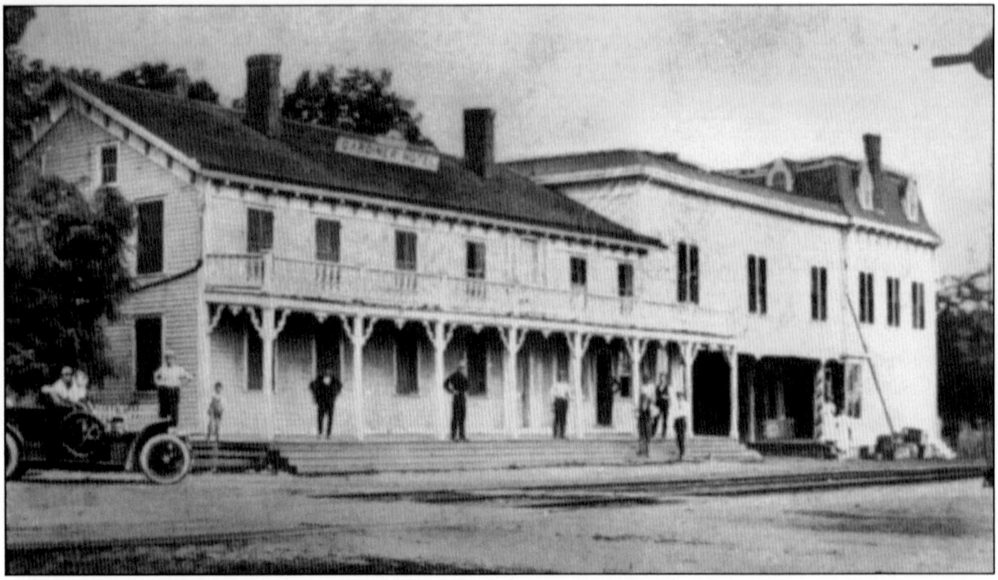

The Gardiner Hotel, shown c. 1910, faced the Wallkill Valley Railroad tracks in the Gardiner hamlet. Floyd S. McKinstry, the railroad's president, built the hotel in 1869, when the railroad reached Gardiner, and he built it small. By 1876, however, the McKinstry-owned complex of hotel buildings, kept by John T. Upright, housed a hardware store, harness shop, millinery shop, and a hall that could seat 600. From 1884, the Gardiner Hotel was for a time called Callahan's Hotel, after its operator, Tom Callahan. (Courtesy of Haviland-Heidgard Historical Collection.)

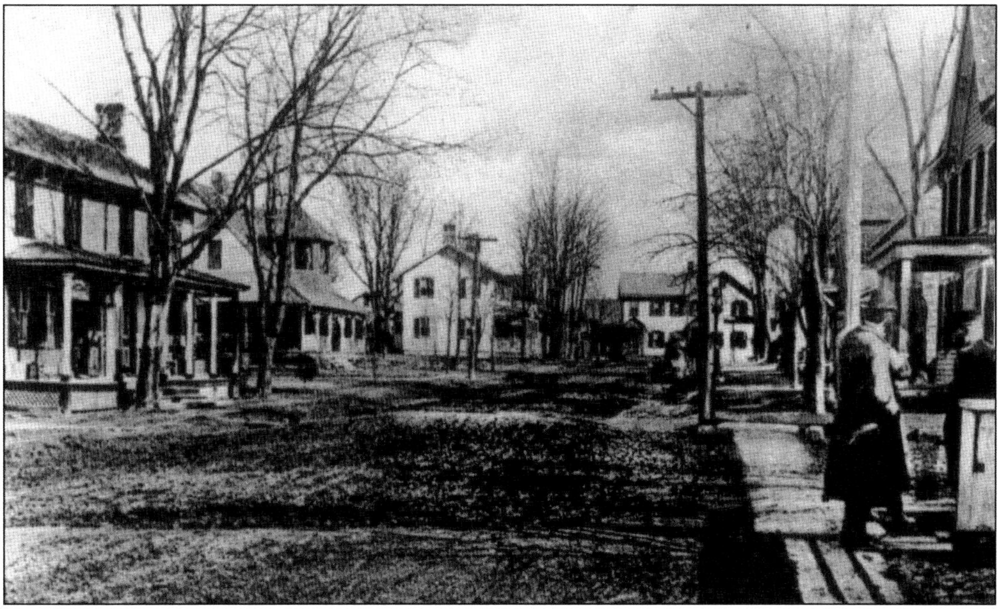

Even if they consist only of boards, sidewalks are available on Main Street in the Gardiner hamlet to help pedestrians get through the mud. In this 1910 view, the porch on the store building at the far left has not been enclosed, as it was by the 1950s, when it was McKinstry's store. A wagon is parked at the upper right; no automobiles are visible. (Courtesy of the Gardiner Library.)

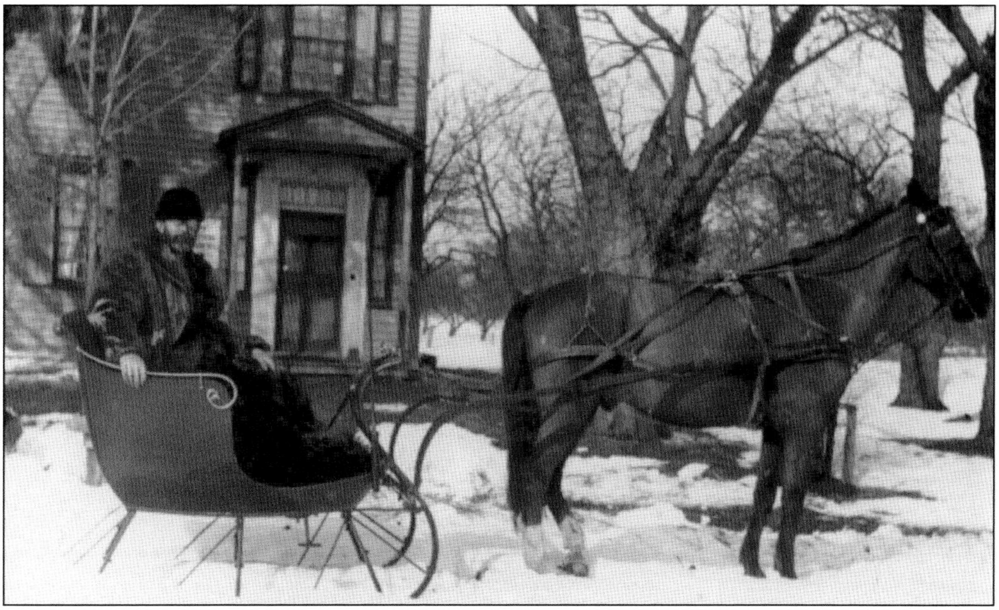

When Dr. Myron E. Stephens first came to Gardiner to practice medicine c. 1890, he was single and boarded in Callahan's Hotel. In this photograph, taken in the late 1890s, the doctor is making his rounds on Farmer's Turnpike, passing the house of Philip and Anna Donahue, whose daughter Betty he was to bring into the world. Stephens visited patients in a wide area, including Modena. He served as medical inspector for all the Gardiner schools and also as Gardiner postmaster. (Courtesy of Carol B. LeFevre.)

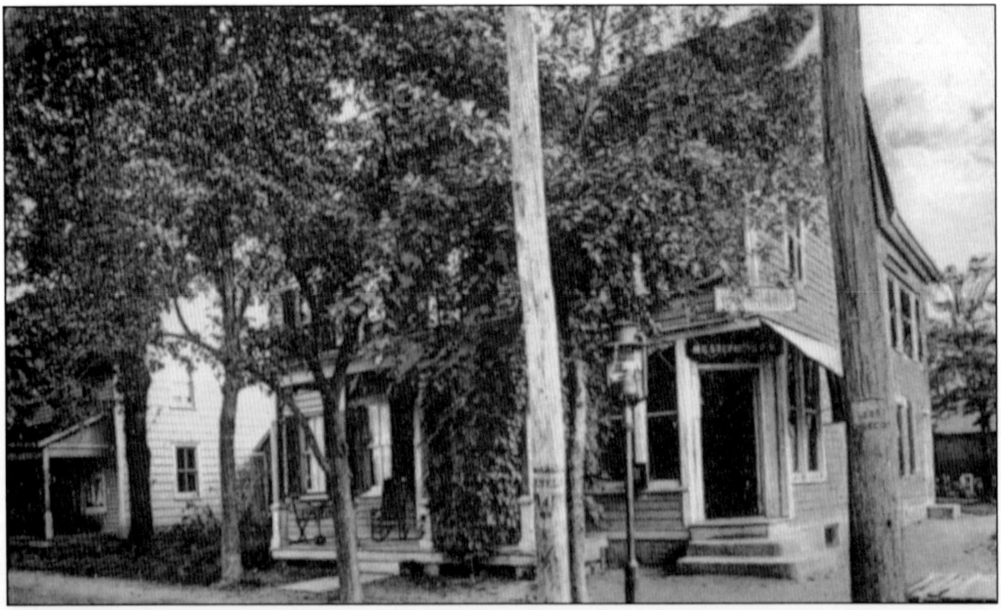

This building housed the Gardiner post office *c.* 1910. It was on the south side of Main Street just east of the Gardiner Hotel, on the corner of what has become Arch Street. As the sign over the door indicates, Dr. M.E. Stephens, a physician, was postmaster. He served from 1899 to 1915. Later, this building housed Cooper's meat market. By the 1950s, it was rented out as apartments, as it still is today. (Courtesy of Daryl P. Carr.)

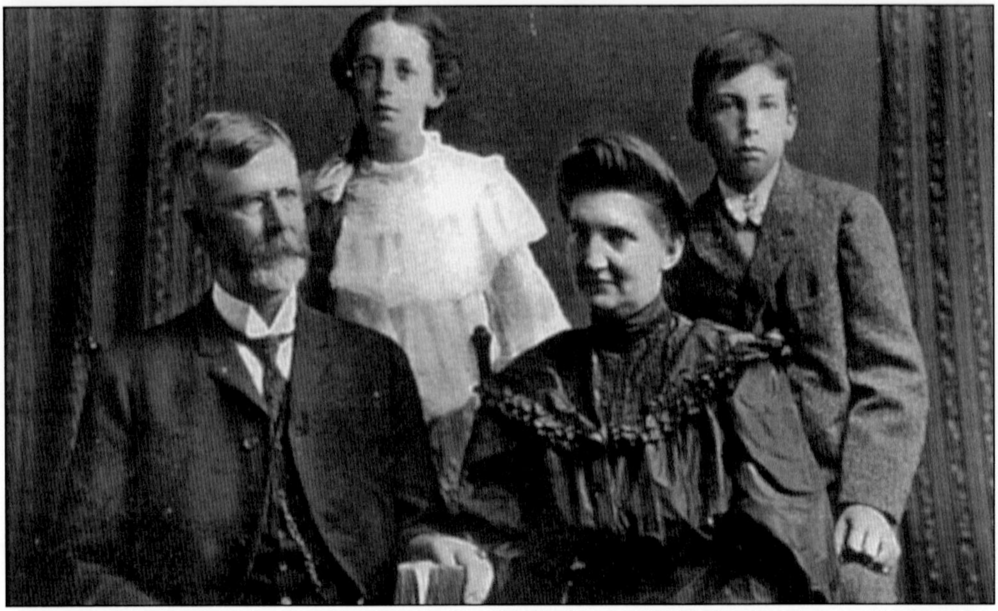

Dr. Myron E. Stephens is shown in 1904 with his wife, Mary LeFevre Stephens, who grew up in Gardiner, his daughter, Lucille, and his son, Homer. Mary Stephens became the organist of the Gardiner Reformed Church and an advocate of women's suffrage. In 1918, during the wartime flu epidemic, Stephens became exhausted caring for flu patients, caught the flu, and died. Homer Stephens became a physician in Walden, and Lucille Stephens became a teacher in Poughkeepsie. (Courtesy of Haviland-Heidgard Historical Collection.)

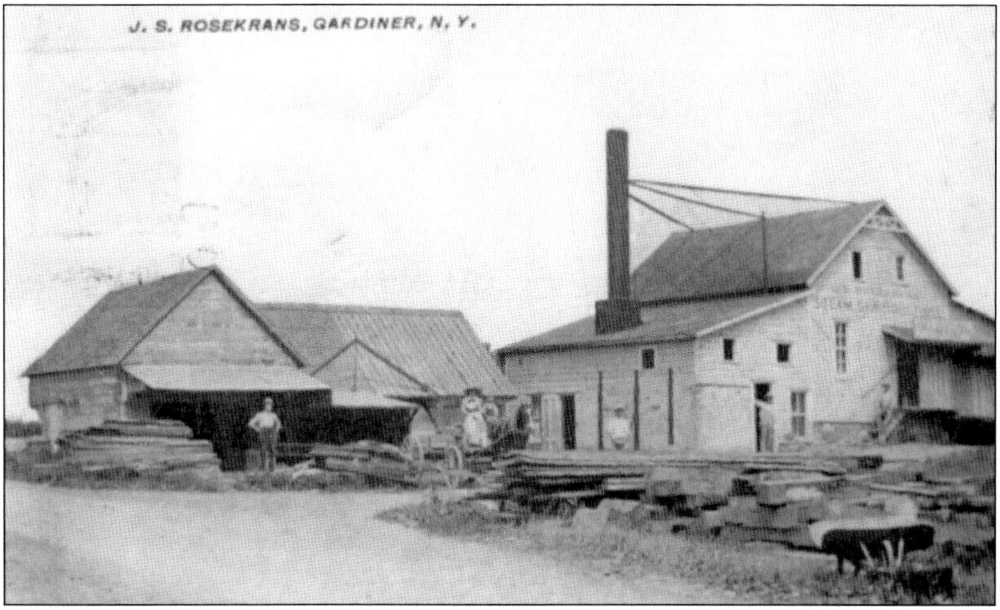

J.S. Rosekrans's steam-operated sawmill was located along the Wallkill Railroad tracks near the center of the Gardiner hamlet, one of several sawmills in the town of Gardiner at the time. Rosekrans, himself, wrote on this postcard, dated July 26, 1915, indicating that he dealt not only in lumber but also in apples: "I need couple cars cider apples this week. Can you help me out. Price 25 cts. per 100 lbs. Tell your neighbors." (Courtesy of William and Carol Majestic Lohrman.)

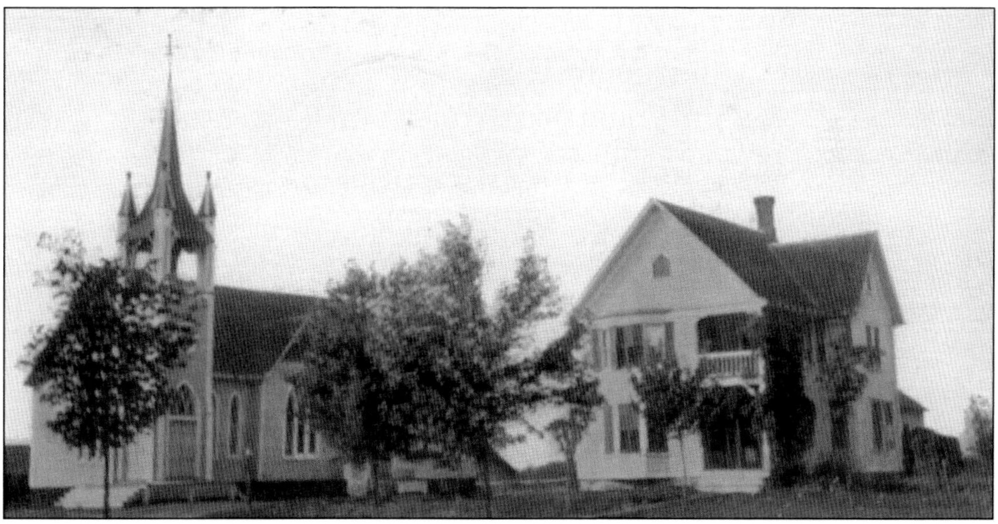

The Gardiner Reformed Church originated as an offshoot of the Guilford Reformed Church. The Guilford pastor first held Sunday school in the Gardiner hamlet, which led to the organizing of the church in 1890. This church, unlike older Reformed churches of the area, never had "Dutch" in its title, which according to its current pastor, was a reflection of the population's increasing ethnic mix by the time of its founding. The church was built in 1892–1893 on land donated by Floyd S. McKinstry, president of the Wallkill Valley Railroad. The accompanying parsonage was built in 1896. This postcard is postmarked 1918. (Courtesy of Daryl P. Carr.)

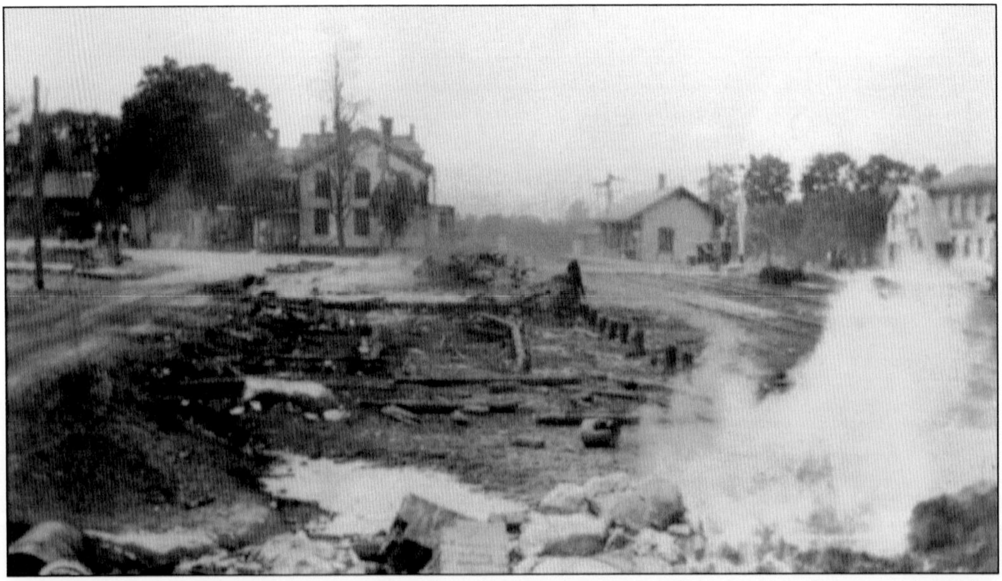

A devastating fire struck the Gardiner hamlet on May 21, 1925. In the foreground of this photograph, taken when the fire was still smoldering, were the remains of a funeral parlor, an icehouse, a feed store, and the Rosekrans sawmill. In the background are the Gardiner railroad station (right of center) and the Gardiner Hotel (left of center), which were hosed with water and covered with wet blankets to keep them from catching fire. (Courtesy of the Gardiner Library.)

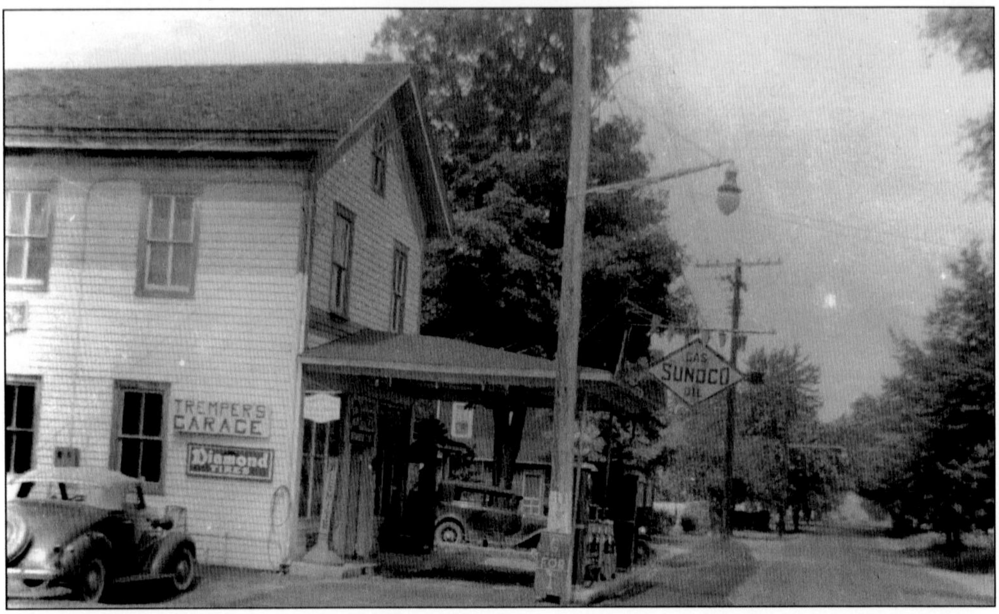

Bob Tremper's Garage, on the south side of Main Street just west of the Gardiner railroad station, was photographed by Harold Marks c. 1937, when he worked there. The car parked at the left was his Chevrolet. He sold gas there at six gallons per dollar, as the sign on the pole indicates. Earlier, the building had housed an Odd Fellows Hall, which sometimes showed movies, including early crude attempts at talkies, with a phonograph playing the sound. By the 1950s, the building had become John Grey's garage. (Courtesy of the Gardiner Library.)

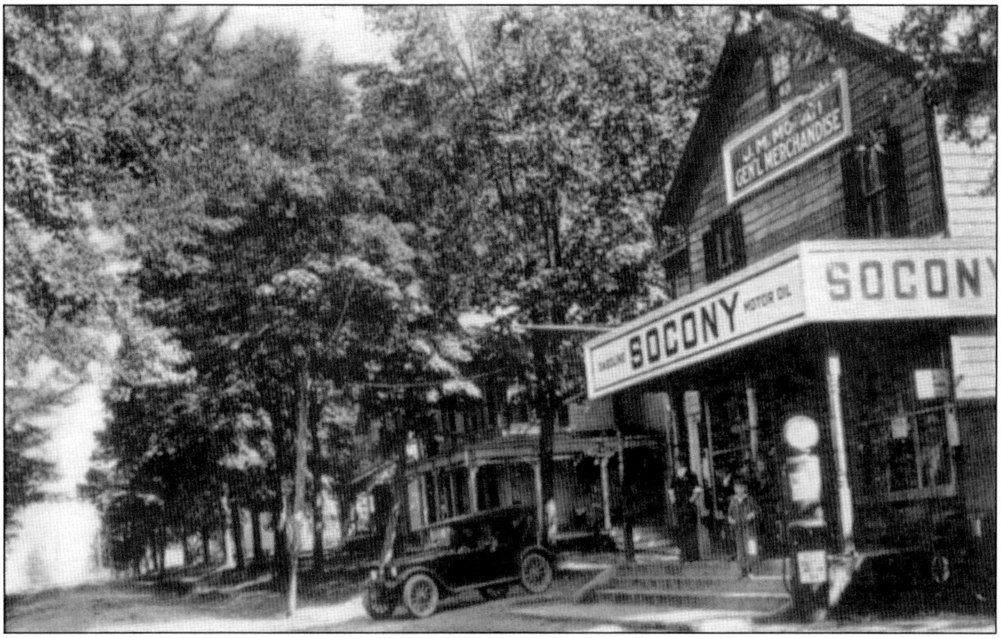

Moran's General Merchandise was located at the junction of Main and First Streets. In its early years, it customarily brought in supplies either by the Wallkill Valley Railroad or by wagon from wholesalers on Liberty Street in Newburgh. In business for over 50 years, the store operated on two floors, offering a wide range of foods and goods, a warm wood stove, and the chance to catch up on the news. After Moran died in 1956, his family tried to continue operating the store, but under pressure from supermarket competition, it closed in 1958. (Courtesy of Betty Moran.)

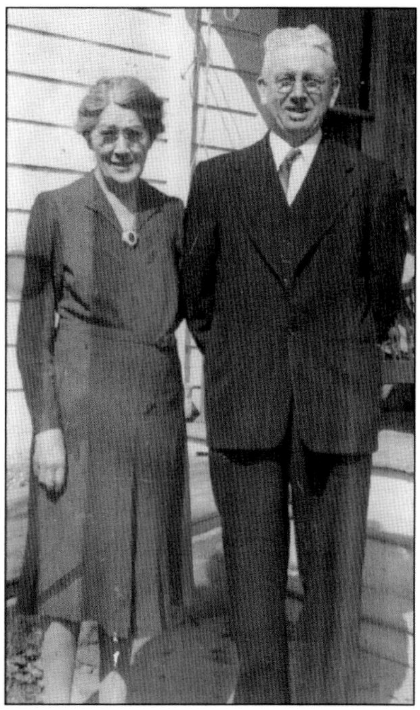

An authoritative figure in Gardiner, John M. Moran stands with his wife, Anna D. Moran. The photograph dates from *c.* the 1940s. Of Irish descent, Moran started out at about 15 years of age working at the general store in the center of the hamlet and eventually became its proprietor. In his store he dispensed advice at the same time that he sold almost everything, from groceries to shoes, hardware, stationery, thread, and candy. In addition to operating the store, he served as town clerk from 1941 to 1956. (Courtesy of Betty Moran.)

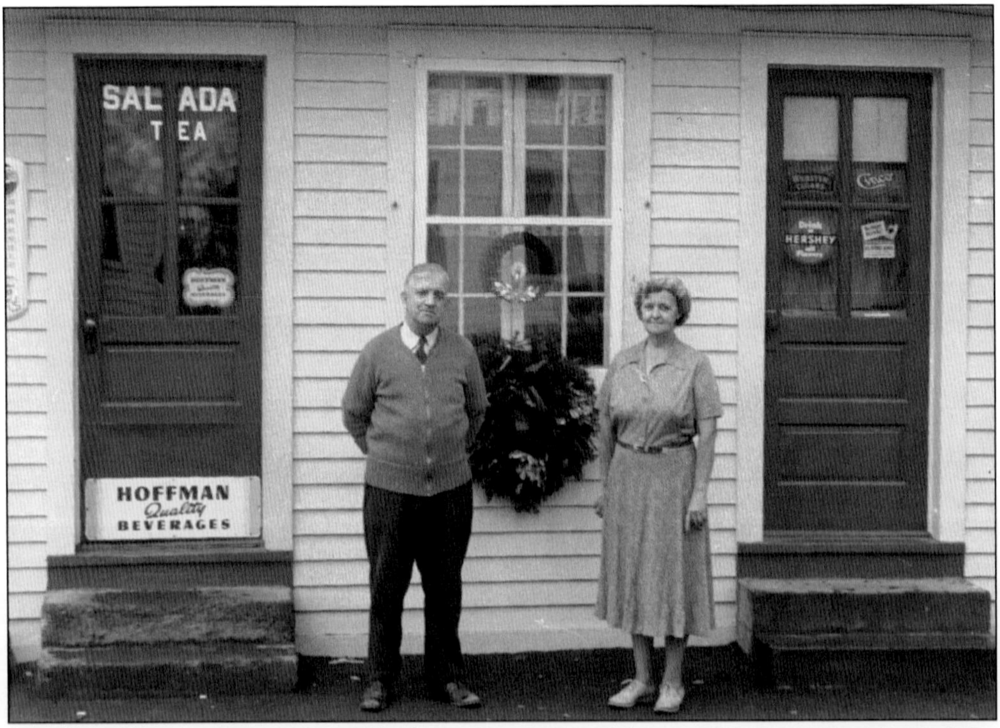

Floyd McKinstry and his wife, Mildred, stand in front of this general store, which included a popular ice-cream parlor, on the north side of Main Street. Shown in the 1950s, McKinstry was the nephew of the Floyd McKinstry, president of the Wallkill Railroad. In 1967, the Robert Gibneys bought it from the McKinstrys and turned it into both a residence for themselves and an antique shop. Still an antique shop, it is now operated by Paul and Mary Ann Osgood. (Courtesy of Gardiner Town Hall.)

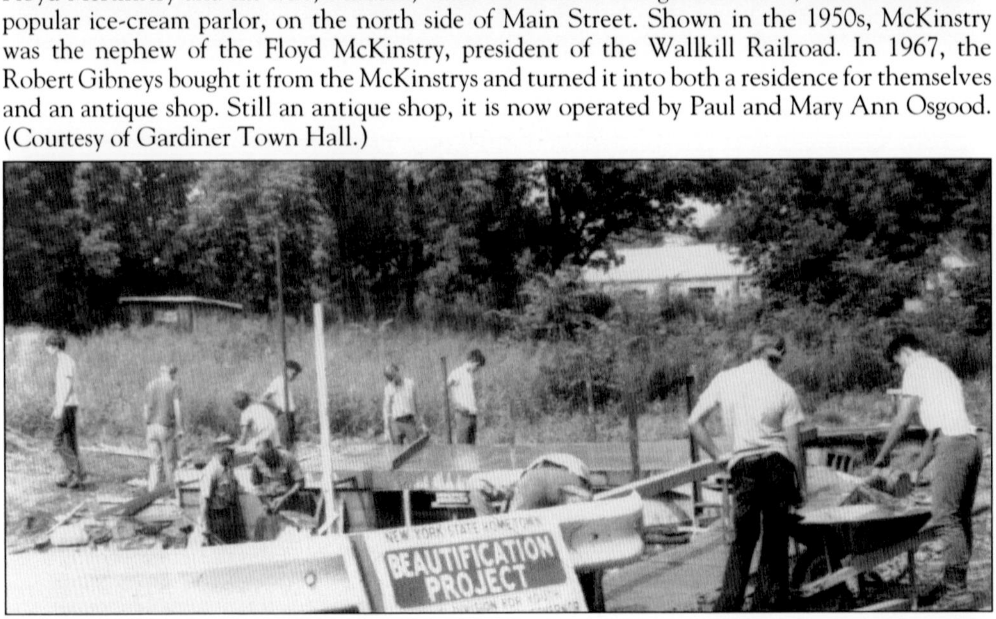

In 1970, Supervisor George Majestic organized a beautification project, funded in part by the state, to employ town youth. Under the supervision of Leo Clinton, town highway superintendent, the young people rebuilt a culvert for a stream to pass under Sand Hill Road near Farmer's Turnpike. Among the youths participating were those from the Baker, Keeping, Lawson, Marks, and Roberts families. The town garage is visible in the background to the right of center. (Courtesy of William and Carol Majestic Lohrman.)

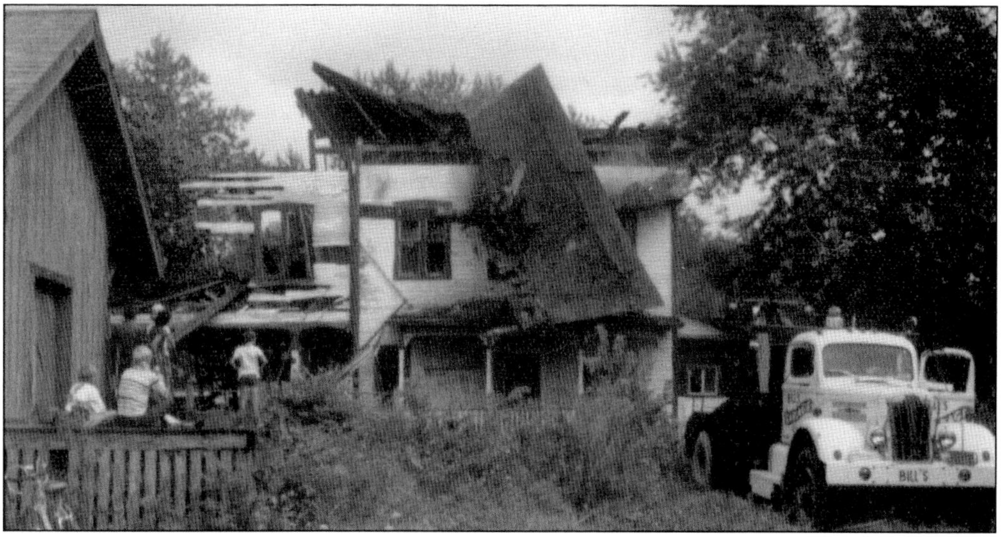

The demolition of the Gardiner Hotel was begun in August 1974 by the Conner brothers, Tom and Bill, the latter being the Bill of Bill's Garage, whose wrecking truck is shown (right). The Gardiner station is also depicted (left). In previous years the hotel had been known for its dances, movies, 10-cent beer, and as a meeting place for the Odd Fellows, the Dairymen's League, and the Gardiner Fire Department's Ladies Auxiliary. Among the more recent operators of the hotel were Thomas Moran (brother of John M. Moran) in the 1930s and early 1940s, Richard or Helen Clinton from 1946 to c. 1971, John Koroky, and Willie Majestic and John Wagner, who arranged its demolition. A pizza restaurant building now stands on the site. (Photograph by Kathleen R. Conner.)

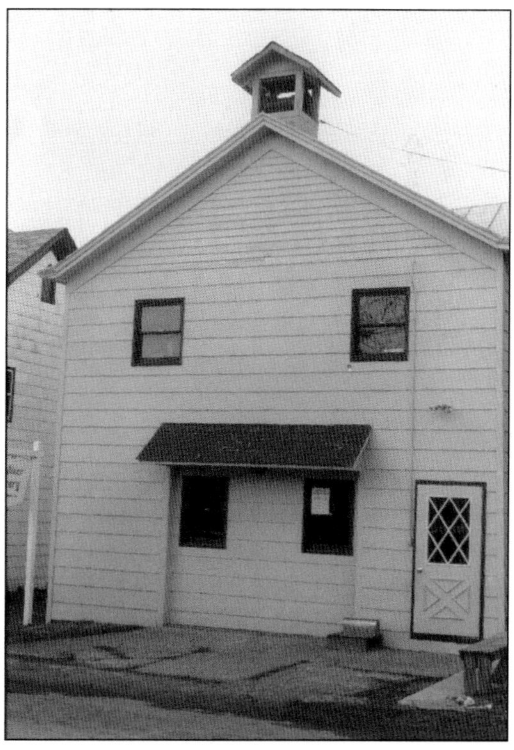

Built in 1909 as the Gardiner Fire House, this structure is located on Station Square opposite the railroad station. Betty Moran recalls that when she was growing up nearby in the 1930s, to learn how the world worked she used to go upstairs to attend the town justice's court. In 1977, after a larger firehouse had been built, the town made this building available to the Gardiner Library. Today, the library, like the earlier fire company, finds the building too small. This photograph was taken in the 1990s. (Courtesy of the Gardiner Library.)

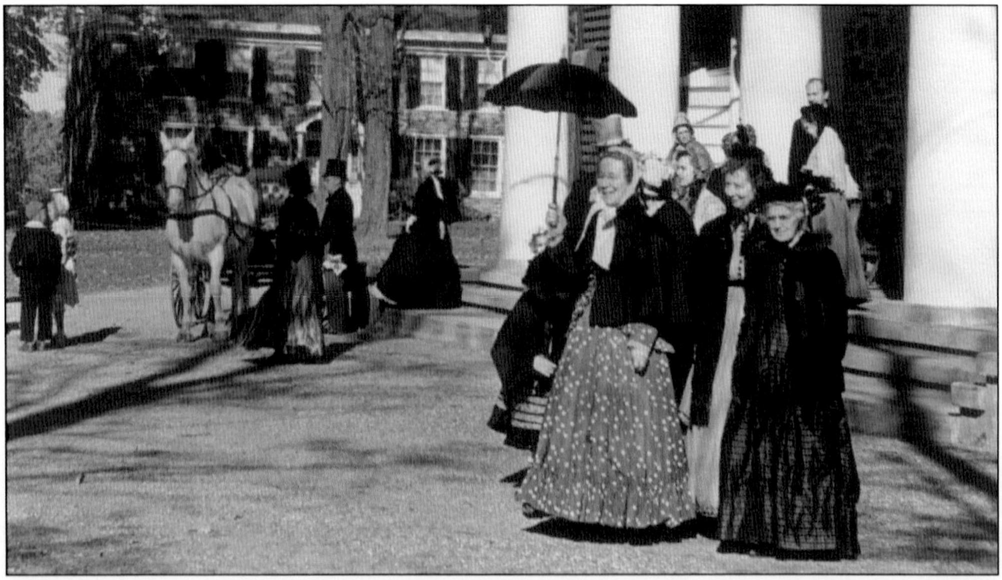

In this 1955 photograph, the Shawangunk Reformed Dutch Church is celebrating the 200th anniversary of its construction, using old costumes and old carriages. Among the costumed children is Kathy Messerschmitt of Albany Post Road in Gardiner. The church is located in Bruynswick in the town of Shawangunk close to the Gardiner border, and it serves people of both towns. The parsonage is visible in the background. (Photograph by Erma DeWitt, courtesy of Haviland-Heidgard Historical Collection.)

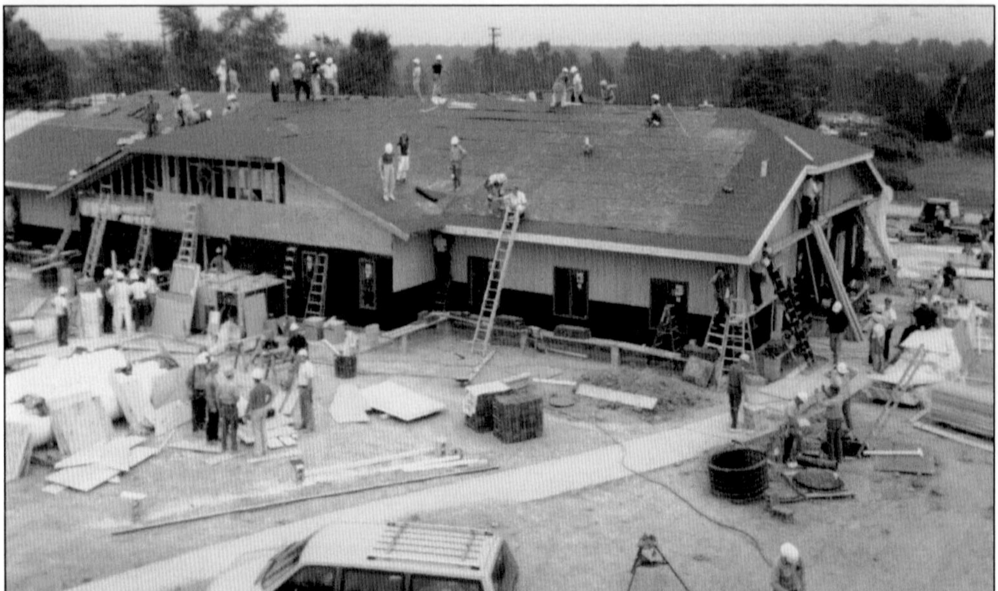

Construction began on a new Jehovah's Witness church in 1996 in Bruynswick over Gardiner's boundary line in the town of Shawangunk on what used to be the Sunny Croft dude ranch. As is customary in building Jehovah's Witness churches, volunteers supplied the labor, coming from as far away as Albany. They included both skilled and unskilled workers, men and women. Within a few years, Jehovah's Witnesses have constructed other new churches in the region, as in Lloyd, New Paltz, and Newburgh. (Photograph by Bob Fisher.)

Laura Dubois of Gardiner and Ellsworth M. Buchanan of Little Britain, in Orange County, pose for their wedding picture. This photograph was taken on January 31, 1906. Ellsworth Buchanan eventually settled on his wife's family farm, located on the edge of Forest Glen near the Wallkill River across from Libertyville, and became a dairy farmer. He shipped out his milk on the Wallkill Valley Railroad, through the Gardiner Creamery in the Gardiner hamlet. (Courtesy of their son, Ralph Buchanan.)

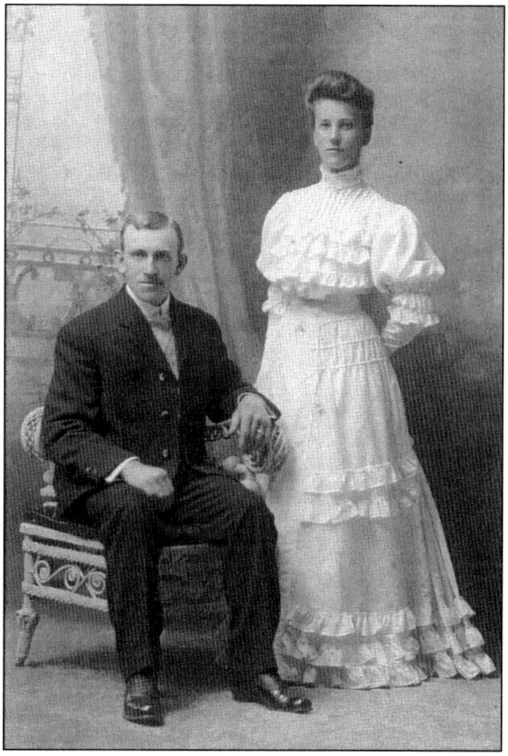

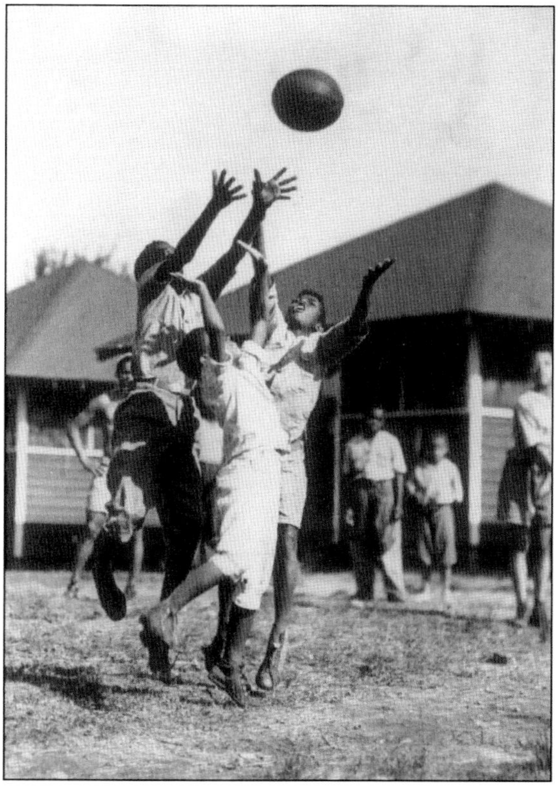

A game was underway at Camp Wallkill, a summer camp operated by the Children's Aid Society. The camp was located on a 444-acre site in Gardiner's Guilford neighborhood, the site of a previous camp operated by St. Phillips Episcopal Church of Harlem. It operated on both sides of Albany Post Road near the Wallkill River from c. 1936 to 1968. Facilities included a crafts building, an Olympic-size swimming pool, overnight camping sites, a dairy farm, and nature trails. The camp offered two or three week sessions for up to 700 children at a time, especially children from Harlem aged 4 to 14, and was run by a staff of 50. (Courtesy of the Children's Aid Society.)

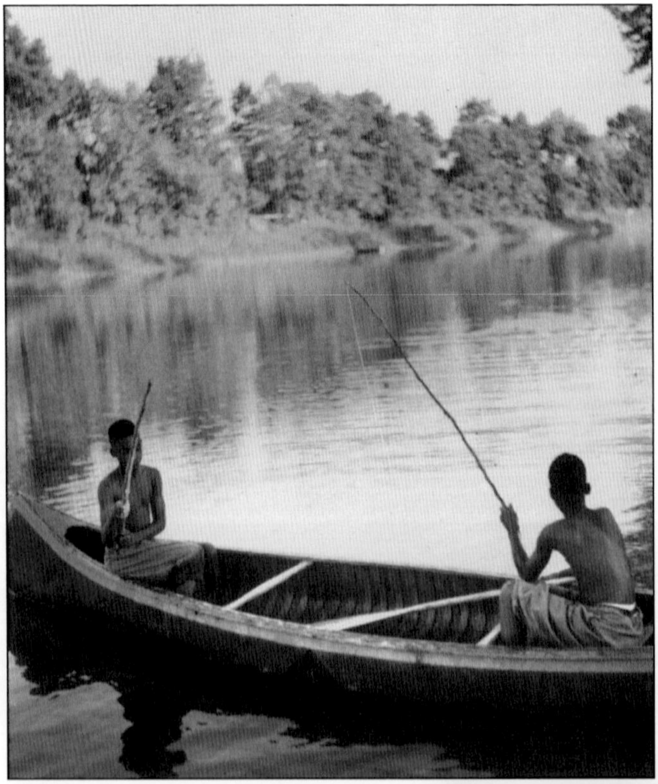

Two Camp Wallkill boys fish from a canoe on the Wallkill River. The camp director from 1940 to 1945 was Julius McLain, who eventually settled in Gardiner. The camp physician was a volunteer, Dr. Virgil DeWitt of Gardiner, who visited daily. Dr. George Bond of the State University of New York, New Paltz, ran a remedial reading program for the campers. One factor that led to the closing of the camp in 1968 was the difficulty of finding staff able to cope with the difficult behavior of the campers. After the camp closed, its pool was used by Gardiner for its recreation program, and some of the buildings and land became the Rivendell Winery. (Courtesy of the Children's Aid Society.)

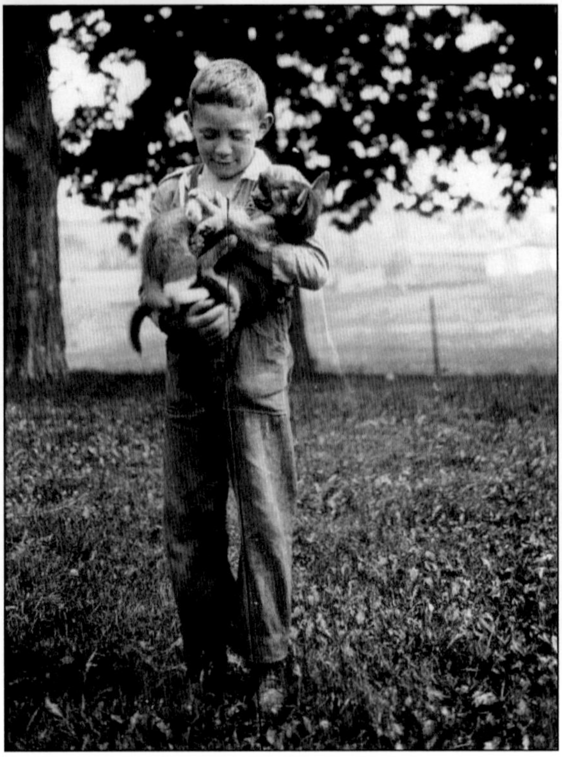

Kenneth E. Hasbrouck, the future historian, is shown here in the 1920s holding a puppy on his parents' farm, located on the western edge of Guilford near Trapps Mountain. He recalled having "stolen" carrots from the garden and climbing up on the coal house roof to eat them. He recalled that when he attended the one-room Guilford school, the teacher disciplined him by rapping his knuckles. He also remembered that blueberry pickers persisted in starting fires on Trapps Mountain to improve the blueberry crop, and the fires spread down the mountain, threatening the family farm. (Courtesy of Alice Hasbrouck.)

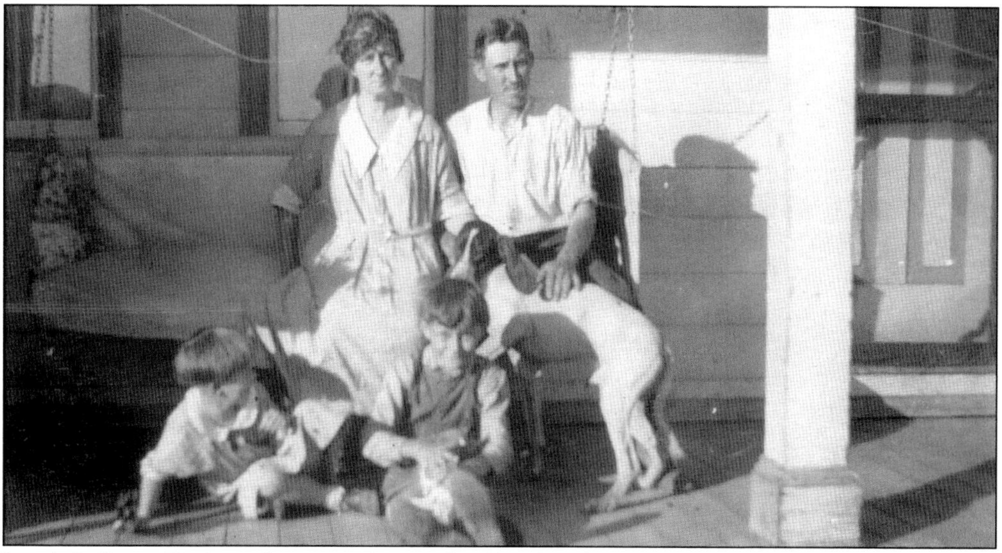

Josiah LeFevre Hasbrouck sits on the porch of his farmhouse on the edge of Guilford, with his wife, Agnes Riley; their son, the future historian Kenneth Hasbrouck (center); and his friend Mildred Radley (left). Josiah Hasbrouck took up farming here at the age of 23 in order to keep the farm in the family. (When Josiah's grandfather Daniel I. Hasbrouck operated the farm, he had supplied the Minnewaska hotels with milk.) A social young man who had attended Eastman Business College in Poughkeepsie, Josiah felt awkward at farming and lonely from living too far out in the woods. In 1927, about two years after this picture was taken, he sold the farm out of his family. (Courtesy of Alice Hasbrouck.)

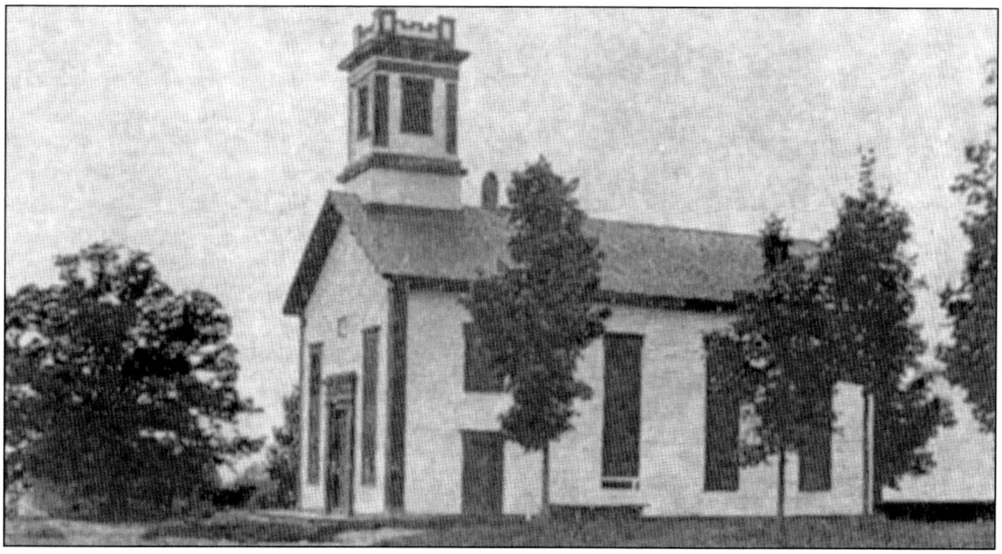

Built in 1833, the Guilford Dutch Reformed Church was the earliest church to be erected in what was to become the town of Gardiner. The builders were primarily descendants of the early Huguenot and Dutch settlers, who located their farms at the corner of the New Paltz–Tuthilltown Road and Guilford School House Road. In time, however, farming declined, Gardiner's population dropped, and a sister Reformed church was built in the Gardiner hamlet. When the Guilford church burned in 1908, it was not rebuilt.(From Kenneth Hasbrouck, *History of the Township of Gardiner*, 1953.)

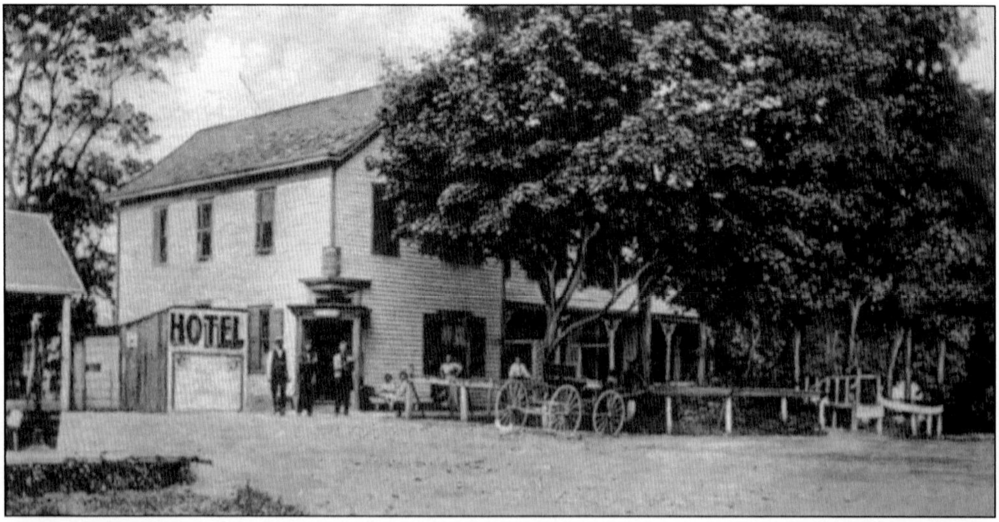

In the 1860s, James Clinton operated a hotel at Ireland Corners. At the time of this postcard, *c.* 1910, the Ireland Corners Hotel was still operated by the Clinton family. By the 1930s, the hotel provided a station for buses on their way from New Paltz to New York City. During the decades the hotel was operated by the Benson family, it catered to sportsmen and organizations planning special dinners. In 2002, after the hotel's longtime operator Paul Benson died, Paul Bart, the son of VirTis president Jerry Bart, bought it. He is continuing to operate its restaurant and considering reviving its function as an overnight hotel. (Courtesy of Shirley Anson.)

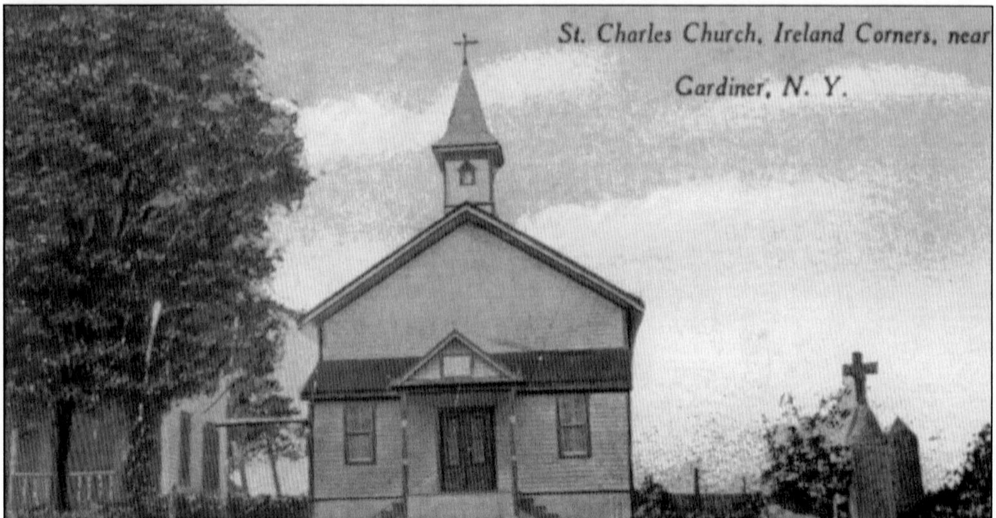

St. Charles Borromeo Roman Catholic Church, depicted here on a *c.* 1900 postcard, originated in the late 1860s in services held in James Clinton's barn, on the hill at the northeast corner of Ireland Corners. In 1882, some of the barn's lumber was used to construct the church just west of Ireland Corners on the road to the Gardiner hamlet, where it has remained. A cemetery was begun at once on the western side of the church, and in 1894, a rectory was built on its eastern side. In recent years the church has been enlarged, its cemetery has been expanded to reach across the road, and a large church hall has been built beside it. (Courtesy of William and Carol Majestic Lohrman.)

The stone house shown in this 1980 photograph was built *c.* 1745 just north of what was later to be called Ireland Corners. It was occupied from 1763 by the Huguenot Daniel Deyo and then by generations of Deyos. By the 1960s, the house had deteriorated. By 1980, two brothers, Charles and Frank Majestic, were reconstructing it from the cellar up, using the original stone and doing much of the work themselves. Here they are restoring a door and windows that face west toward woods where generations of Deyos are buried in a family cemetery. (Photograph by William B. Rhoads.)

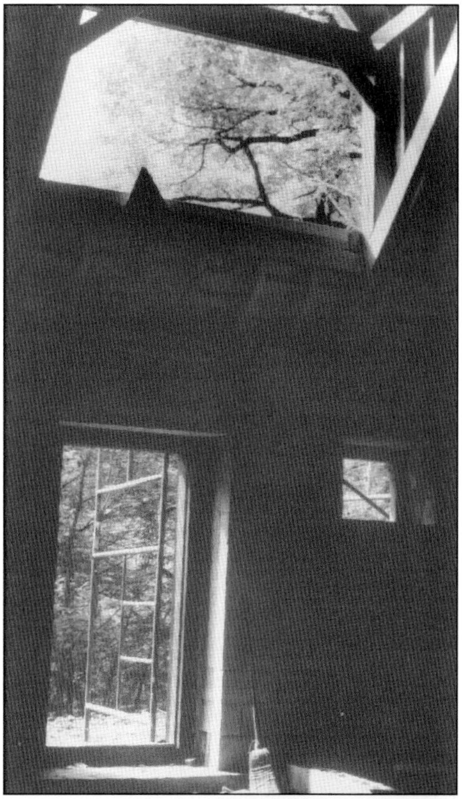

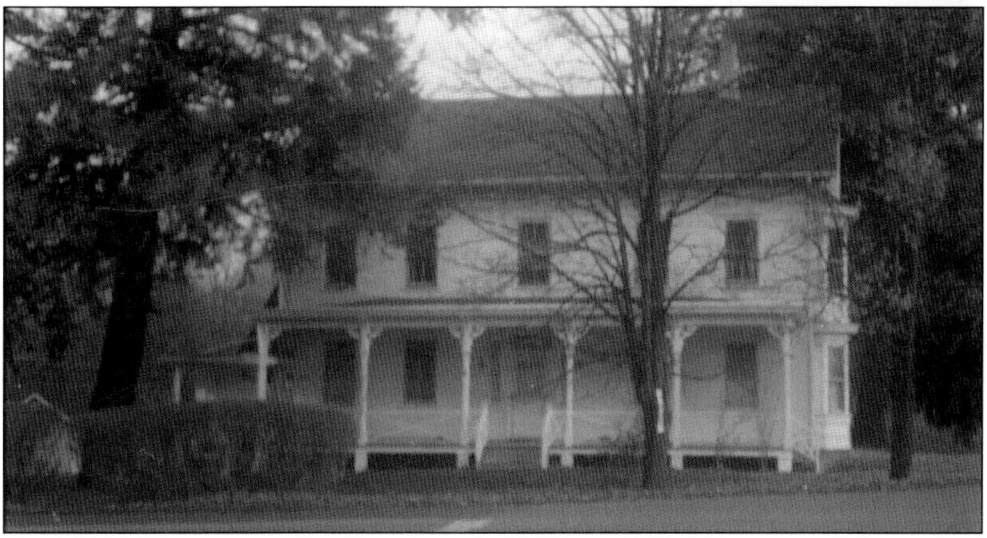

Dr. Abraham Deyo's farmhouse, on the northwest corner of Ireland Corners, was built *c.* 1840. He was a grandson of Daniel Deyo, who settled in the stone house just to the north. Abraham Deyo practiced medicine from 1851 to 1871 and then devoted himself to farming. By 1881, he had acquired several farms and was shipping milk by wagon to the Borden condensery and fruit by rail from the Gardiner station. By the 1990s, the house was owned by Michael Clinton, of the Clinton family long associated with Ireland Corners, and rented out as apartments. (Courtesy of Haviland-Heidgard Historical Collection.)

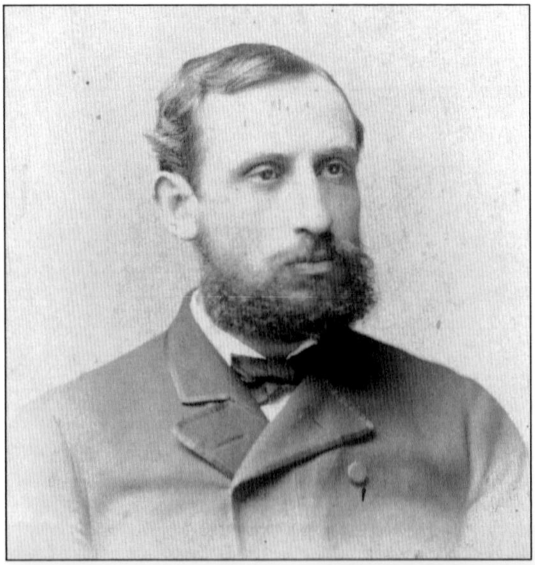

Solomon LeFevre Deyo grew up in the farmhouse built by his grandfather Nathaniel Deyo on the Ireland Corners–Modena road. He attended Kettleborough School and graduated from Union College as a civil engineer. After directing construction for various railroads, he became the chief engineer for building New York City's first subway system, the Interborough, in 1900. After the subway opened in 1904, he remained its chief engineer. He retained ties to his family's Gardiner farm, which was operated by his brother, Gardiner Supervisor A.L.F. Deyo. Solomon infused funds into the farm and kept a pony there for his daughter. (Courtesy of A.L.F. Deyo's grandson John K. Jacobs.)

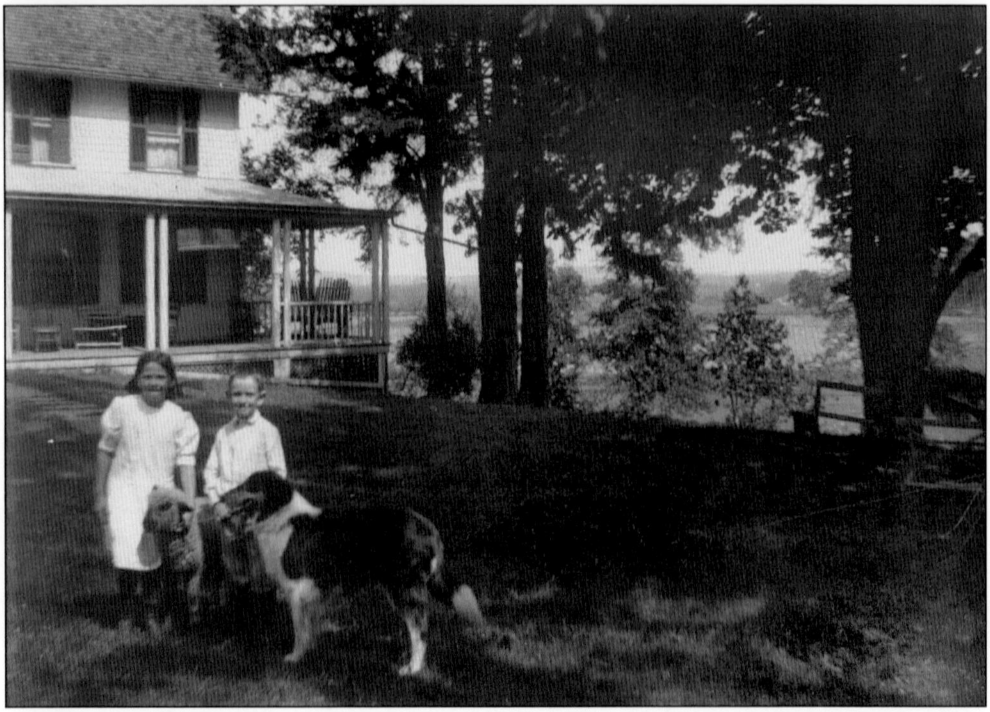

Dorothy and Andrew Deyo stand in front of the house of their grandfather A.L.F. Deyo, Gardiner supervisor. Their father, Joseph Deyo, grew up in this house, located on the Ireland Corners–Modena road. The two children grew up in the next house to the west, which was built for their father and is now the office of Foster and Schmalkuche, accountants. Joseph Deyo became a Gardiner justice and assisted his father on the family farm. Andrew Deyo also worked on the farm; eventually, however, he abandoned farming and became a county welfare agent. The house, shown *c.* 1912, was occupied continuously by Deyos until 1965, by which time the family had sold off the farmland and sold the house to the Mabees. (Courtesy of John K. Jacobs.)

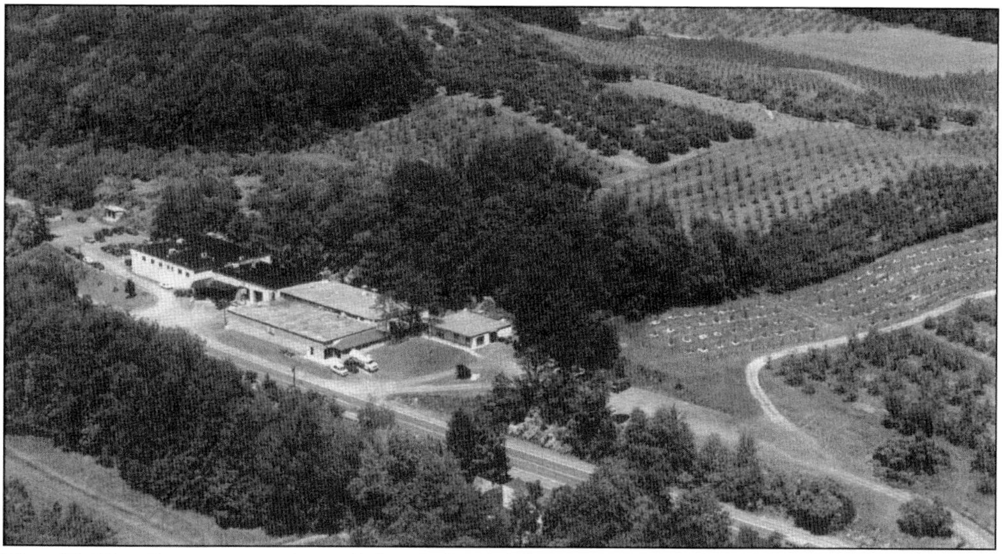

The VirTis Company makes of biomedical laboratory research equipment for hospitals, universities, and pharmaceutical manufacturers. VirTis was founded in 1953 as a part-time enterprise in a basement in Yonkers. In 1955, it became full-time. In 1957, it moved to Gardiner. There, it took over and later enlarged an abandoned International Harvester sales building on Route 208, about two miles south of Ireland Corners. This photograph, taken in 1995, shows the VirTis plant, with a portion of the Wright orchard behind it. (Courtesy of VirTis Company.)

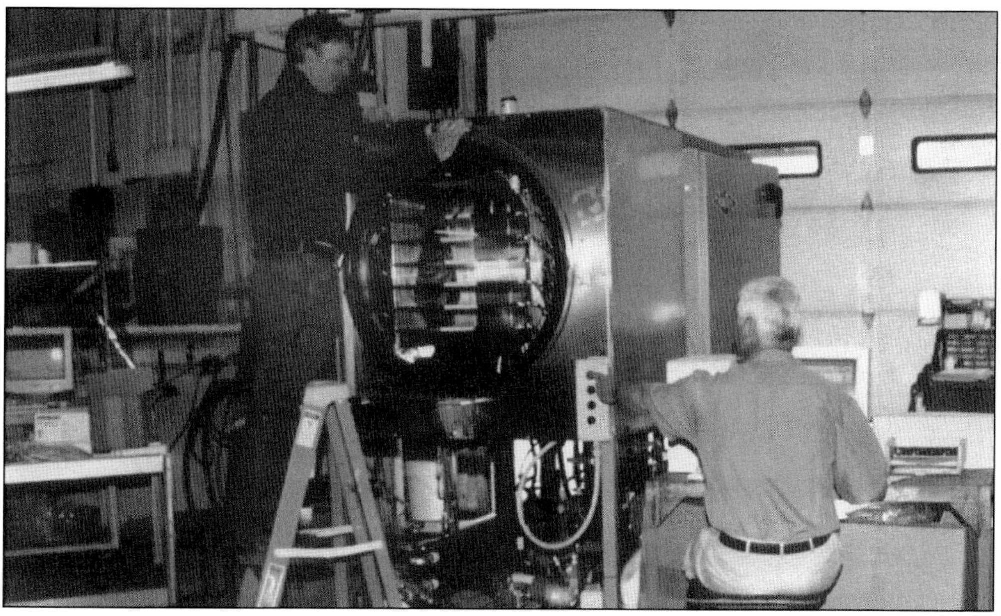

At the VirTis plant, refrigeration technician John Winters and vice president for marketing Ken Tenedini work on equipment the company produces. The company name is a contraction of "viruses" and "tissue," the materials its equipment often handles. The company has approximately 85 employees. Its president is Siegfried "Jerry" Bart, an engineering graduate of Rensselaer Polytechnic Institute, who has been with VirTis since 1967. This photograph was taken in 2001. (Courtesy of VirTis Company.)

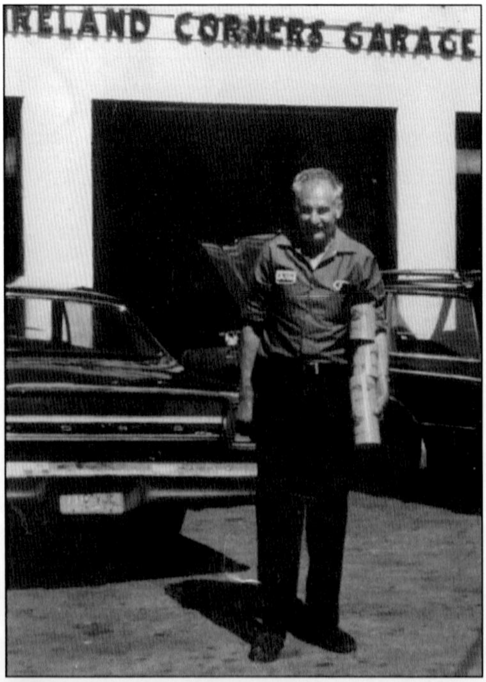

Jacob Honold balances cans of motor oil in front of his Ireland Corners Garage on the west side of Route 208, in this c. 1980 photograph. With his wife, Annette Schiro Honold of Louisiana, he raised three children, William, Caroline, and Jacob "Jay" Jr. Jay Honold followed his father in operating the garage, relocating it to the east side of Route 208. In 2000, he relocated it again, this time directly on the corner of Ireland Corners, and in the process upgraded it into a magnificent building, a palace. (Courtesy of Jay Honold.)

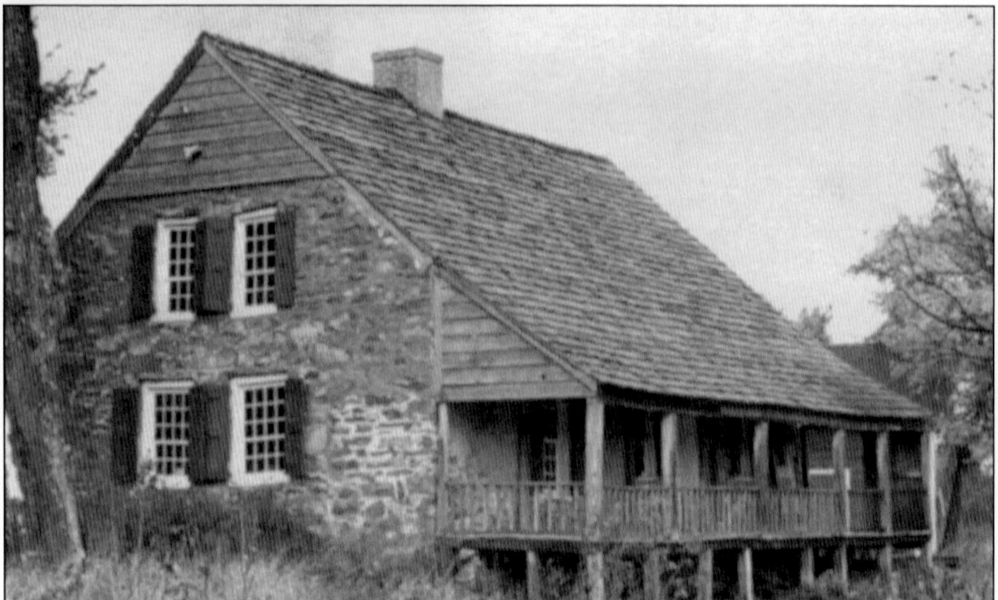

Built in 1738, this stone house, is understood to be the oldest existing house in Gardiner. Located on Route 32 near Jenkinstown, it overlooks Plattekill Creek. It was built by Dutch settler Evert Terwilliger and his wife, French Huguenot Sarah Freer Terwilliger. In the 1790s, when the Terwilligers were financially pinched, the house was bought by Congressman Josiah Hasbrouck to live in while he built an imposing mansion next door. Afterward, the house served the Hasbroucks as a tenant house. Since 1958, the Huguenot Historical Society has preserved both the imposing mansion and the modest tenant house beside it. (Courtesy of Haviland-Heidgard Historical Collection.)

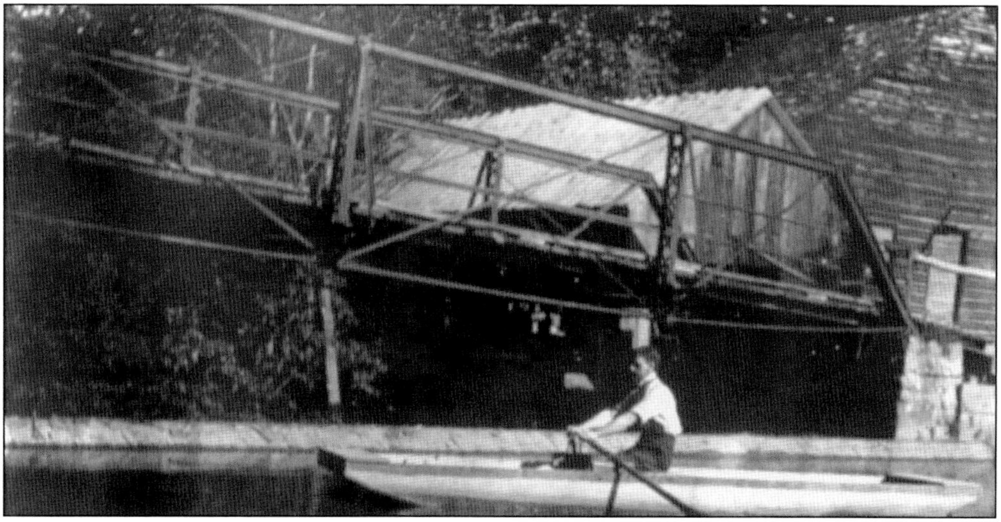

From c. 1798 to 1925, the Jenkins family, of English origin, operated grist and saw mills in Jenkinstown, a hamlet named after them. The mills were on Plattekill Creek. They were small, and the Jenkinses employed only two or three men to run them. This photograph, taken c. 1900 looking north, shows the mill buildings, the wooden milldam, possibly Lambert Jenkins rowing on the mill pond, and an iron bridge that carried a road running from Jenkinstown Road northeast to Dubois Road. In 1925, a heavy storm washed out both the bridge and the dam, emptying the pond and stopping the mills. The town replaced the bridge. The need for the mills having declined, the Jenkins family did not replace the dam. The town demolished the bridge and abandoned the road c. 1970. (Courtesy of Gladys P. DuBois.)

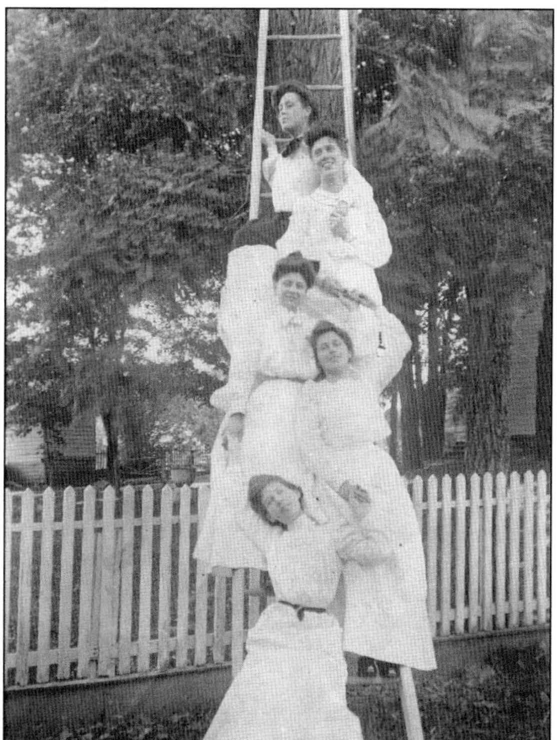

The Jenkins sisters pose teasingly on a ladder, probably in the 1890s. The daughters of Johannes Jenkins, they lived on Jenkinstown Road on the family farm, located near the family mills. The sisters were Emert, Georgia, Margaret, Rachel, and Rita. From c. 1900 to 1910, Rachel Jenkins taught at the nearby Kettleborough School, driving there by horse and wagon. According to family tradition, she did not like teaching. Boys annoyed her by being absent too often, saying they were needed for farm work. She quit. (Courtesy of Gladys P. DuBois.)

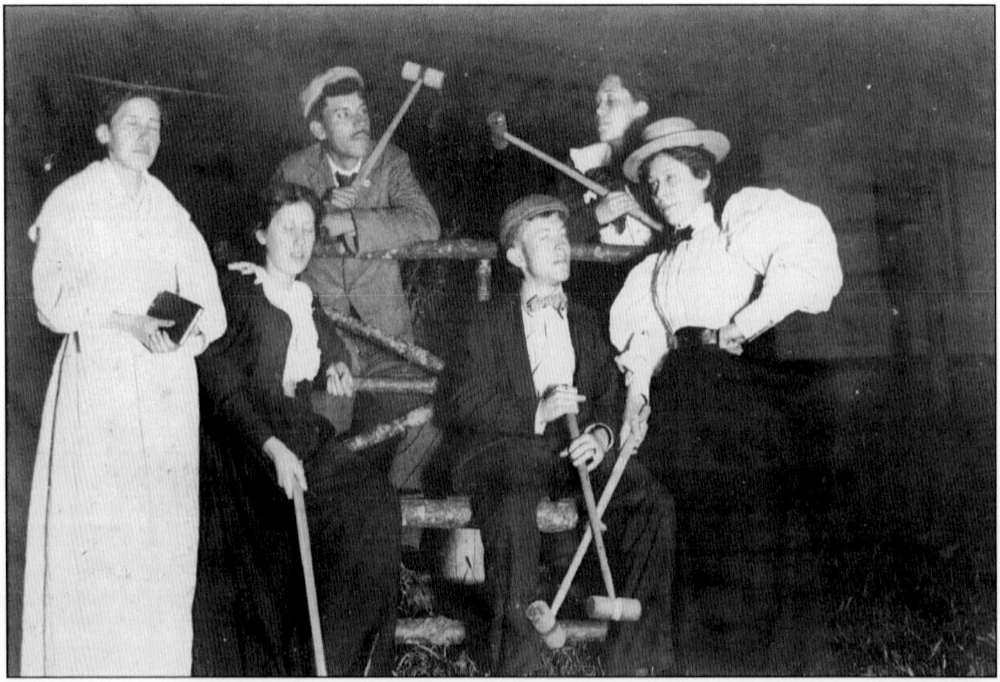

A Johannes Jenkins family group clowns with croquet mallets, probably in the 1890s. Descendants of the Jenkins family believe that the two men in the photograph are the sons, James and Lambert Jenkins. James Jenkins attended Cornell University and became a lawyer and county judge, living in Kingston. Lambert Jenkins stayed home to run the family farm and mills. The mills are now gone, but the farm is still occupied by descendants of the Jenkins family. (Courtesy of Gladys P. DuBois.)

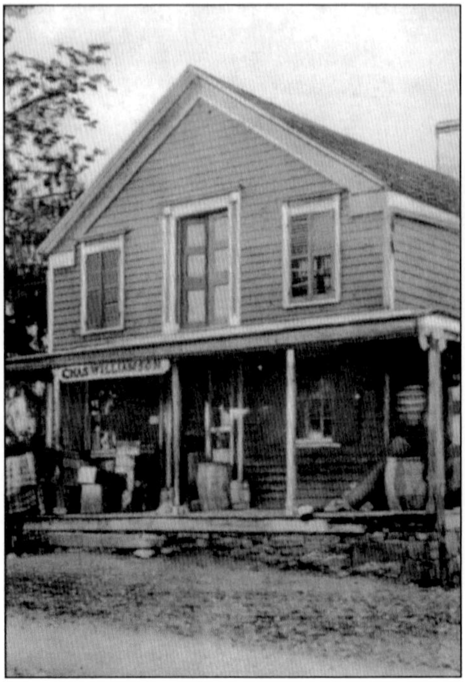

This general store was in Jenkinstown on the north side of Jenkinstown Road near the Jenkins sawmill and gristmill. In the 1890s and early 1900s, Charles Williamson, whose name appears on the store in the postcard reproduced here, was its proprietor and probably lived with his family in the building. When Betty Moran was growing up in the early 1920s in the Gardiner hamlet, she remembers being taken to the store to buy shoes. Afterwards, however, when the store was being operated by Howard and Otto Cashdollar, it attained a reputation for providing prostitutes, cockfighting, and illegal liquor (it was during Prohibition), and was raided by state troopers. (Courtesy of Gladys P. DuBois.)

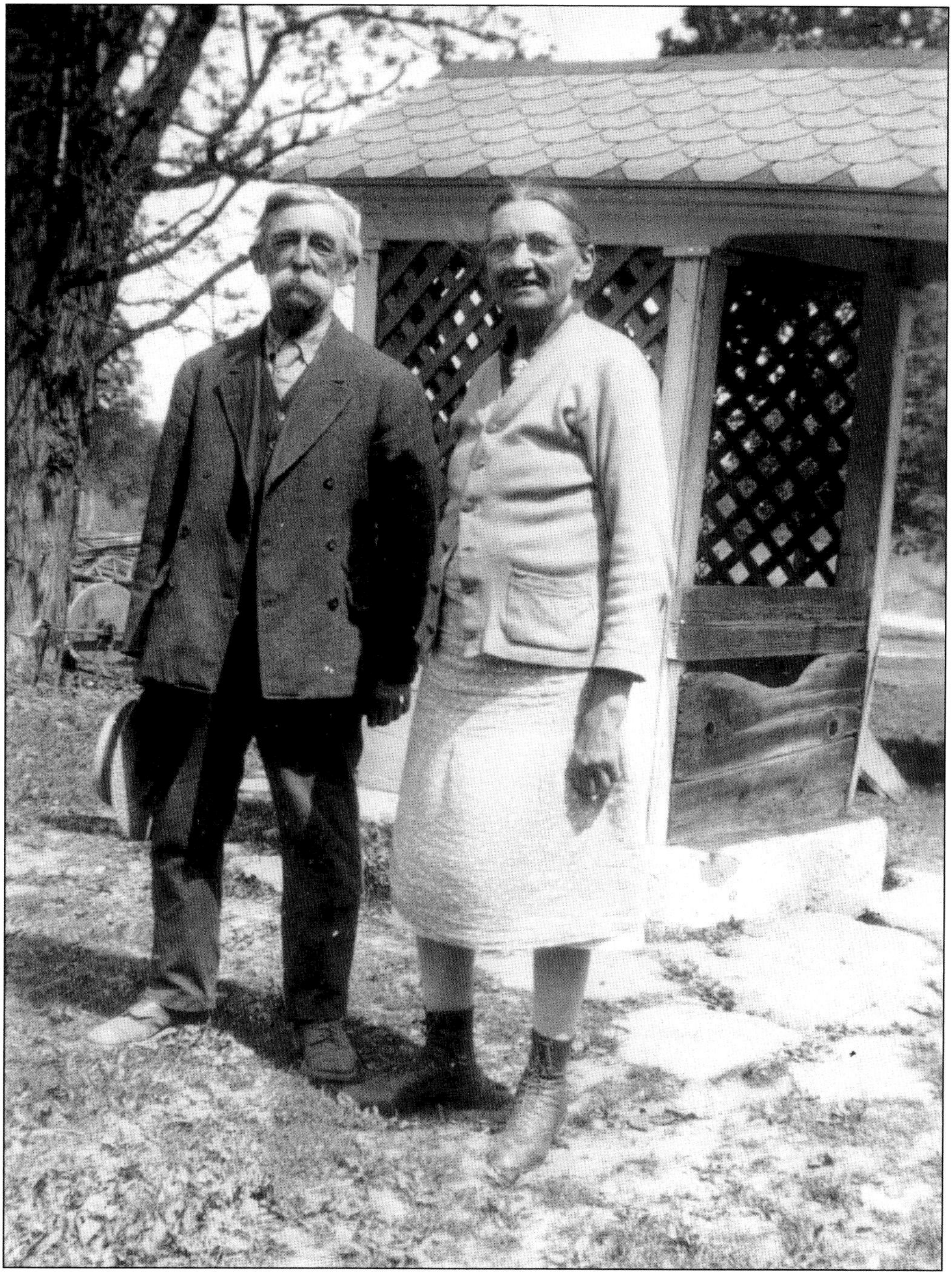

Johnston Hasbrouck and his wife, Sarah LeFevre Hasbrouck, stand by their farm's well house, in Kettleborough on Route 208. The neighboring one-room Kettleborough School, because it lacked a water supply of its own, sent children to this well house to fetch water. The house was originally built of stone in 1772 by John A. LeFevre, assisted by slaves who afterward lived in the cellar. As a descendant of the LeFevres, Sarah Hasbrouck, along with her husband, were given this house and farm when they were married in 1878. They spent most of their lives living there and farming its land. (Courtesy of Alice Hasbrouck.)

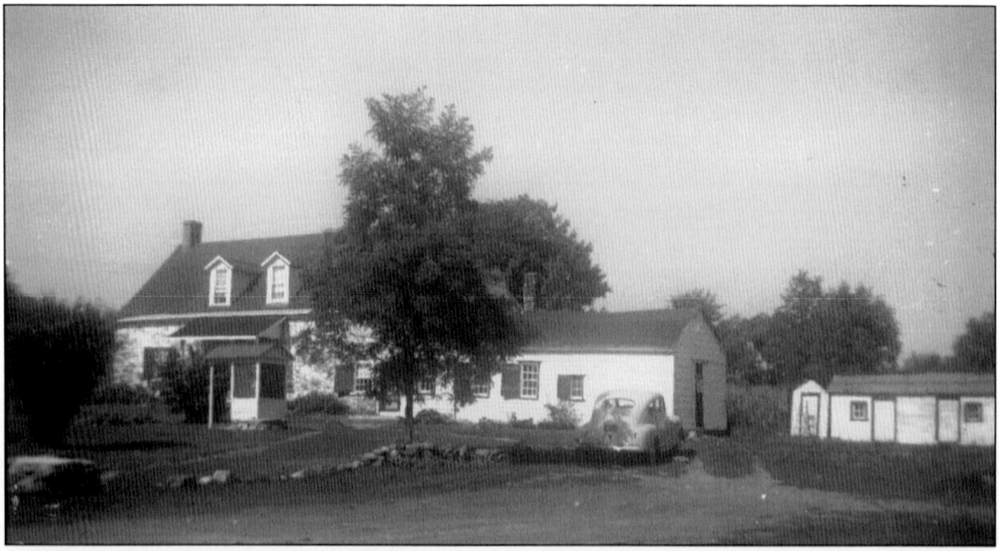

The house of Johnston and Sarah Hasbrouck, in Kettleborough, was occupied from 1948 by their grandson Kenneth E. Hasbrouck and his wife, Alice. Kenneth Hasbrouck, who was the Gardiner town historian and the head of the Huguenot Historical Society in New Paltz, enhanced its landscape. He preserved the old stone part of the house but tore down the deteriorating wooden addition, shown here in 1949, rebuilding it with a modern kitchen. He died in 1996. (Courtesy of Alice Hasbrouck.)

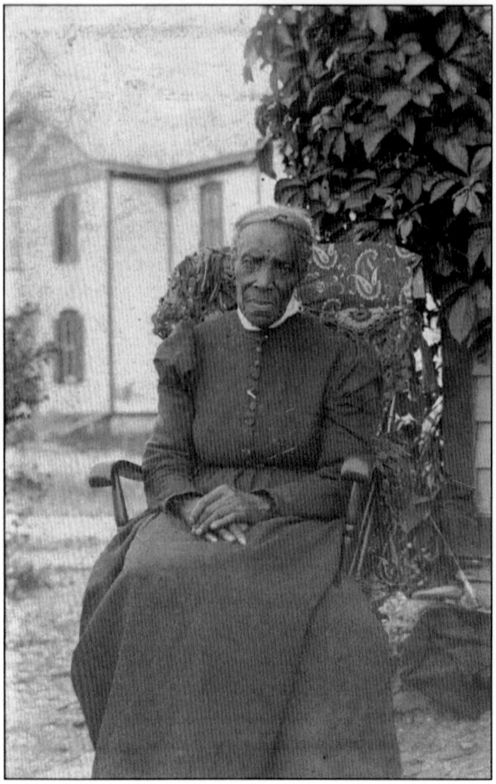

As a child, Judy Jackson lived as a slave on Libertyville Road in New Paltz, but as an adult she was given by Philip LeFevre of Kettleborough, to his son Andries P. LeFevre when the young man married. She remained a slave of the LeFevre family until 1827, when all slaves in the state were freed. Long known for her delight in singing religious songs, she died in New Paltz at the age of 98. While slavery was legal in the state of New York, it was common for substantial farm families in the region to have two or three slaves for such work as farming, cooking, and childcare. (Courtesy of John K. Jacobs.)

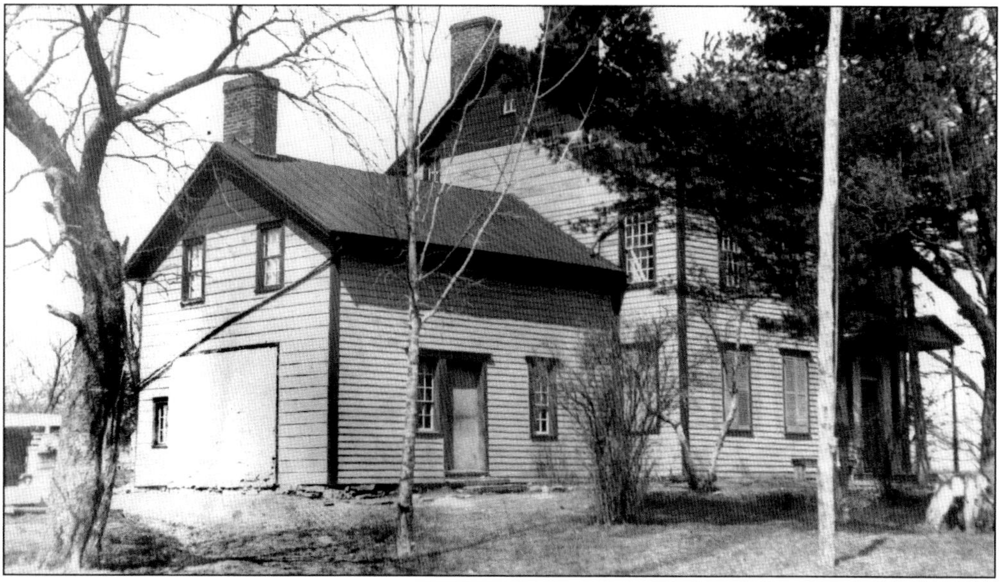

A Christian school for boys called the Industrial Colony was established in the 1890s at the John H. Wurts farm (now the Arthur McCord farm), shown here. It was situated in Kettleborough a mile north of Ireland Corners on the road to New Paltz. The school was for underprivileged boys from the "slums" of New York City and Brooklyn. According to the June 4, 1897 New Paltz *Independent*, the colony gave preference to boys who were "street Arabs" with "bad reputations." (Courtesy of Carol B. LeFevre.)

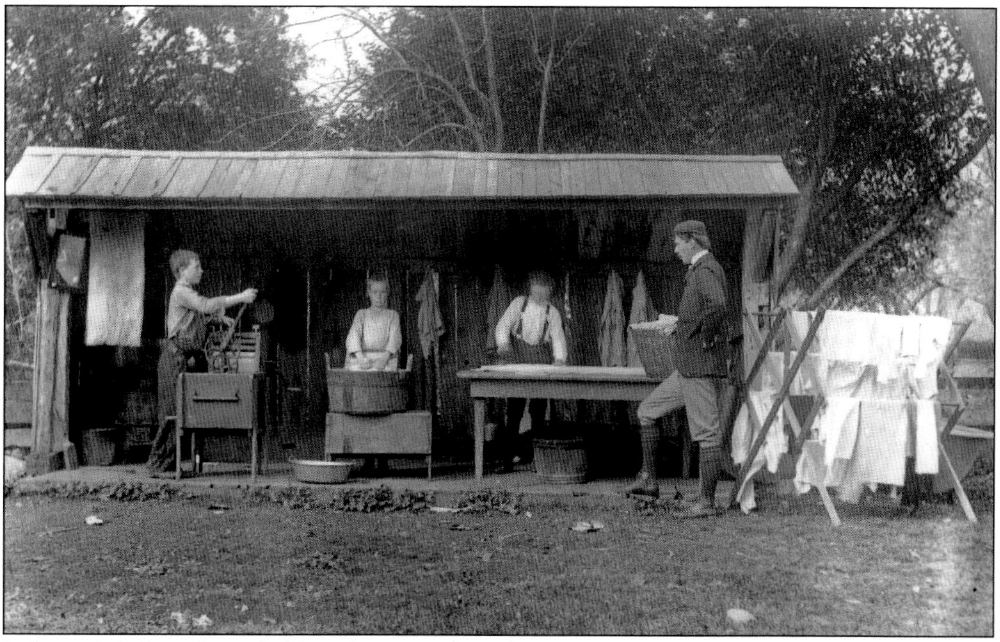

Industrial Colony boys did laundry. Social work theory at the time emphasized the value of learning practical "industrial" skills in a small "colony" setting rather than a large institutional one, preferably in the country rather than a city. The colony accepted no more than 30 boys at a time. It operated year-round in Gardiner from *c.* 1897 to 1900, supported by churches in both metropolitan New York and the Gardiner region. (Courtesy of Carol B. LeFevre.)

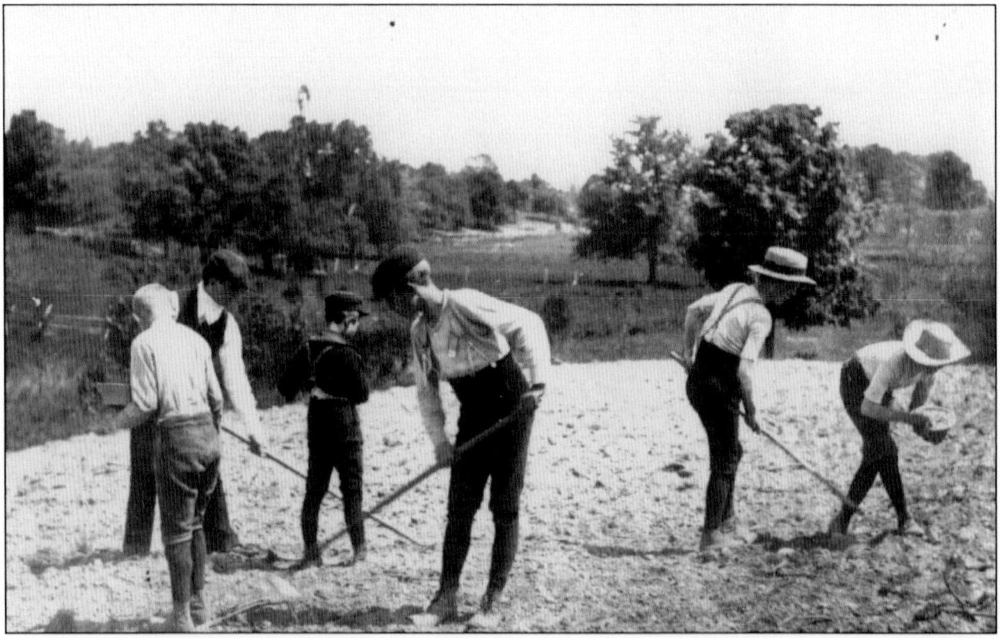

Colony boys planted corn by hand in a stony field, with adult help. The Colony assigned the boys such work—and paid them only if they worked. In accordance with the custom of the 1890s, the boys tended to wear hats, knickers, stockings, and high shoes. (Courtesy of Carol B. LeFevre.)

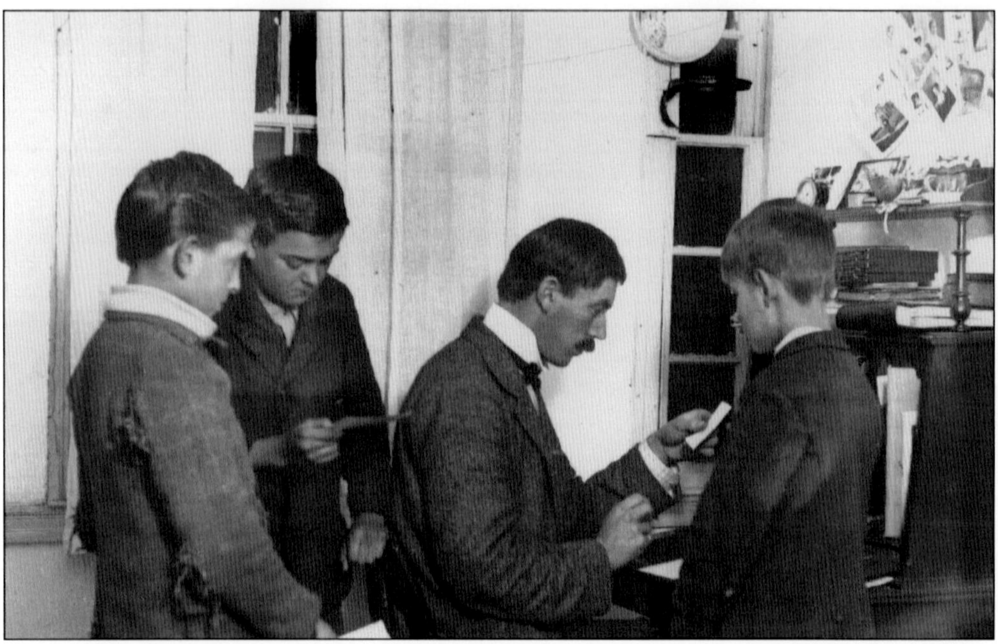

The Industrial Colony paid the boys for the work they did in special Colony money. In turn the Colony expected the boys to use the money they earned to pay for the food, lodging, and clothes they received. If the boys noticed the contrast between the elegant dress of the paymaster and their own rough clothing, the staff hoped this would motivate them to work harder to enable them to buy better clothing. (Courtesy of Carol B. LeFevre.)

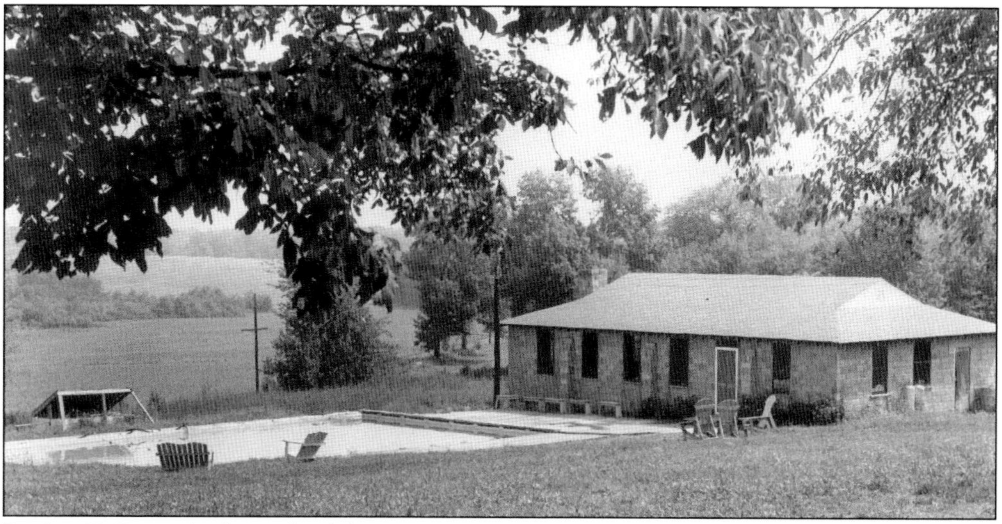

Booker T. Pierce built much of the swimming pool (left) himself. A Fisk University graduate, he came to Gardiner as a social worker for the Children's Aid Society's camp. Liking the area, he bought a farm on the edge of Libertyville, off Yankee Folly Road (named after Fowler, a Yankee who lived there), in the late 1930s. Pierce tried to farm the land but lacked agricultural experience. This photograph was taken in the 1950s. By then, Pierce was employed as a laboratory technician for IBM in Poughkeepsie, and he and his family began to develop his land into a resort for blacks, offering swimming, tennis, dancing, and views of the Shawangunk Ridge. (Courtesy of Booker T. Pierce's daughter, Diane Smith.)

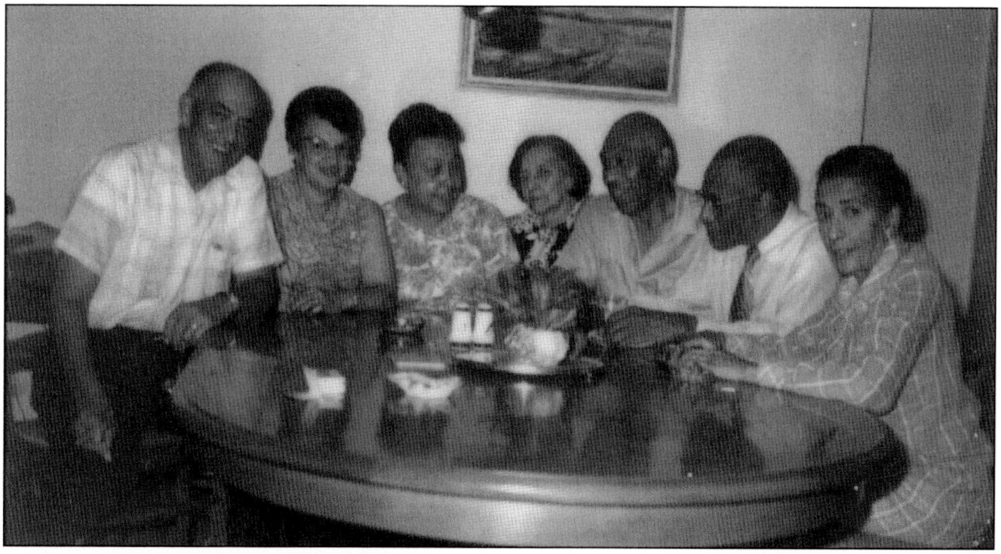

Booker T. Pierce (fifth from the left) began to close his resort and sell off his farmland c. 1970. In doing so, he created a new street off Yankee Folly Road, Pierce Lane, and built a house there. Shown with him in his new house, from left to right, are his brother-in-law Eugene Bass of Florida; Reba Coleman of Newburgh; his sister-in-law Anita Bass; his wife, Ann Pierce, a teacher at Highland Training School; and Julius and Helen McClain of Albany Post Road—a former director of the Children's Aid Society's Camp Wallkill and a psychiatric social worker for the State Hospital in Poughkeepsie, and an executive in the antipoverty program in Poughkeepsie, respectively. (Courtesy of Diane Smith.)

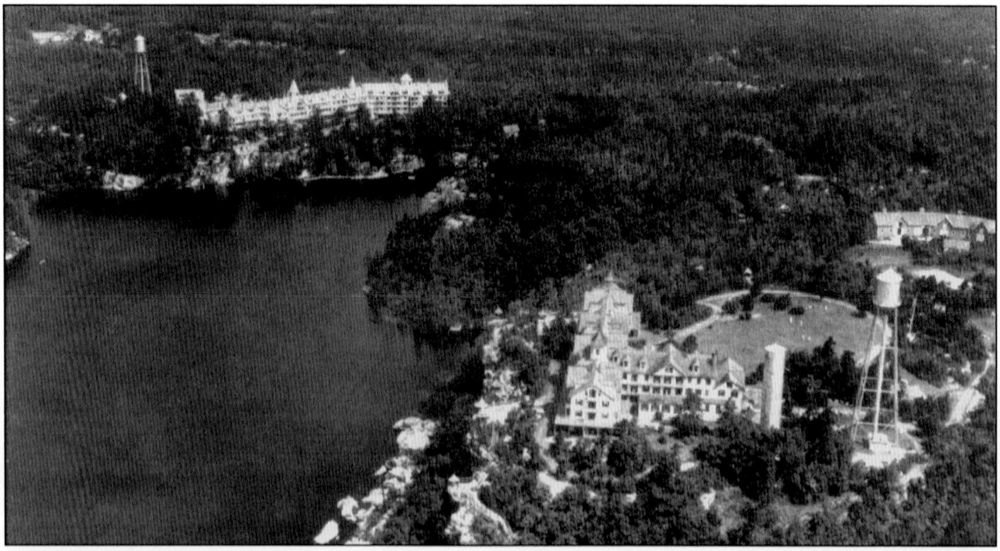

Two resort hotels overlooked Minnewaska Lake, Wildmere House (left) at the lake's northern end, and Cliff House (right) on its eastern side. Cliff House accommodated more than 200 guests, and Wildmere House more than 300. All together, the Minnewaska resort employed 213 people in the summer of 1925. It employed slightly more, 243, in the summer of 1963. Many long-term employees lived nearby, as in the Trapps neighborhood of Gardiner; temporary employees were often students brought in from a distance. (Courtesy of Minnewaska State Park Preserve.)

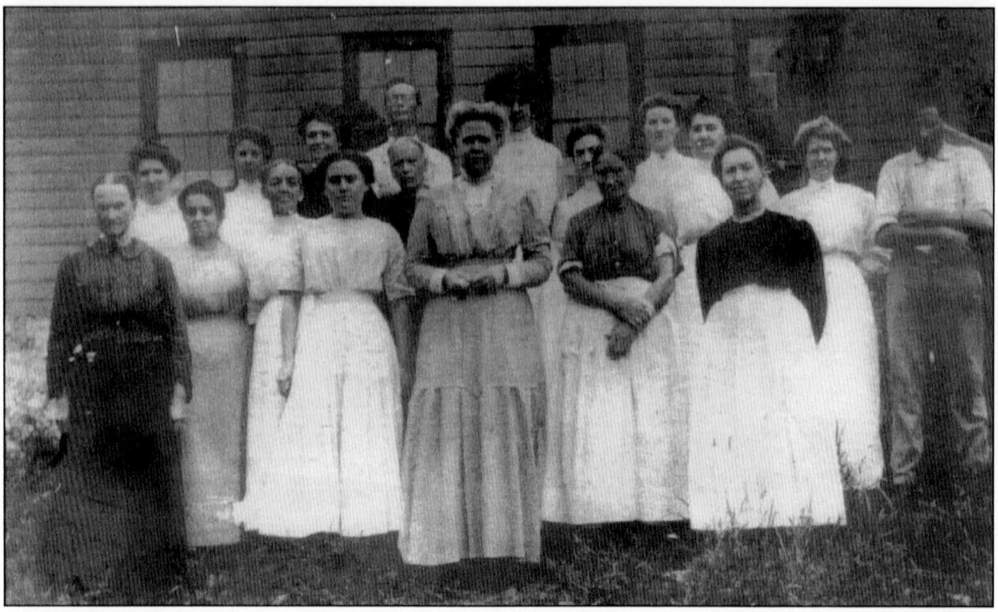

Minnewaska's laundry crew poses by the laundry building west of Wildmere House. In this c. 1907 picture, the tallest young woman in the center of the back row is Anna Elizabeth Enderly, whose family ran the sawmill at Split Rock in the Trapps. Since Minnewaska did not have a central heating system, the two men shown probably managed a separate steam system that both heated the laundry's water and powered the line shaft that ran the laundry machines. (Courtesy of Joan Wustrau.)

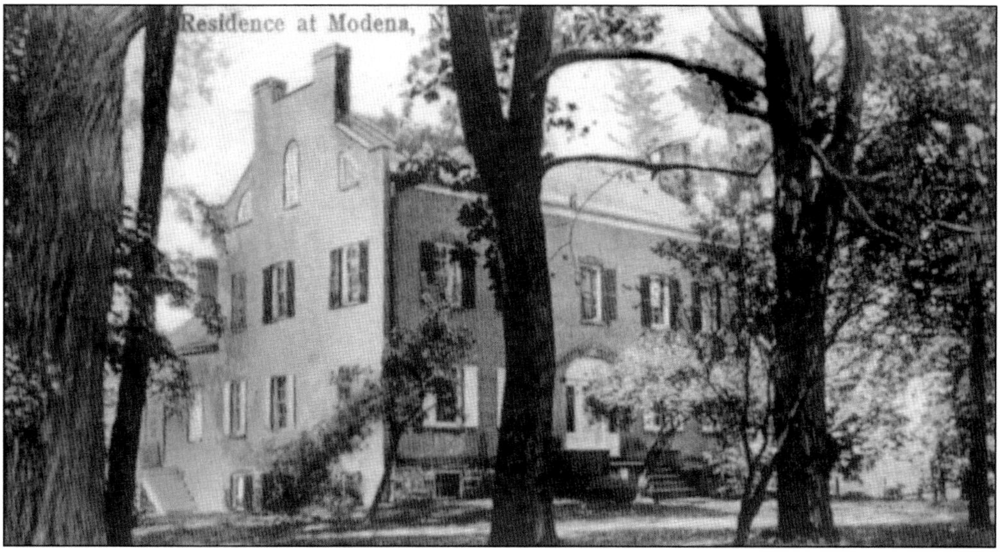

The Cole-Hasbrouck-Delamater house in Modena is imposing but restrained. Predominantly red brick, it is located on the west side of Route 32 just north of the center of Modena. The family that has long occupied it operated key Modena enterprises. Originally built c. 1820 as a small house, it was enlarged by John C. Cole, who farmed, practiced law, and ran a sawmill. It was further enlarged by Joseph E. Hasbrouck Sr., who married into the Cole family, and built up a lumber business. This postcard is postmarked 1905. (Courtesy of Haviland-Heidgard Historical Collection.)

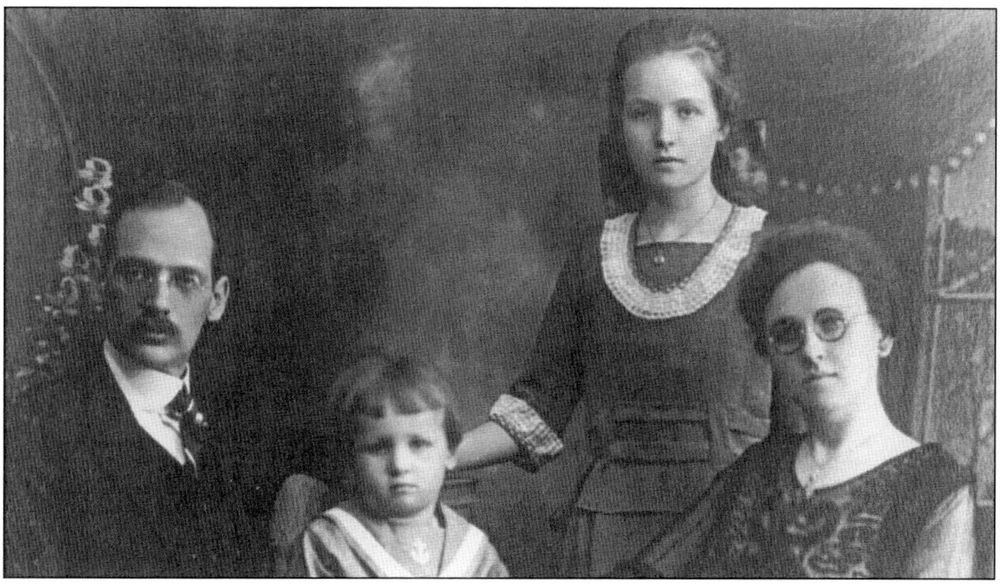

Joseph E. Hasbrouck Jr. was a Modena lumber dealer and postmaster. He is shown here c. 1920 with his wife, Sara Van Orden Hasbrouck of Gardiner's Forest Glen, and their children, Leah and Joseph O. At the time, the family lived in a modest two-story house, built for them in Modena, across the street from the large brick house of Joseph E. Hasbrouck Sr. Leah Hasbrouck married into the Delamater family and, with her husband, occupied the big house. Her son, John O. Delamater, a New York City lawyer, now occupies the big house. (Courtesy of Office of Plattekill Town Historian.)

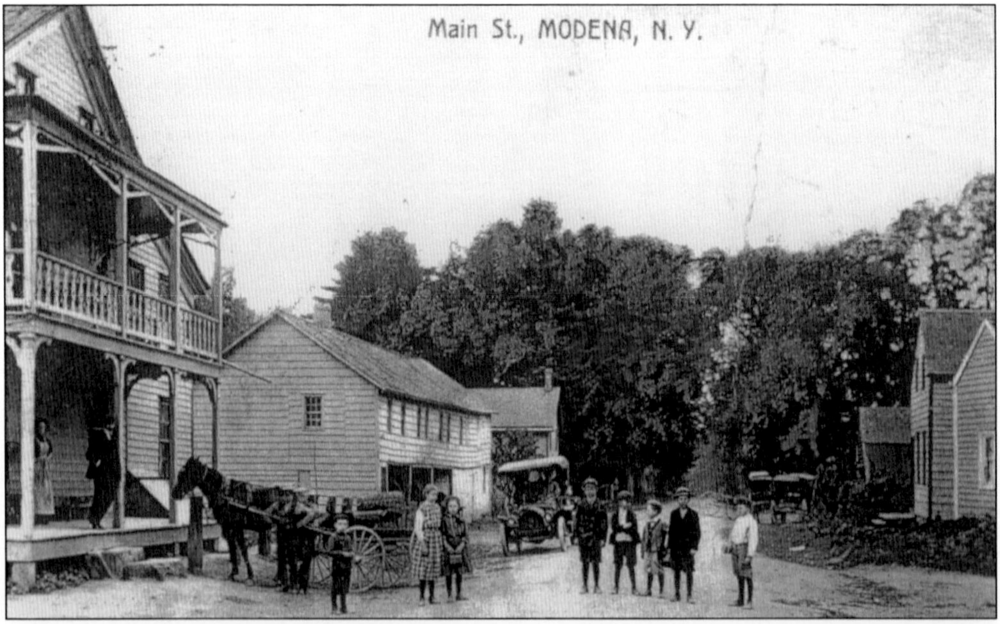

These buildings were erected by the Cole family and later owned by the Hasbrouck family, which married into the Coles in 1872. From left to right in this *c.* 1910 view are the Modena hotel, the long stable-garage, and the store. In recent decades, the hotel's first floor has served as the Modena post office. As the building aged and parking for its customers increasingly became a problem, a new post office building was built a mile north of this site and opened in 1996. Since then, the historic hotel building, still owned by Hasbrouck descendants, the Delamaters, has been empty. (Courtesy of Office of Plattekill Town Historian.)

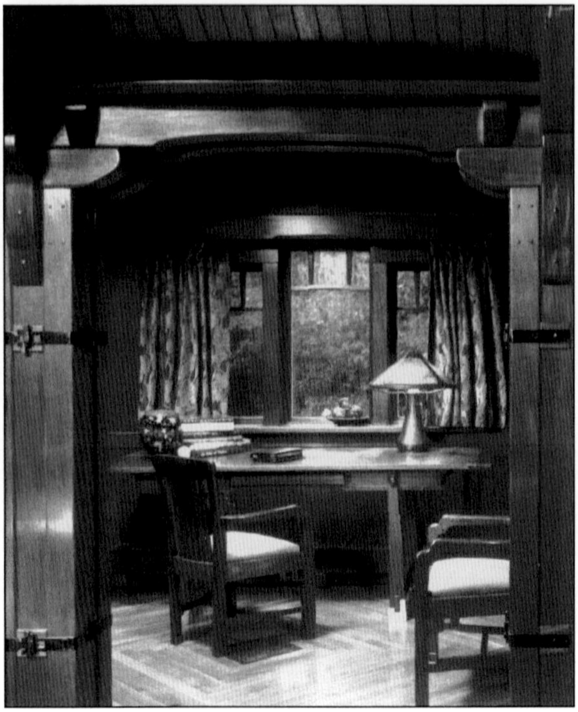

Matthew Bialecki, a Gardiner architect, designed the interior of this house on North Mountain Road, owned by Julian Studley, a Manhattan real estate developer. The design won an award in 1996 from the American Institute of Architects. Bialecki, California-raised and educated, discovered the Gardiner area when he came here in the 1980s to rock climb. As an architect, he avoids designs that are coldly functional and adapts a mix of styles. In the study room shown, he adapted the Japanese tori for the doorway. (Courtesy of Matthew Bialecki.)

The Whites pose in front of their house, Orchard Hill, in New Hurley, soon after they acquired it in 1906. From left to right are family friend Aunt Caltoni; Titus C. White and his wife, Emma Klein White; their daughter Marie White Hemingway and her husband, William E. Hemingway. (Courtesy of the Whites' great grandson Richard Tuman.)

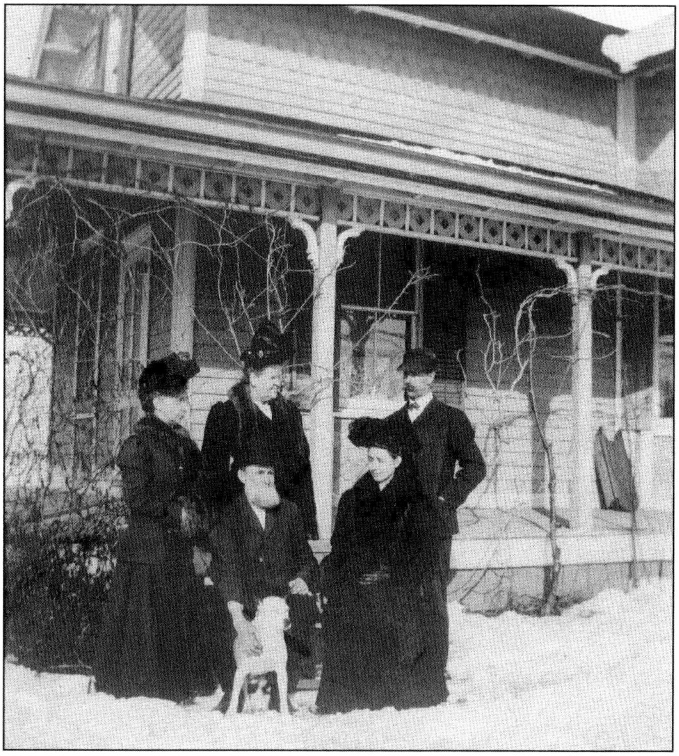

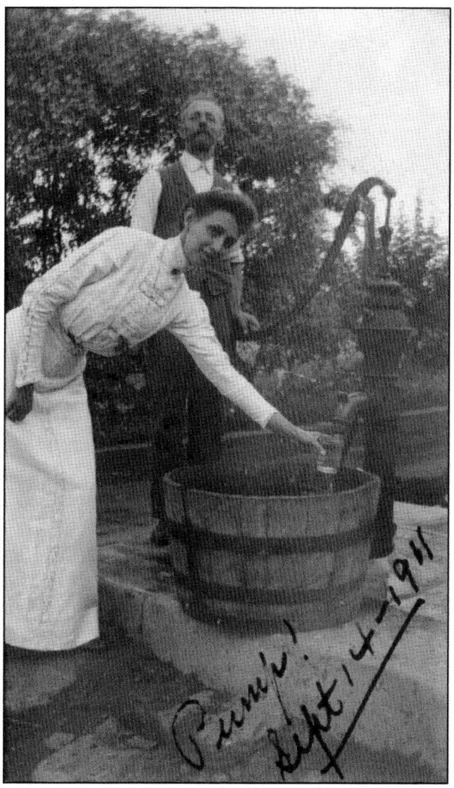

The Hemingways of Orchard Hill farm in New Hurley visit their well pump on September 14, 1911. While haughty-looking William E. Hemingway pumps, his wife, Marie White Hemingway, with a gentler demeanor,reaches for a glass of water. (Courtesy of Richard Tuman.)

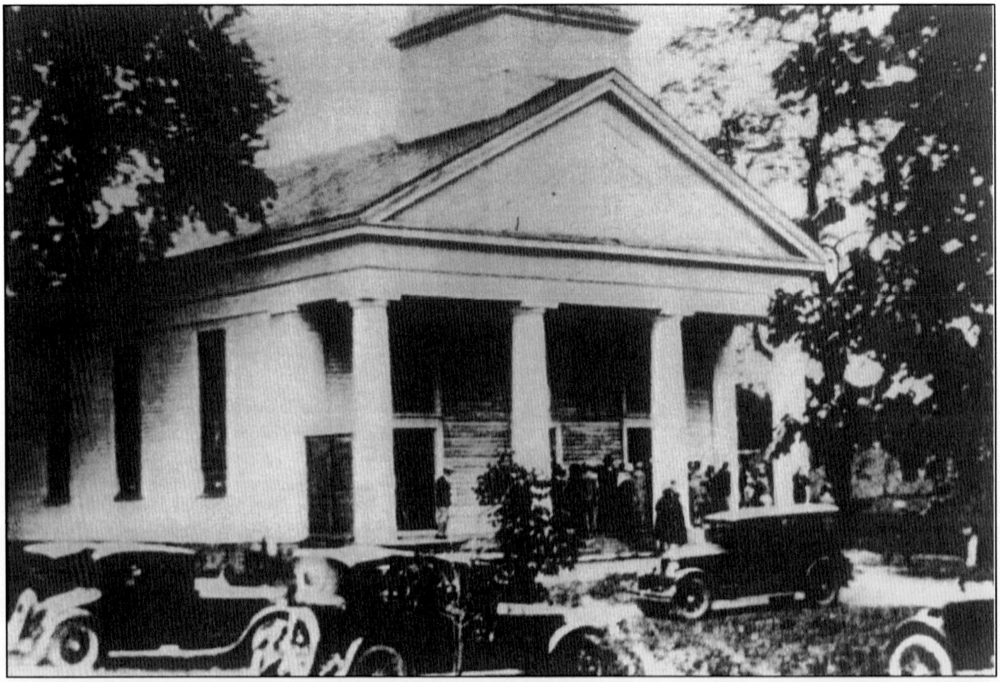

The Reformed Dutch Church of New Hurley, photographed in 1927, was organized in 1770 by the Dutch, who predominated in the area. This building was constructed in 1835 on a site in Plattekill in the rural New Hurley community, which straddles the towns of Gardiner, Plattekill, and Shawangunk. Having become ethnically mixed, the church has long since dropped the word "Dutch" from its title, calling itself simply "Reformed." For the historically minded, however, the name "Dutch" lingers. (Courtesy of Office of Plattekill Town Historian.)

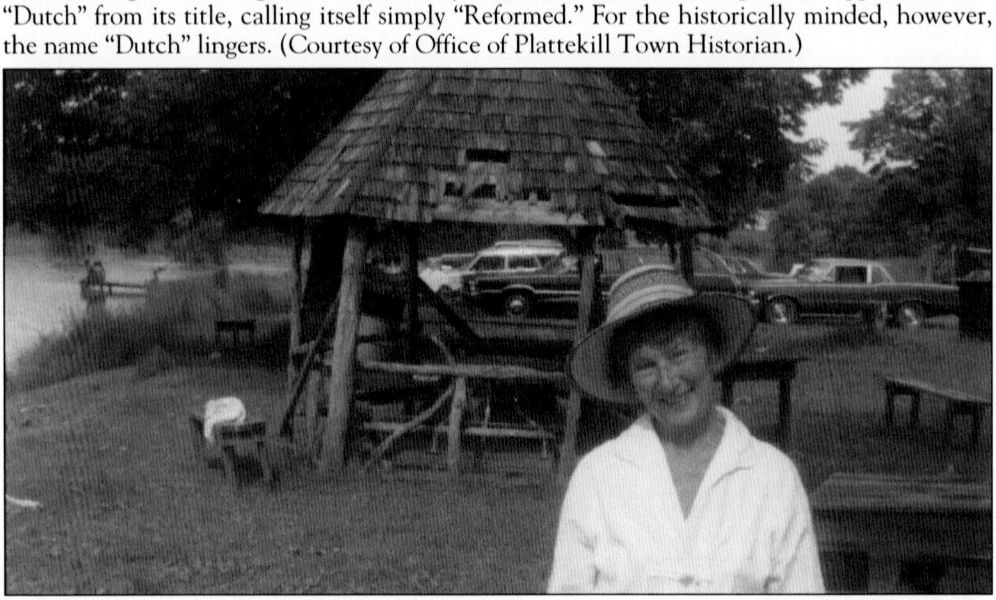

Tillson Lake, in the Rutsonville neighborhood, was artificially created in 1929, when H.A. Tillson dammed the Palmaghatt Kill. It became a popular resort, with diving boards, picnic tables, a golf course, gazebos patterned after those at Minnewaska and Mohonk, and a renowned roller-skating rink. By the 1970s, however, when Dorothy Felshin brought her family here, one of its gazebos seemed neglected. (Courtesy of Annie Felshin O'Neill.)

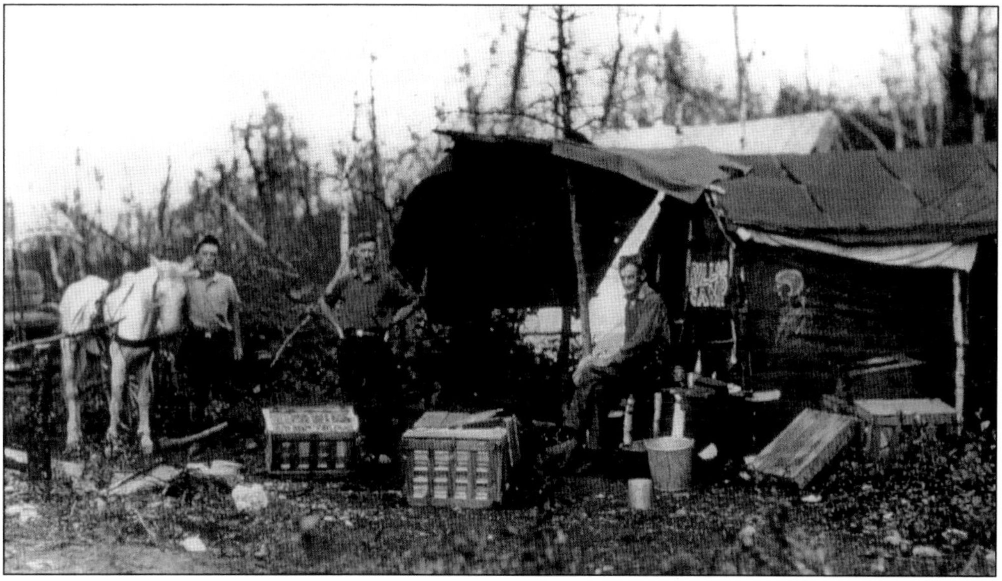

Huckleberry picking was common in the Trapps-Minnewaska-Ellenville mountain region. In berry season, berry pickers might stay in a rough camp such as this for weeks at a time. Shown here *c.* 1920 with his horse and wagon is Arthur Van Leuven at a huckleberry camp on the Old Smiley Road, west of Lake Awosting. The son of Eli and Anna Van Leuven of the Trapps, Arthur Van Leuven may have been there to deliver supplies and pick up berry crates such as those visible on the ground. (Courtesy of Harold Van Leuven.)

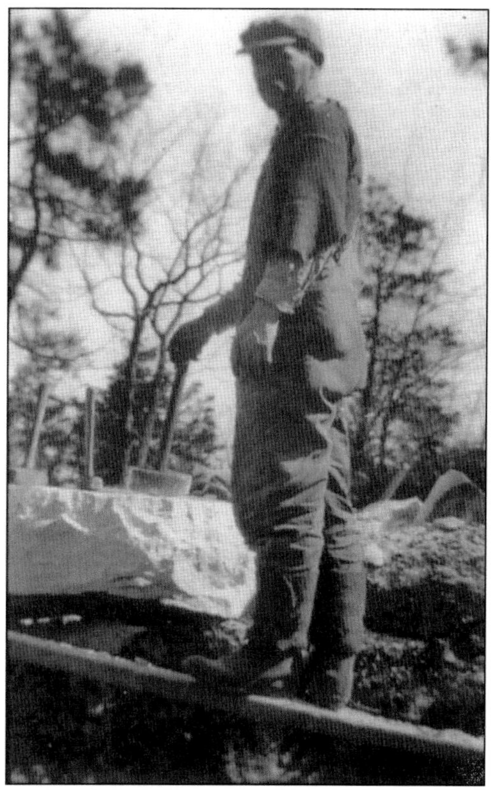

Not far from his home near Dickie Barre Mountain, Simon Coddington cuts millstones. To ship the stones out, cutters might slide them downhill on stone sleds, draw them by wagon to High Falls, and then send them on by railroad. Pictured here *c.* 1910, Coddington also cut stone for Minnewaska carriage roads. When he died in 1917, it was said to be from stone dust complications. His daughter, Evelyn Coddington DeWitt, worked as a waitress at Minnewaska and played the organ at the Trapps Chapel. (Courtesy of Mohonk Preserve.)

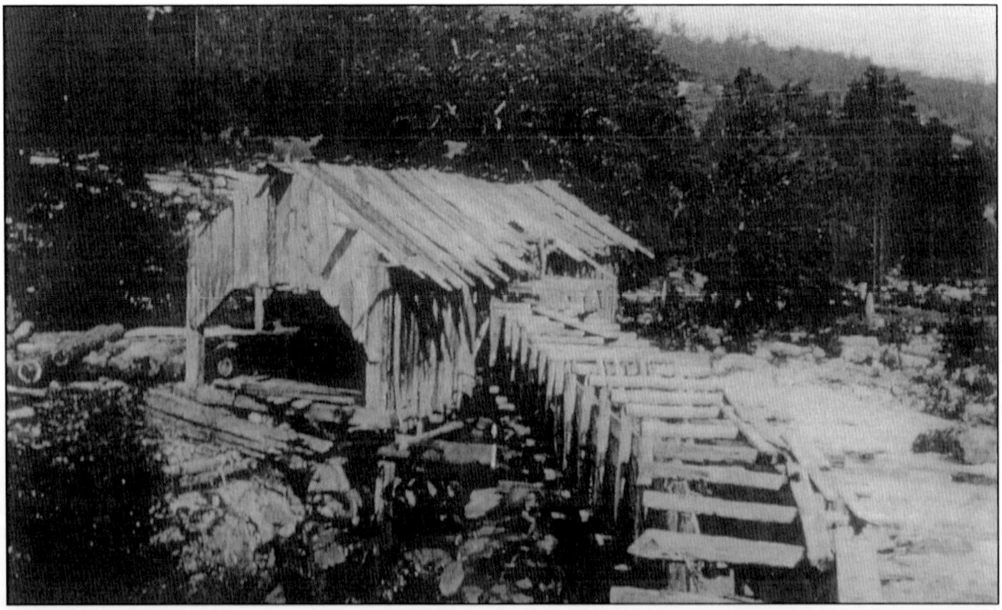

The Enderly Sawmill, operated by the Enderly family from soon after 1801, was located at the site known as Split Rock, on the Coxing Kill in the Trapps neighborhood of Gardiner. Although the mill's waterwheel was placed in the split between two rocks, the wheel was not powered by the stream flowing through the split but by water from an upstream pool fed through a sluiceway above the split. The sluiceway, as shown in this *c.* 1910 view, was a wooden trough with pieces of slab wood nailed across it to hold it together. The spot is now a picnic site that is open to the public. (Courtesy of Mohonk Preserve.)

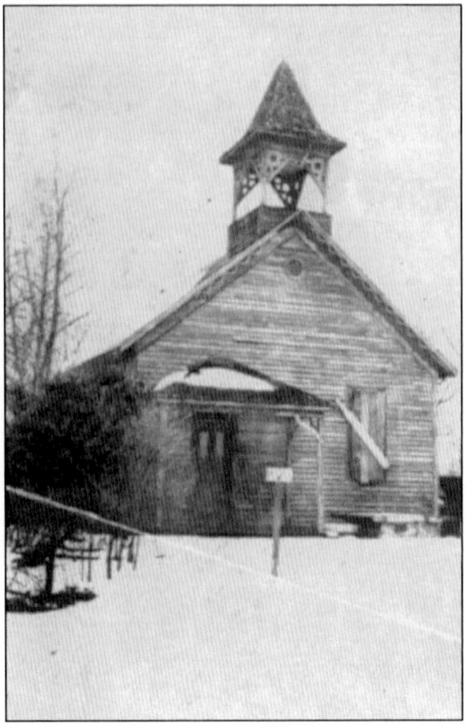

The Trapps Chapel, built *c.* 1881, was on the east side of Trapps Road near where the Minnewaska Trail (Route 44–55) later crossed it. It was built with the help of Alfred Smiley of the Minnewaska resort and resort guests. Alfred's son, George Smiley, was often the chapel's Sunday school superintendent. The chapel being independent, it was sometimes served by Methodist ministers from Alligerville, sometimes by Reformed ministers from Guilford. If no minister was available, a member of the Smiley family might speak. (Courtesy of Haviland-Heidgard Historical Collection.)

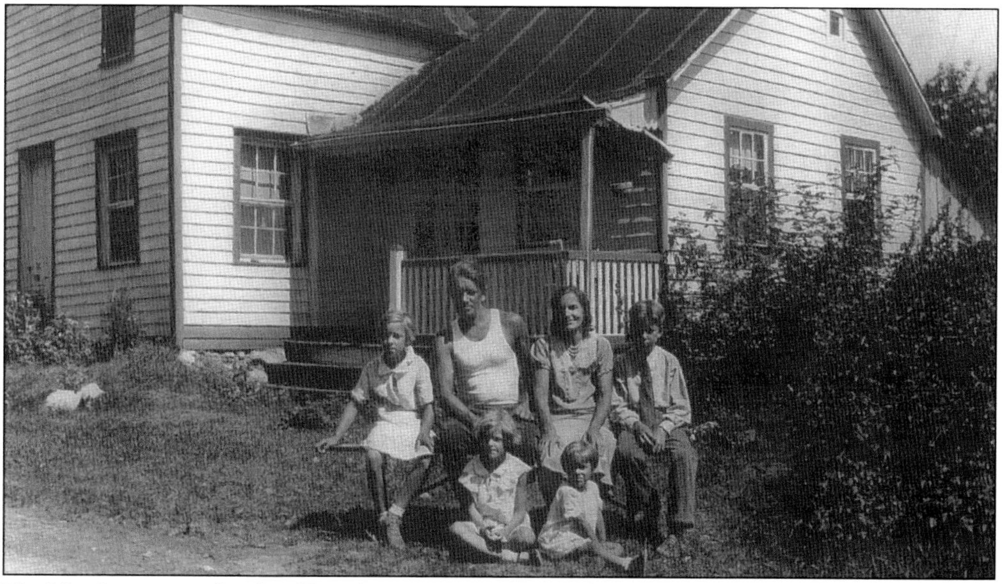

The Van Leuvens, a family of Dutch origin, were among the residents who had lived in Gardiner's mountain neighborhood, the Trapps, since before the Civil War. They were often small farmers, blueberry pickers, hoop makers, woodcutters, millstone cutters, or maintenance staff at the nearby Minnewaska hotels. Shown here c. 1940 are Winslow and Bertha Veres Van Leuven, with their children Doris, Ethel, Alice, and Roger, in front of their house on Trapps Road. (Courtesy of Doris Van Leuven Hall.)

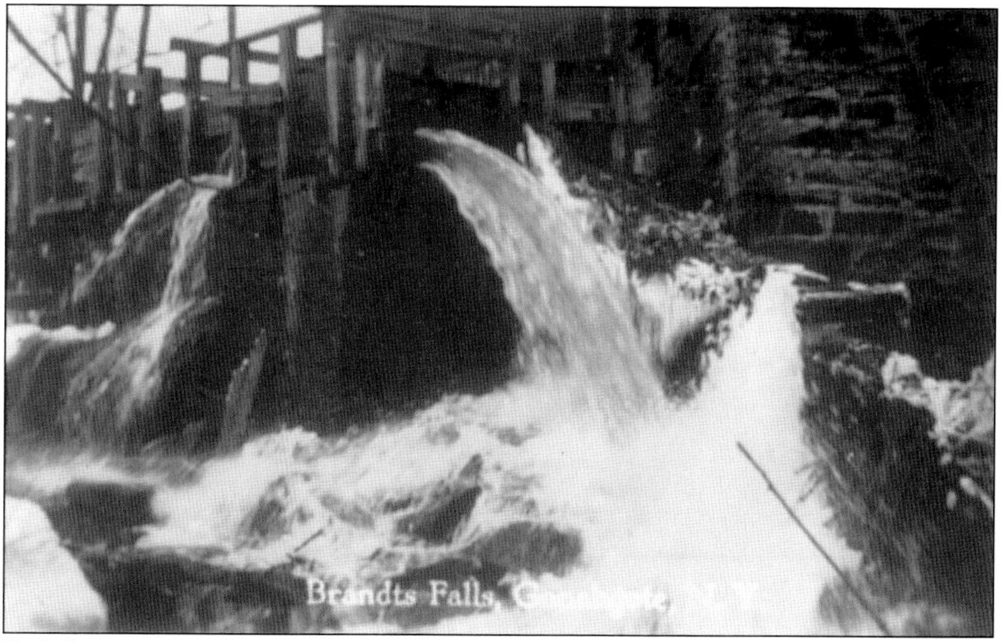

Tuthilltown Grist Mill is traditionally believed to have been built on the Shawangunk River by Selah Tuthill in 1788, with great beams held together by wooden pegs. The mill, which has operated almost continuously since then, was a center around which the Tuthilltown neighborhood developed. This postcard calls the water pouring out of the mill "Brandt's Falls," after Ludwig Brandt, who operated the mill from 1900 to 1941. (Courtesy of Daryl P. Carr.)

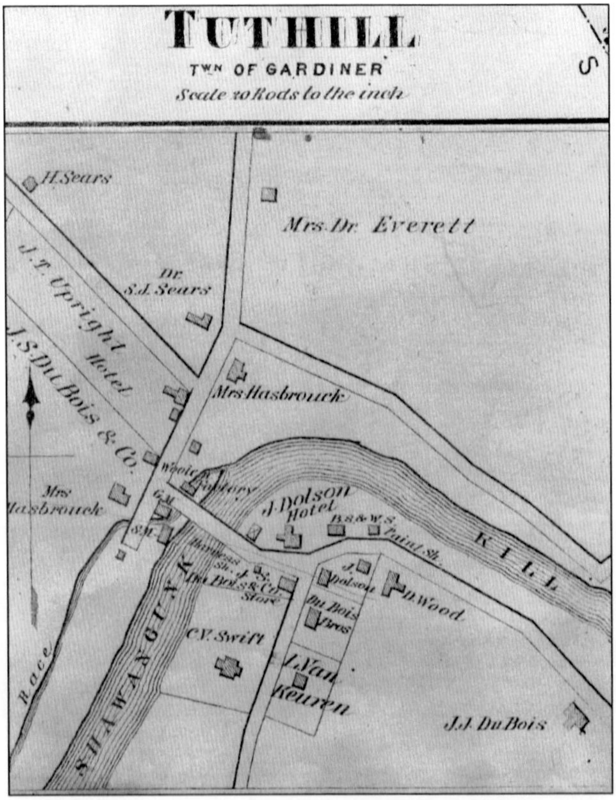

This 1875 map of "Tuthill" (Tuthilltown) indicates the location of a gristmill ("GM") and a sawmill ("SM"). It marks the sites of two Sears family houses: one belonging to Dr. Sears, physician, and the other belonging to Sears's son Hector Sears, who was later to found Gardiner's only newspaper. It also marks the sites of Dolson's Hotel (center), which by the 1950s, was known as Bunk's, and the DuBois store (center), which later became Meinecke's. (From F.W. Beers *Atlas*, 1875.)

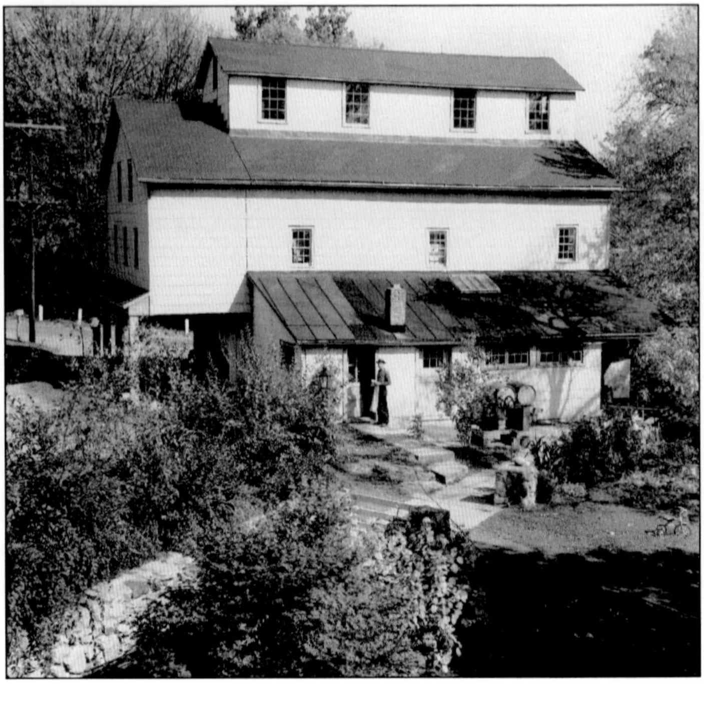

George Smith is shown *c.* 1949 standing by his Tuthilltown Mill, wearing a hat and apron. After he bought the mill in 1941, Smith, who was raised on a farm in Modena and educated to be a teacher, added an extra story to facilitate the installation of modern machinery and improved the millrace by lining it with stone. However, Smith discovered that he could not support his family by operating the mill and eventually took a full-time job teaching in the Highland schools. (Courtesy of Dan Smith.)

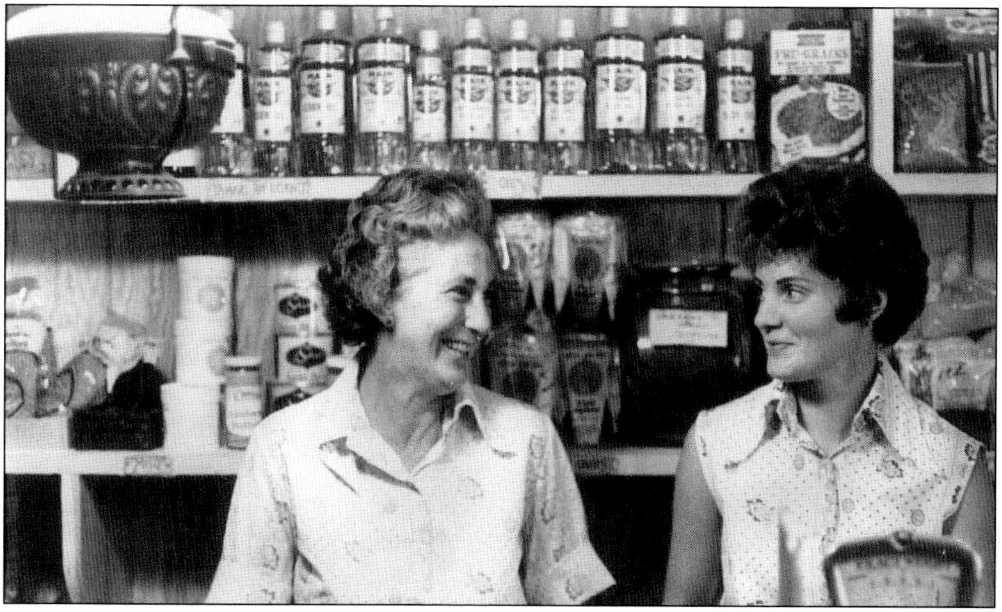

Eleanor Smith (left), wife of George Smith Sr., and Elza Smith, wife of George Smith Jr., are ready for customers in their Country Store, in the Tuthilltown Mill. Pictured *c.* the 1980s, they sold the flour ground in their mill, as well as other foods. The bottles on the shelves included corn and soy oils, nuts, peanut butter, and cashew butter. In her own kitchen, Eleanor Smith prepared doughnuts, which she sold at the mill store and delivered to restaurants in New Paltz, until a doctor warned her that she was overdoing. (Courtesy of Dan Smith.)

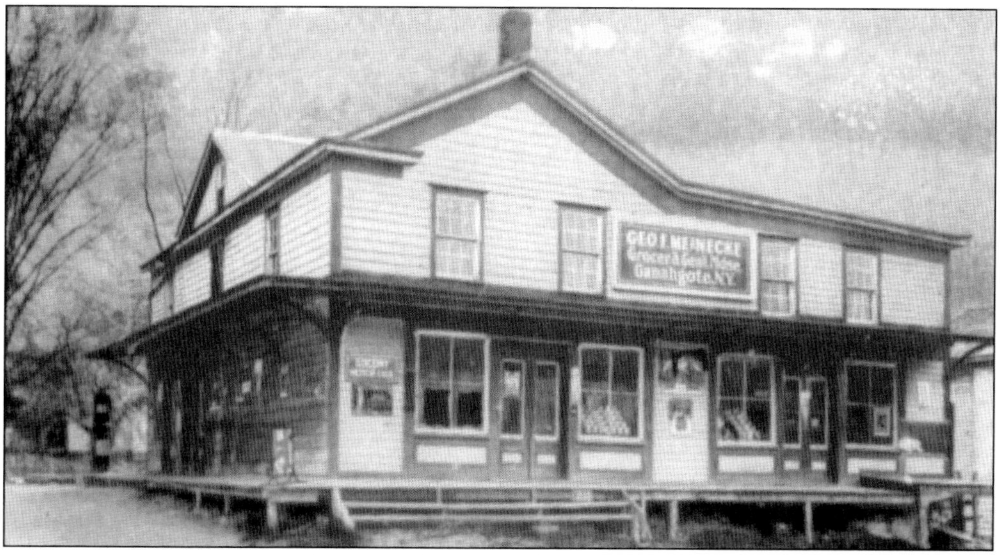

This Tuthilltown store, on the east side of the Shawangunk Kill, is pictured *c.* 1900, when it sold groceries and "Gen'l Mdse," as its last proprietor, George F. Meinecke, advertised. Earlier, the store housed a post office, presided over by Mrs. Jim DuBois, who chose to call the post office Ganahgote, a supposed Native American name, producing confusion then and since. The community has long since reverted to the traditional name of Tuthilltown, honoring Selah Tuthill, the original builder of the gristmill. (Courtesy of William and Carol Majestic Lohrman.)

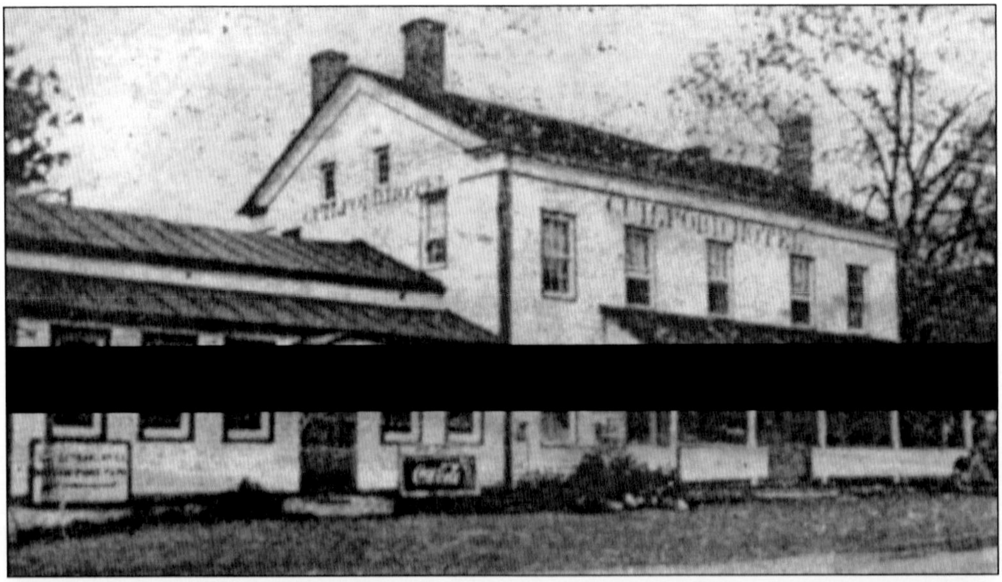

Over time, this Tuthilltown hotel went by a variety of names. In 1875, it was the Dolson Hotel. Later, it became the Guilford Hotel (at a time when Guilford had been stretched to include not only the original Guilford but also both Tuthilltown and the Gardiner hamlet). In the early 1950s, it was known as Bunk's Hotel and offered "home cooking," bathing and fishing next to the hotel in "Shawangunk Creek," and dancing "every night." By the 1960s, the hotel was known as Connie Jordan's. (Bunk's Hotel Flier, courtesy of the Gardiner Town Hall.)

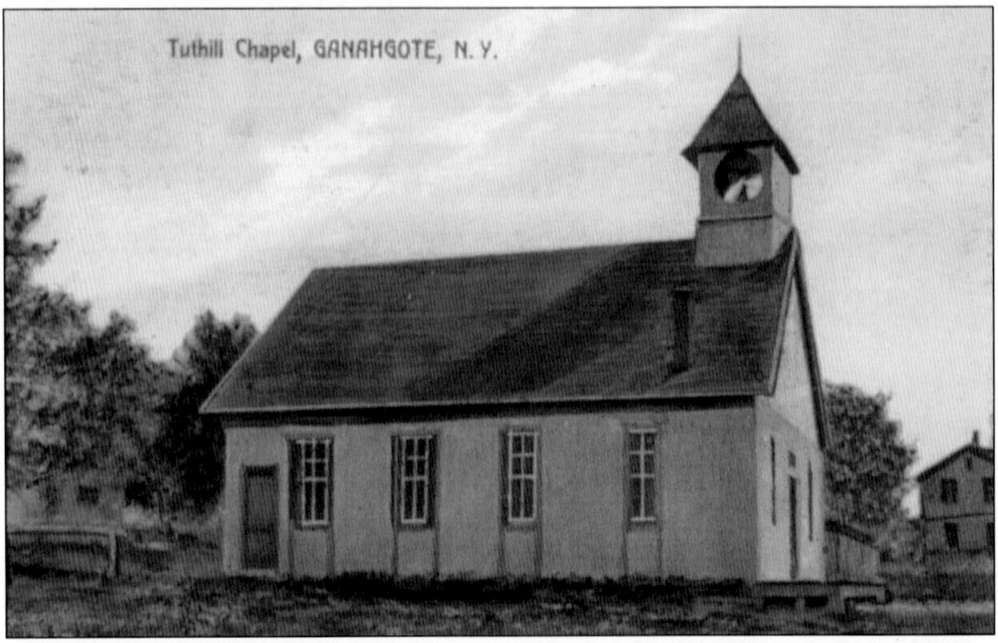

The Tuthilltown Chapel, shown here on a postcard postmarked 1910, was built in 1895 as a branch of the Guilford Reformed Church. Located centrally in Tuthilltown, it was across the Shawangunk River from the Tuthilltown Grist Mill. As the growth of the Gardiner hamlet drew population away from Tuthilltown, attendance dwindled and the chapel closed c. 1925. (Courtesy of Daryl P. Carr.)

Margaret A. Collins was born in Kentucky but lived in New Orleans, Louisiana, where this photograph was taken. On July 20, 1865, she married Hector Sears while he was in the U.S. military service. The couple had five children: Edward J., who became an electrical engineer in New York City; William H., who became a conductor for the West Shore Railroad; Edith; Estelle; and Ida. (Courtesy of Haviland-Heidgard Historical Collection.)

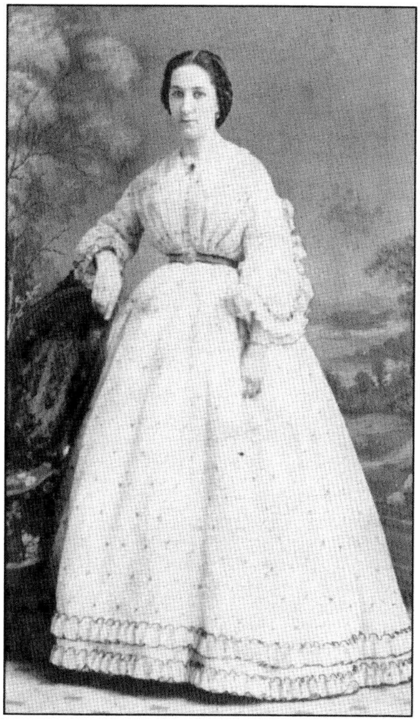

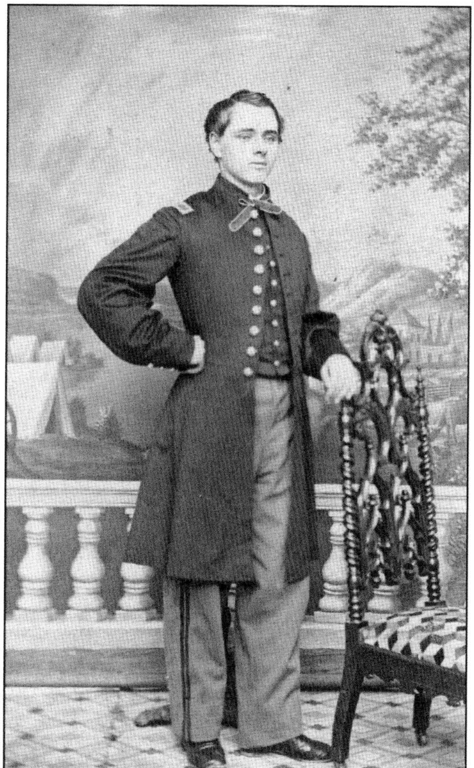

Hector Sears, born in Pine Bush in the town of Rochester, was photographed in Washington, D.C., near the end of the Civil War, in his Union uniform. After being wounded at Port Hudson, Louisiana, in 1863, he was hospitalized in New Orleans. Later, he became provost marshal for several counties in Virginia. Leaving the army by 1869, he settled near his father, a physician, in the Tuthilltown neighborhood of Gardiner, studied law with his uncle in Montgomery, and then established a law practice in Gardiner. In 1882, he founded the only newspaper Gardiner ever had, the *Gardiner Weekly*. (Courtesy of Haviland-Heidgard Historical Collection.)

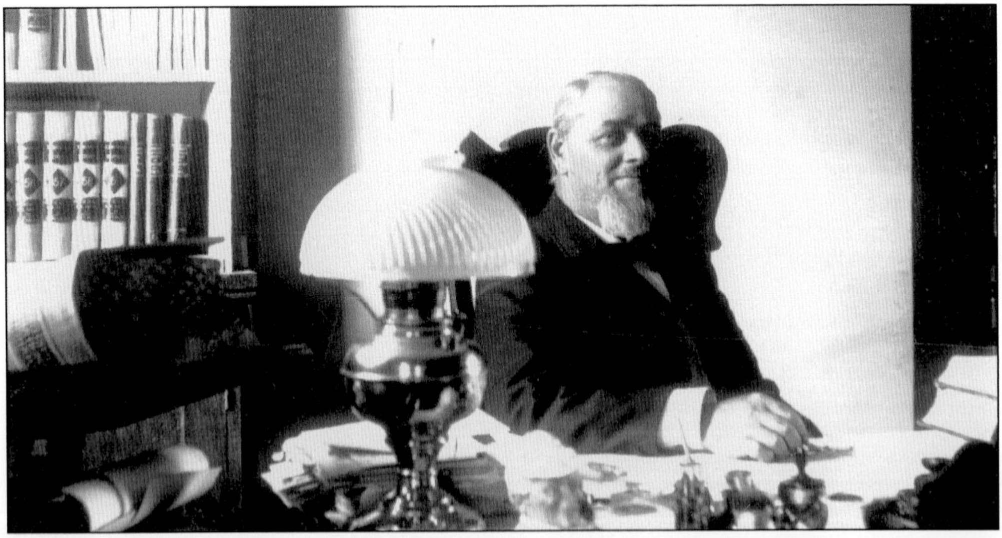

Hector Sears, who combined such roles as insurance agent, journalist, printer, and attorney, is shown here in his office in the late 1890s. Although he lived in Tuthilltown, for a time he kept both his law office and print shop in the Gardiner Hotel next to the station. He served Gardiner at various times as justice of the peace or supervisor. He founded two newspapers, the *Gardiner Weekly*, which he ran himself, and the *Highland Post*, which his sister, Carrie W. Sears, ran for him. He printed both of them in his own print shop in the Gardiner hamlet. (Courtesy of Carol B. LeFevre.)

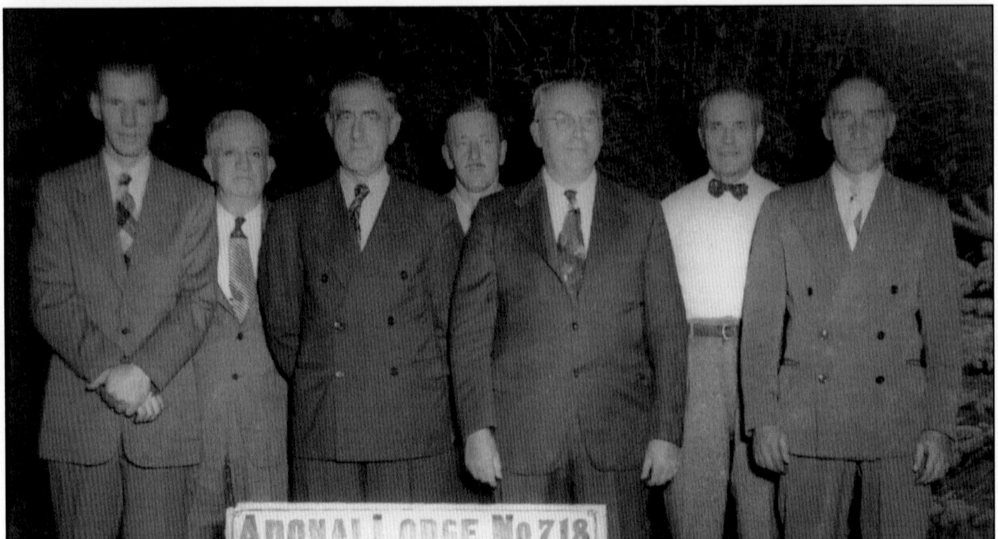

The Masons of Tuthilltown, founded in 1872 and shown here c. 1954, sometimes met at the house of German-born Jacob Honold, on Albany Post Road at Tinker's Lane. From left to right are Harold Marks, industrial photographer for DeLaval of Poughkeepsie; Floyd McKinstry, grocery proprietor on Main Street; Jacob Honold, retired New York City patrolman whose son Jake, from 1945, was the proprietor of the Ireland Corners Garage; Art Kurtz, fruit farmer on Route 208 north of Ireland Corners; Myron Wells, Gardiner station agent; Frank Donda, farmer on Burnt Meadow Road; Ransom Freer, ironworker whose wife, Hillie Freer, taught at Gardiner School. (Courtesy of Marybeth Majestic.)

Four

Schools

In the 1790s, the state of New York began to foster public schools by providing matching grants for them. It was then that the Kettleborough School was founded, the first known school in what was to become the town of Gardiner. By the 1830s, when public schools were becoming common in the state, the future town had additional schools, as at Tuthilltown and Libertyville. After the town of Gardiner had been created, in 1874, Gardiner was officially reported to have nine one-room schools, three east of the Wallkill River (Kettleborough, Maraback [later the Gardiner School], and New Hurley), and six west of the river (Tuthill, Guilford, Libertyville, Schoonmakers [Benton's Corners], "Traps," and Rutsonville). Each school had its own district, with boundaries that sometimes crossed town lines. Each had its own trustees and its own right to levy taxes.

By the 1920s, schools in the state were being centralized, according to the theory that larger schools meant more efficient education. While local residents often resisted the change, believing that for small children small schools were healthier, beginning in the 1930s all the remaining Gardiner school districts were absorbed into centralized school systems and gradually closed. Schools on the southern edge of Gardiner, those that served Bruynswick, Rutsonville, and New Hurley, closed in 1943 and were absorbed into the Wallkill system. The last two Gardiner schools to close were absorbed into the New Paltz system. Those two were the Tuthilltown school, which closed in 1959, and the Gardiner School in the hamlet of Gardiner, the only one of the town of Gardiner's schools to have grown larger than a one-room school, which closed in 1981. Since then, Gardiner has had no public schools, which has weakened its sense of self.

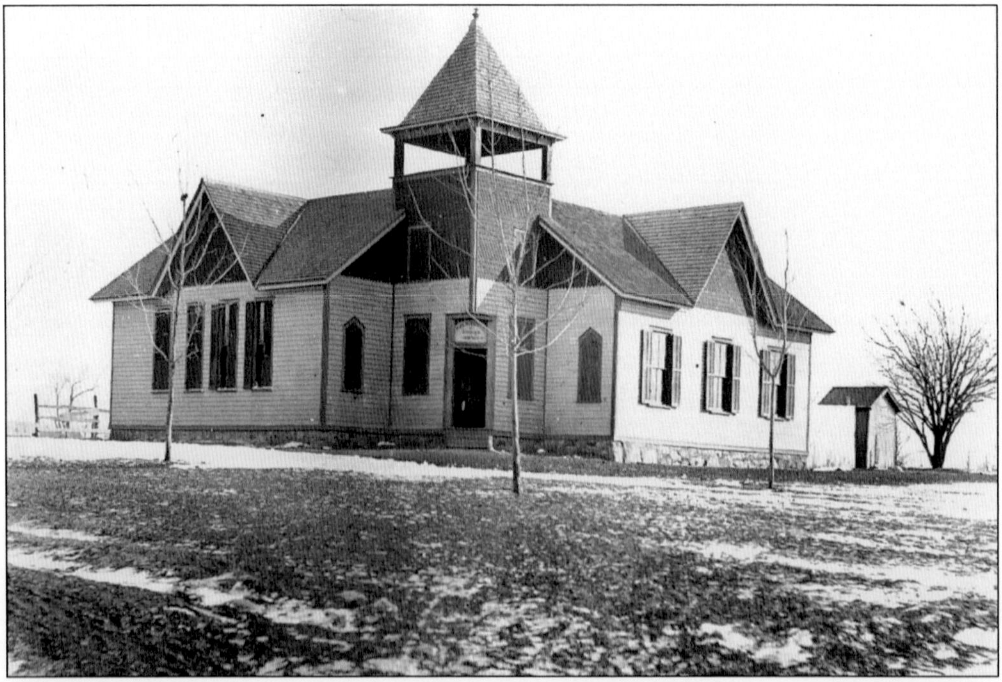

The school building for the district that included the Gardiner hamlet was at first located on Marabac Road, two miles southeast of the hamlet. By 1874, the Gardiner hamlet had grown so that most of the children attending the school were from the hamlet. Thus, the parents pressed for the school to be relocated to the hamlet. After a long struggle, the district built a school in the hamlet in 1880 (it did not move the old Marabac school building to the hamlet in 1875, as has been claimed). In 1895 (not 1893), the school was enlarged from one room to two rooms. This photograph, the earliest one of the school known, was probably taken *c.* 1897, soon after the school's enlargement. (Courtesy of Carol B. LeFevre.)

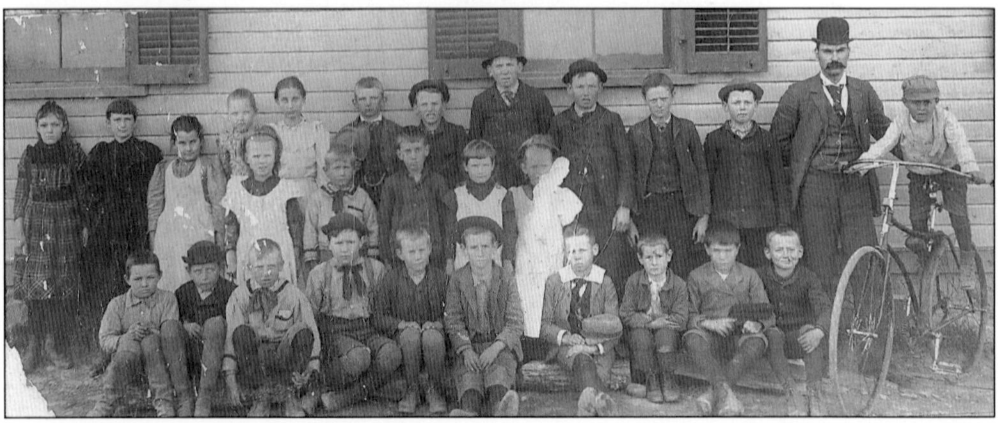

Teacher Lester H. Decker (right) appears imposing as he stands by his pupils at the Gardiner School in the 1890s. At that time, nearly one third of the teachers in the Gardiner area were men. The older boys often wore hats and long trousers, the younger boys, knickers and stockings, and the girls, long dresses protected by pinafores. The fashion of the day did not allow for either boys or girls to show bare legs. Decker and his wife both studied at New Paltz Normal School; she taught at Guilford School, and he later became a White Plains real estate dealer. (Courtesy of Vivian McCord.)

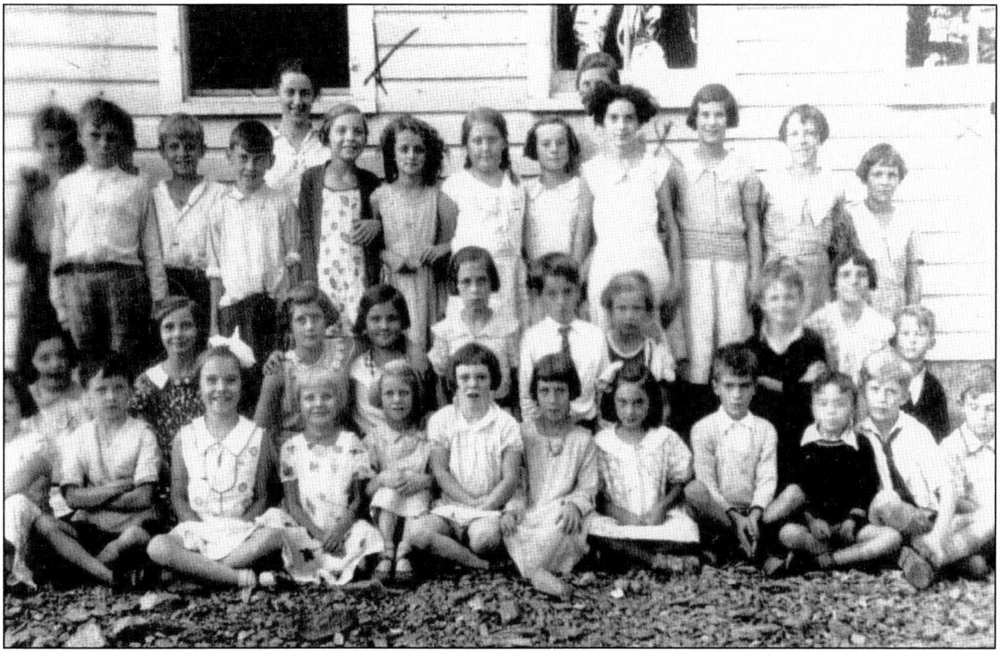

Gardiner School students pose in front of teachers Margaret Carroll (left) and Jennie Alsdorf. Among those pictured in this 1933 photograph is Paul Donahue (front right). A comparison with the 1890s class pictured on page 68 reveals that neither class is wearing high shoes; however, in 1933, the boys are no longer wearing hats, the girls are no longer wearing pinafores, and many bare legs are showing. (Courtesy of Paul Donahue.)

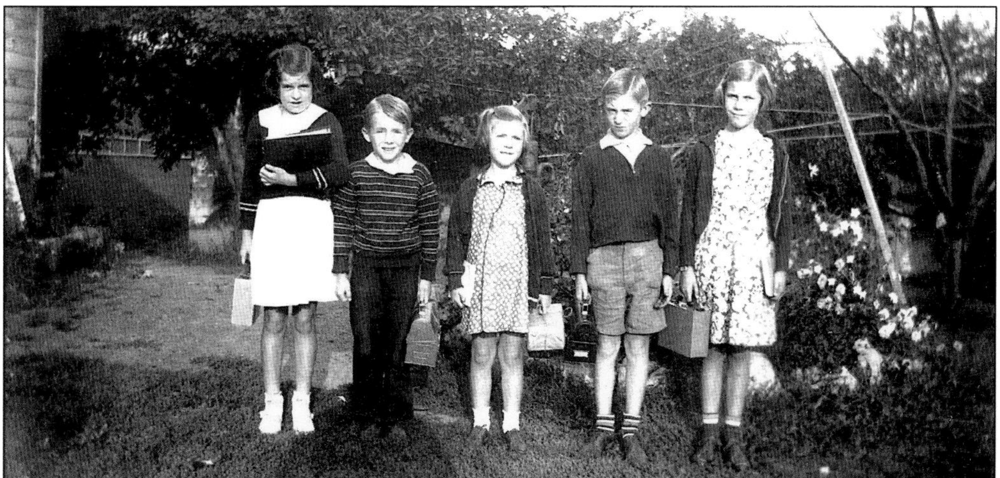

Carrying their lunches, these children from the Clinton and Wells families set out to walk a mile from Ireland Corners to the Gardiner School. Shown here in September 1937, they usually took a shortcut behind St. Charles Catholic Church. Once, after they had reached the school yard and were playing baseball, Joan Wells (center) recalls, one of the boys swung his bat too far, hitting her head and causing it to bleed. The boy, Henry Majestic, ran in distress to the Gardiner railroad station to tell the girl's father, station agent Myron Wells, that he had "killed" Joan. However, Joan Wells still lives in Gardiner, as does one of the others in this photograph, Donald Clinton (second from left). (Courtesy of Joan Wells Decker.)

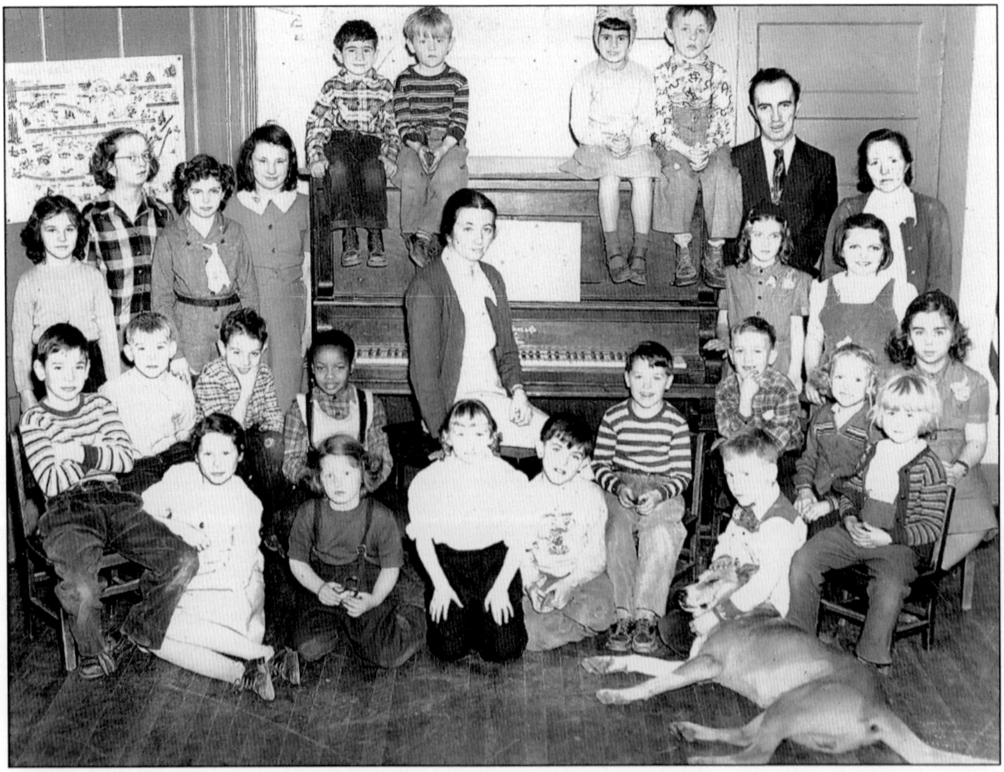

Gardiner School pupils pose with teachers Janet Bracken (at the piano) and Jason Goumes and Marie Dodd (back right). Richard Hoppenstedt, son of the hamlet veterinarian, hugs Rex, the Linz family dog, who enjoyed school. The children loved having Rex, as shown c. 1949, and the teachers accepted him as an asset. (Courtesy of Haviland-Heidgard Historical Collection.)

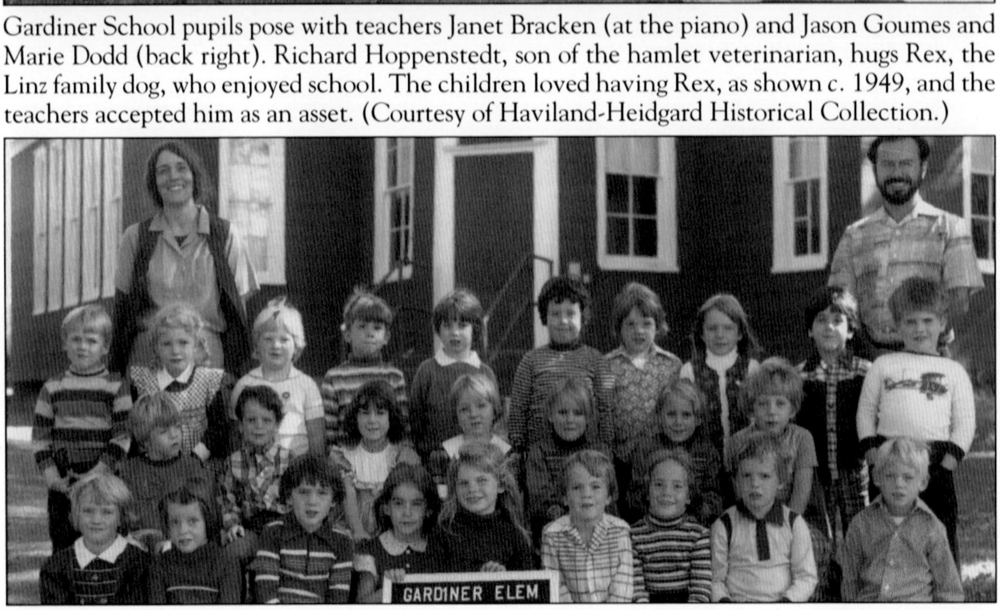

The kindergarten class poses in front of the Gardiner School with teacher Gail Slotwinski (left) and a practice teacher from the State College at New Paltz. In September 1978, the building, which had long been painted white, had recently been painted red and housed kindergarten and first grade. When Gardiner's population was smaller, the school included up to grade eight. New Paltz Central School District officials were pushing to close the school, while the parents club and Gardiner town board were struggling to keep it open. (Courtesy of Gail Slotwinski.)

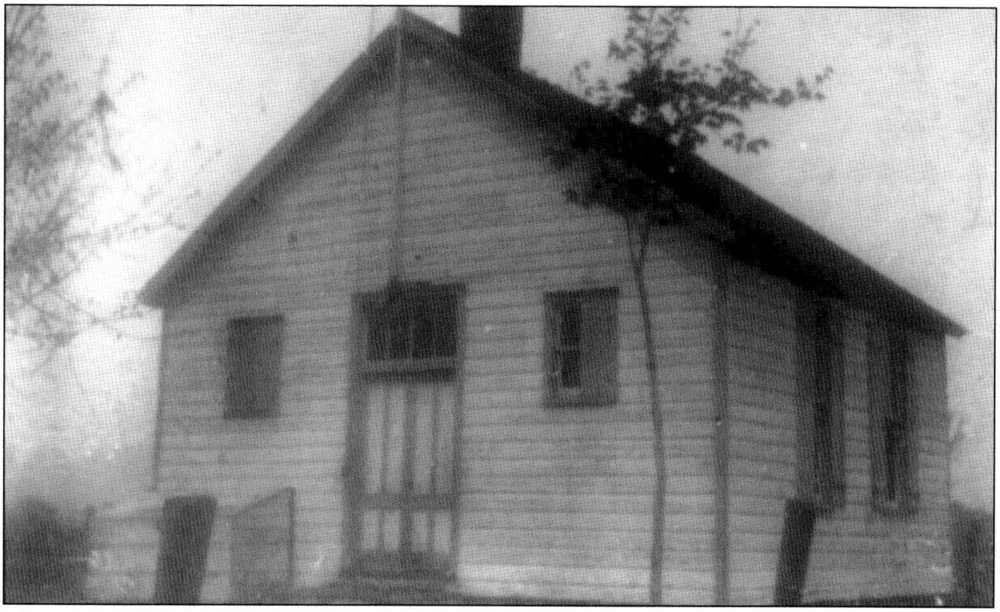

The Benton's Corners School was created c. 1850. When it was depicted on this postcard postmarked 1908, it had been painted red, but having faded, it was called the Pink School. After it was moved to a site north of the corner on the west side of Bruynswick Road c. 1928, it was painted white, invalidating its popular name. In 1939, it was merged into the Wallkill School District. From the 1940s to 1950s, boys walking to the school carried shotguns to hunt squirrels along the way, and students such as the Conner children, Thelma, Skeeter, and Tom, took turns fetching water for the school from Miske's store, nearby at the corner. The school closed c. 1956, the artist Leonard George being its last teacher. (Courtesy of William and Carol Majestic Lohrman.)

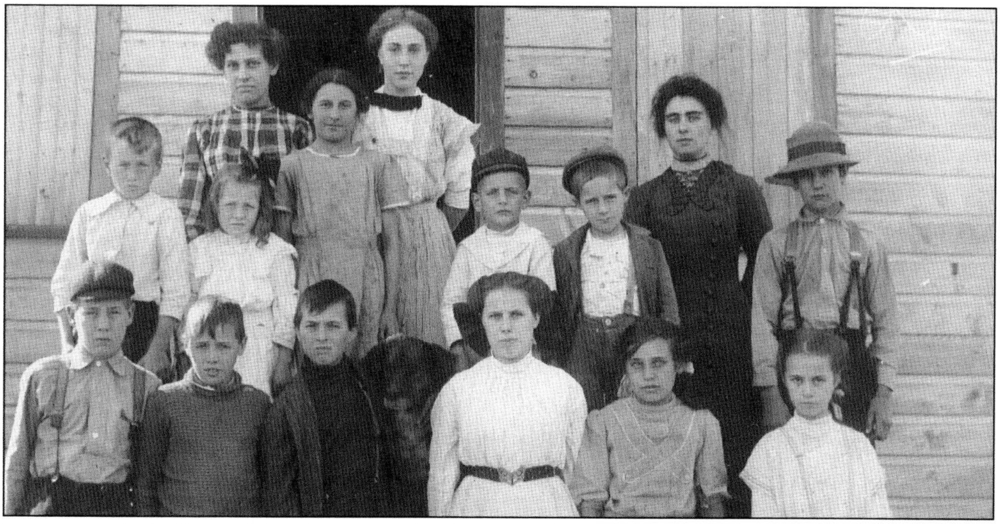

Students of Guilford School pose with their teacher Anna Heaney (back right). Pictured c. 1910, the school was on Guilford School House Road west of the Hasbrouck Road junction. It is now used as a residence. Heaney, who graduated from New Paltz Normal School in 1908, also taught in New Hurley. In 1917, she married Philip H. Donahue, and the couple ran a farm on the southern edge of the Gardiner hamlet. (Courtesy of Anna Heaney's son Paul Donahue.)

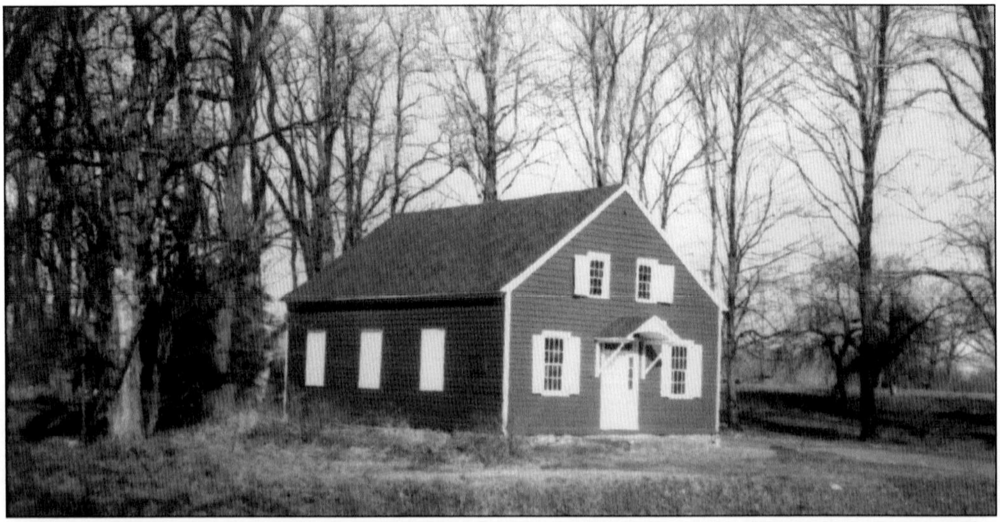

Kettleborough School, on the Ireland Corners–New Paltz Road, was established by the 1790s. The building shown here was built in 1835. In the 1850s, many students were of long-settled Huguenot families, and others were of Irish immigrant farm-labor families. The school closed in 1932. Later, Kenneth Hasbrouck, the historian who lived next door, acquired the building, preserved it, added its door canopy, and painted it, not its traditional white, but red. Recent owner Mike Boylan has also preserved it and kept it painted red. It has become a beloved Gardiner landmark. It is shown here *c.* 1989, when it and the neighboring Hasbrouck house became a National Historic Place. (Courtesy of Alice Hasbrouck.)

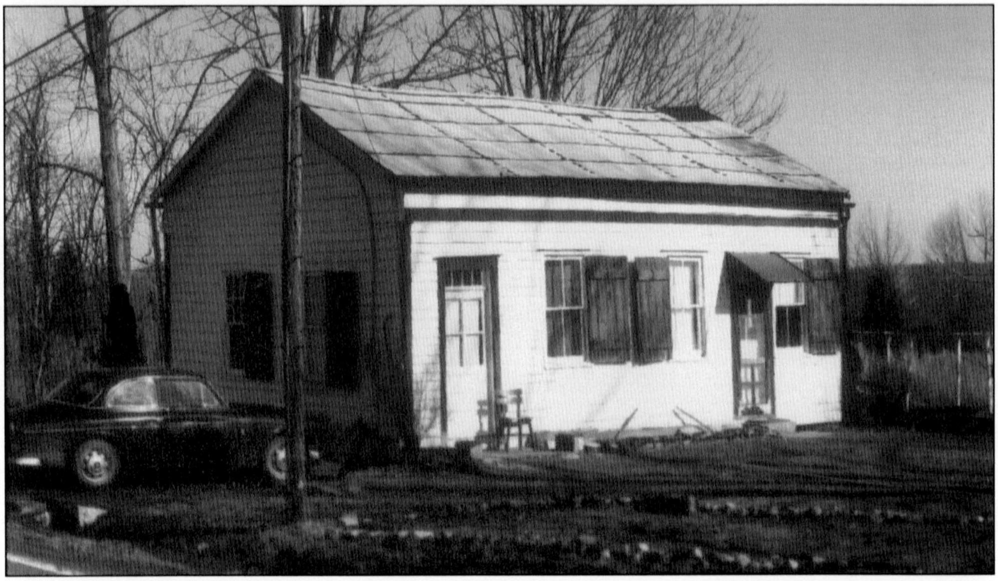

The one-room Libertyville School, built in 1838, was located on the Wallkill River's west side, on Libertyville Road near where it joins Albany Post Road. In 1856, a total of 64 students were enrolled, some of whom lived over the town border in New Paltz. The school's district extended across the river, and students who lived on the other side had a holiday anytime they were unable to ford the river. The building ceased to be used as a school in 1929. When William Rhoads photographed it in 1977, it was occupied as a residence. It still is. (Courtesy of William B. Rhoads.)

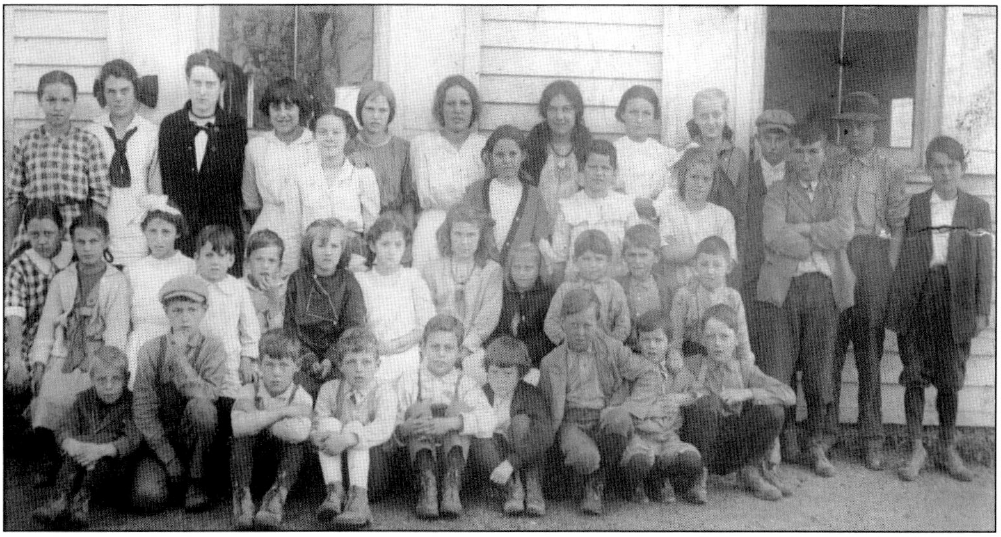

The Libertyville School's attendance appears large in this photograph taken in 1915. Among families likely to be represented among the students were Lutins, newcomers who ran a summer boardinghouse, and the longer-settled farm families, Quicks, Jansens, and Deckers. David M.W. Decker might be among the youngest students shown here. He was born in 1910. (Courtesy of Mary Tubbs Decker.)

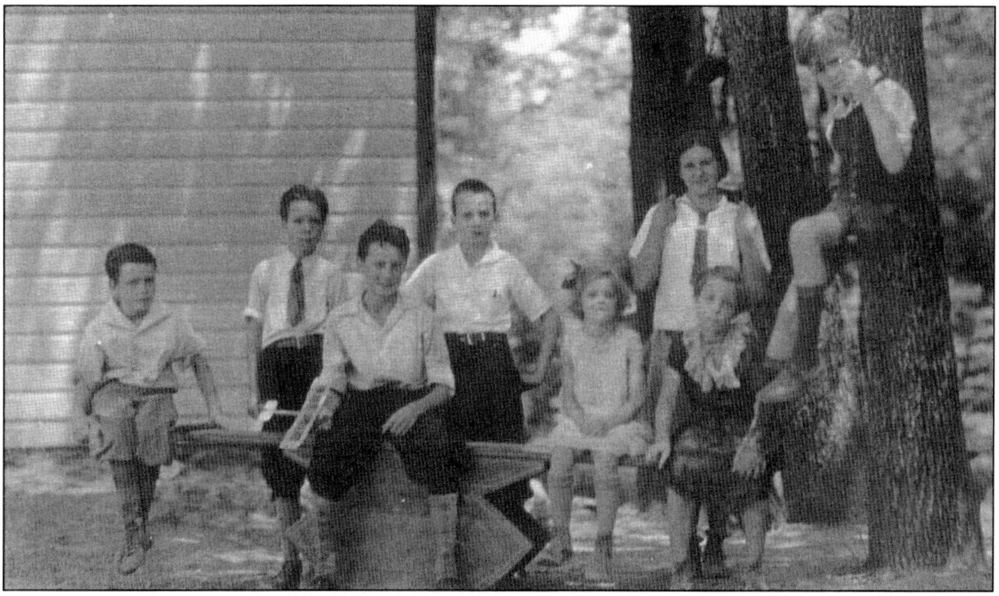

The first Trapps School building on this site on Trapps Road was built in 1850. From 1887 to 1890, one of its three trustees, Edward A Smiley, the son of Minnewaska founder Alfred H. Smiley, led the effort to build a new school on the same site. When this photograph was taken c. 1937, the Trapps population was declining and the attendance was so small that the school threatened to close. According to former student Roger Van Leuven (second from left), the desks were double, two children to each desk, and the students built some of them. Wood for the stove came from Minnewaska resort, and it was split by the students. The school finally closed in the mid-1940s, and the students were absorbed into the New Paltz school system. (Courtesy of Mohonk Preserve.)

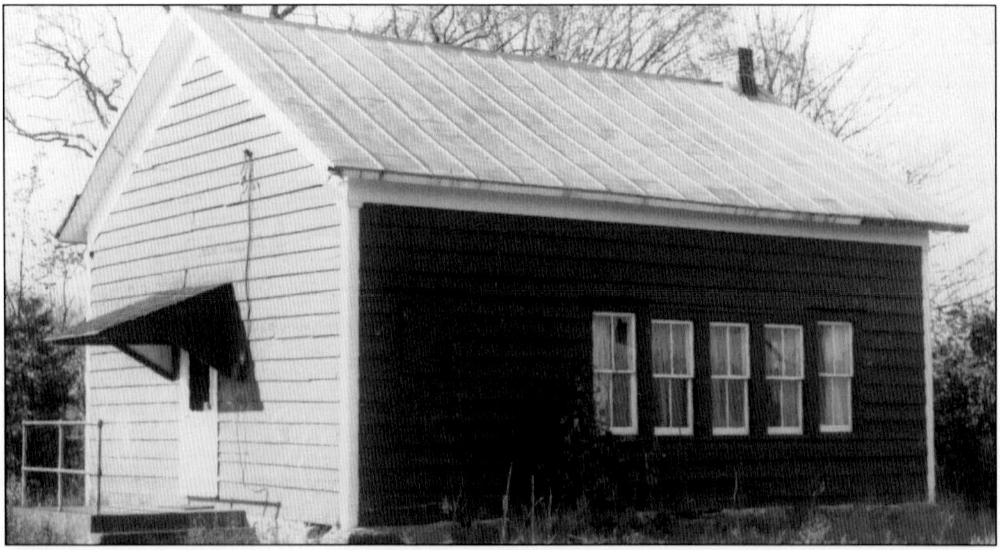

When Kathy Messerschmitt Weiss was a student at the Tuthilltown School on McKinstry Road, children played a knife-throwing game in the school yard without fear that anyone would be hurt. Weiss said a high point of the day was when teacher Vira Atkins read aloud, as from Laura Ingalls Wilder books. Because the teacher taught many different grades, the scholars were forced to learn independently, becoming self-reliant. Pictured in 1986, the school closed in 1959 and has recently served as artist Ron Schaefer's painting studio. (Photograph by Marion Ryan, courtesy of Haviland-Heidgard Historical Collection.)

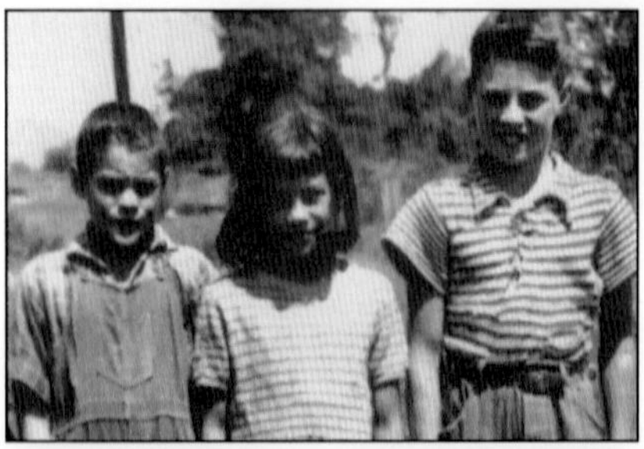

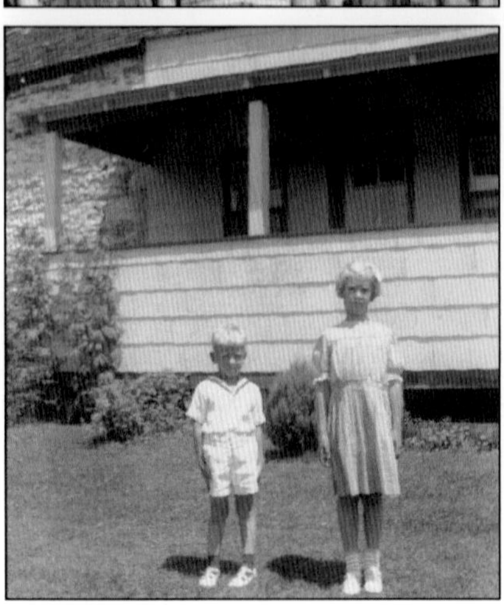

The three Togna children (upper left) lived off Burnt Meadow Road. Their father, Tony Togna, an immigrant from Italy, worked long hours as a farm laborer, and their mother was often hospitalized. The children had to get themselves up in the morning, prepare their own lunches to carry, and walk three miles to the Tuthilltown School. By the time this photograph was taken in 1940, the eldest child Enrico, aged 11, had been given a key to the school. He walked there early to start the wood stove. The two Ruger children, Smith "Smitty" and Vivian (lower left), lived on a farm on Tuthilltown Road just west of the Wallkill River. Their father, Floren Ruger farmed the land and ran a gas station by this house. When this picture was taken *c.* 1940, Vivian was attending Tuthilltown School, as her little brother did later, when he was old enough. She married Frank McCord in 1952 and served as town clerk from 1966 to 1995. (Upper photograph courtesy of Enrico Togna; lower photograph courtesy of Vivian R. McCord.)

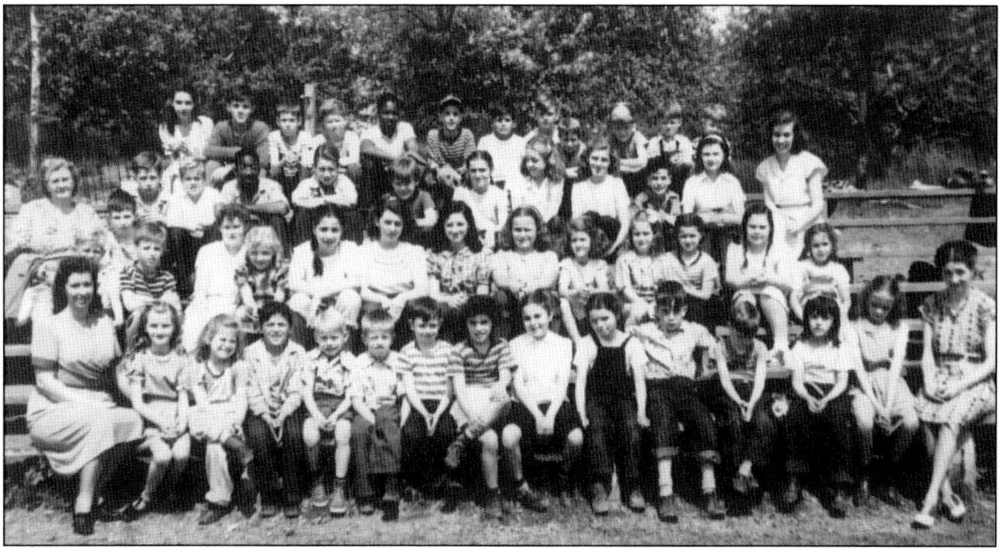

Three small schools of the New Paltz Central School District join together for an annual field day. While most of the small schools in the district had closed by then, the three represented here c. 1952 were still open: the one-room Plutarch School in New Paltz, the one-room Tuthilltown School in Gardiner, and the two-room school in the Gardiner hamlet. These three schools held their field day jointly at the Gardiner School because running water and generous field space were available there, as they were not at the other two schools. (Courtesy of Haviland-Heidgard Historical Collection.)

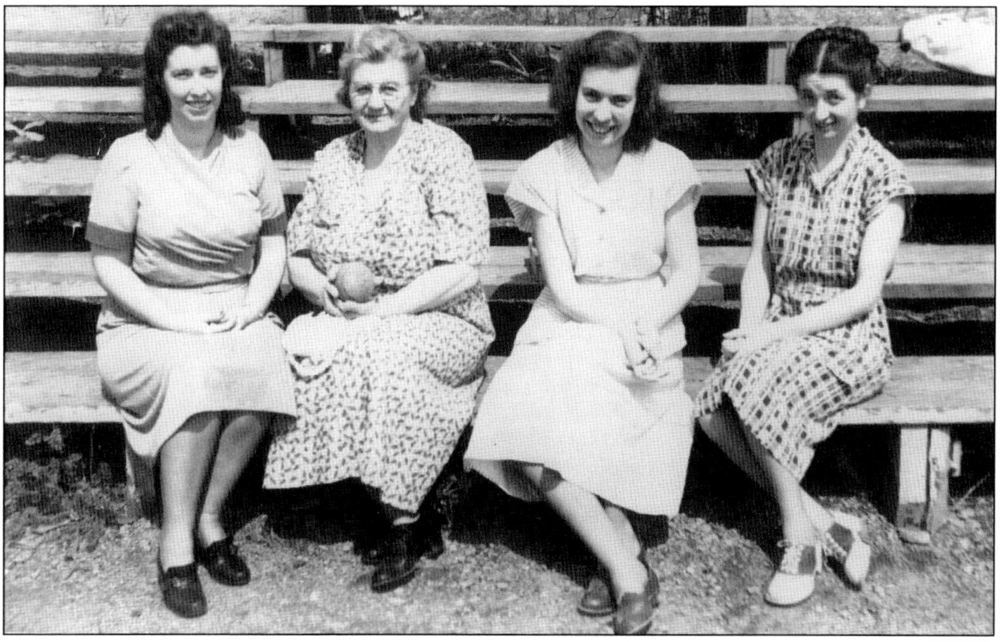

Four teachers sit on the bleachers at the New Paltz Central School District's annual field day. From left to right in this c. 1952 photograph are Genevieve Boland of the Plutarch School, Vira Atkins of the Tuthilltown School, and Mary Jenkins Nichols and Janet Bracken of the Gardiner School. Nichols was a member of the Jenkins family who operated a fruit farm on Yankee Folly Road. (Courtesy of Haviland-Heidgard Historical Collection.)

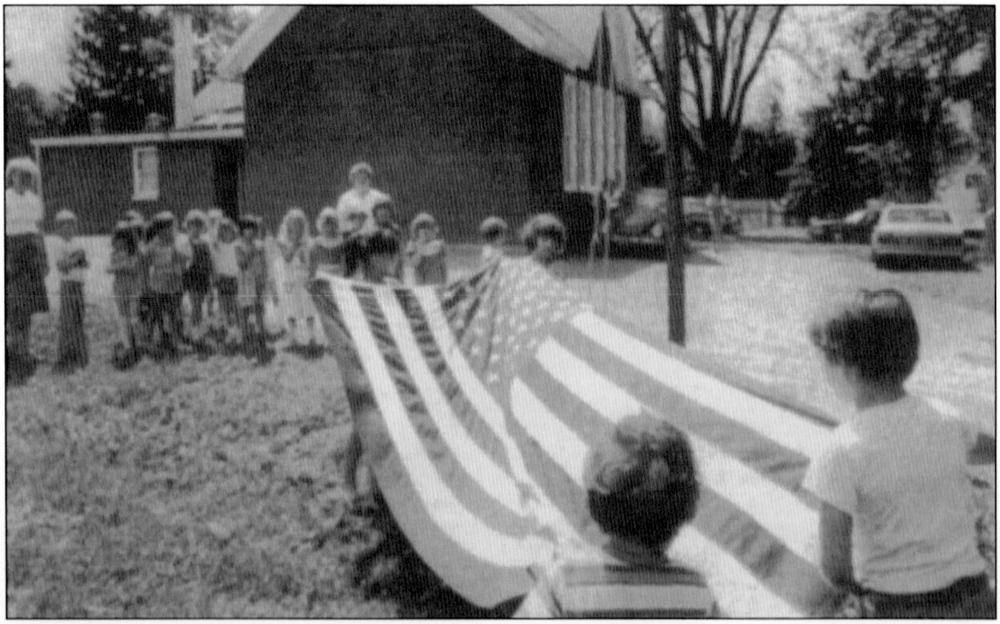

After the Gardiner School has held its last class, four children fold the flag while the rest of the students, teacher Lois Baker (left), and teacher's aide Margaret LaMark look on. The school closed in June 1981—the last of Gardiner's former district schools to close. While many parents argued that for small children small schools are better than large ones, officials of the New Paltz Central School District argued that it would be more efficient to educate these children in a larger school in New Paltz, in accord with a long-term trend for closing small schools throughout the state. In a referendum, voters of the New Paltz School District chose to close the school. (Photograph by Mike Carey, courtesy of the *Times-Herald-Record*.)

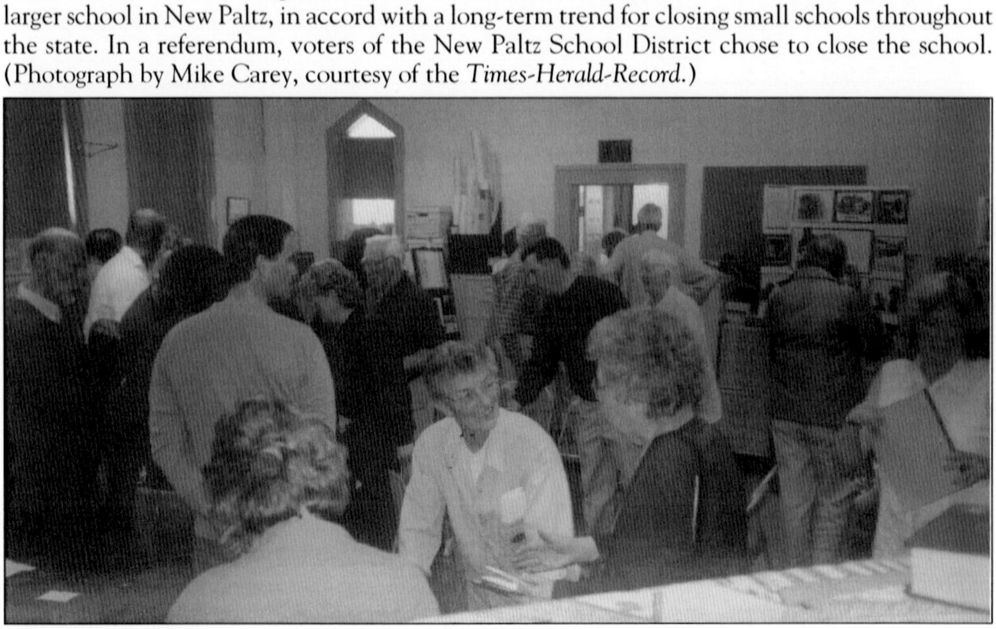

The Gardiner Historical Society meets at the former Gardiner School (then serving as the town hall) to remember the school 21 years after it closed. Among those shown on May 4, 2002, are Lynn Gorton (center), head of the school's parents association; Marybeth Majestic (far right), head of the historical society; and Paul Donahue (beneath the pointed window), a former Gardiner School student. (Photograph by Laura F. Walls.)

Five

Aqueducts

New York City constructed two great aqueducts to bring in water from the Catskill Mountains: the Catskill Aqueduct, built from 1909 to 1915, and the Delaware Aqueduct, built from 1937 to 1945. Both aqueducts passed through the town of Gardiner. Both still provide New York City with water.

In the Gardiner region, when the Catskill Aqueduct encountered such obstacles as the Shawangunk Mountains in the Bonticoe neighborhood or the Wallkill River in the Libertyville-Forest Glen neighborhood, it passed deep under them. Elsewhere, parts of the Catskill Aqueduct were constructed of concrete conduits placed in the ground in shallow cuts, covered with only a thin layer of soil. In contrast, the later Delaware Aqueduct passed deep under the Shawangunk Mountains near Lake Minnewaska and also deep under Gardiner's Wallkill Valley and stayed deep in the ground. The Delaware Aqueduct did not emerge close to the ground surface anywhere in or near Gardiner.

The ceremony beginning the construction of the whole Delaware Aqueduct was held in Gardiner in 1937, with New York City Mayor Fiorello LaGuardia speaking. Gardiner's present town garage is built near the ceremony site on fill excavated for the aqueduct tunnel that had been brought to the surface through a nearby shaft.

As dangerous as building the aqueducts was, several Gardinerites dared to work inside the aqueduct tunnels, among them Leonard Dewyea, Ransom Freer, Chet Hoffman, Walter Hoppenstedt, Patrick Powers, Ike Williamson, and brothers Frank, George, and Charles Majestic. Some of these men still live in Gardiner and still remember.

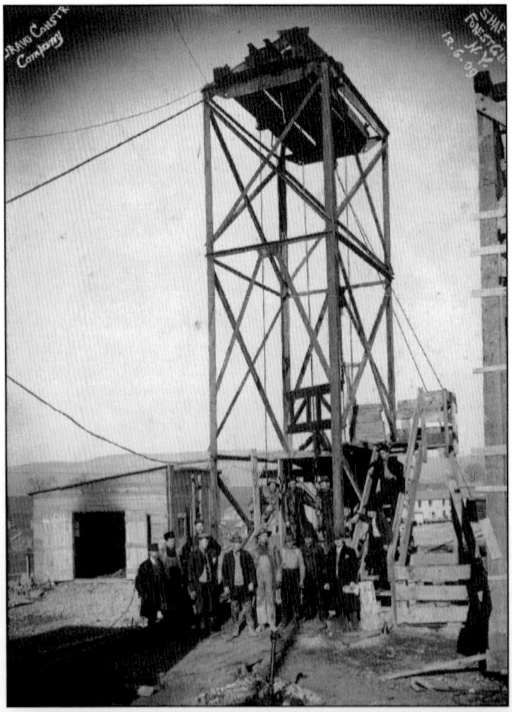

As pictured on December 6, 1909, the Catskill Aqueduct's Shaft No. 4 was near the northwest corner of Forest Glen and Old Ford Roads in Gardiner. The shaft reached down into the aqueduct tunnel that was being constructed to pass deep under the Wallkill River. The shaft was used both to lift earth out of the tunnel as it was excavated and to lower supplies and workmen down to the tunnel. A tragedy occurred when three men were being lowered in a bucket and the bucket fell. The men were killed. (Courtesy of Haviland-Heidgard Historical Collection.)

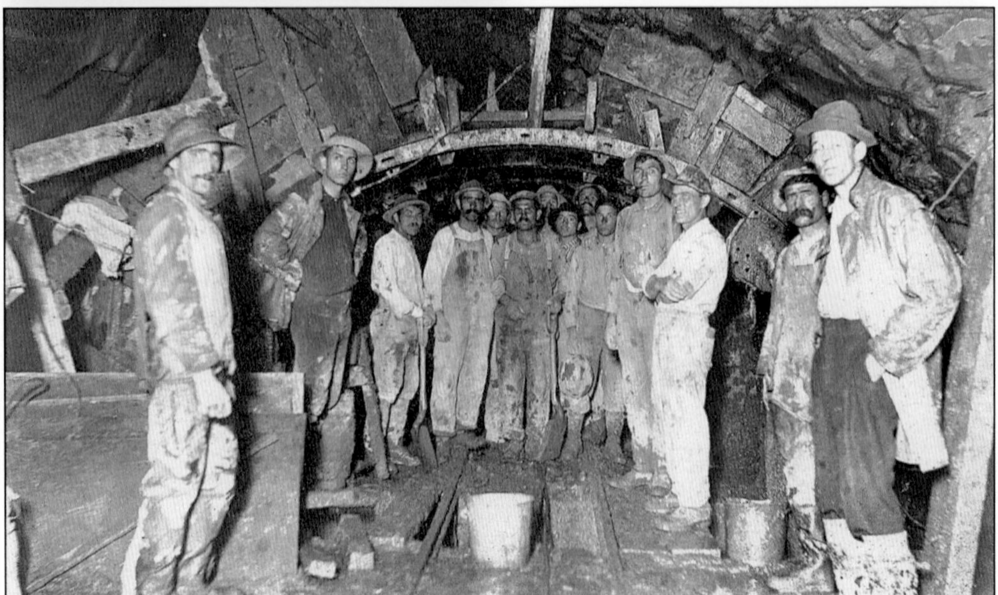

These workmen are constructing the Catskill Aqueduct's tunnel, a 14.5-foot diameter concrete conduit, deep underground at Forest Glen. They were assisted, as the track shown in this July 25, 1911 photograph suggests, by small work trains running through the tunnel. One young Gardiner resident who operated such trains was Walter Hoppenstedt, father of the future Gardiner veterinarian, Clifford Hoppenstedt. Many such workmen were immigrants with what long-term residents considered to be "jaw-breaking" names: Italian, Russian, Polish, Croatian, and the like. (Courtesy of Haviland-Heidgard Historical Collection.)

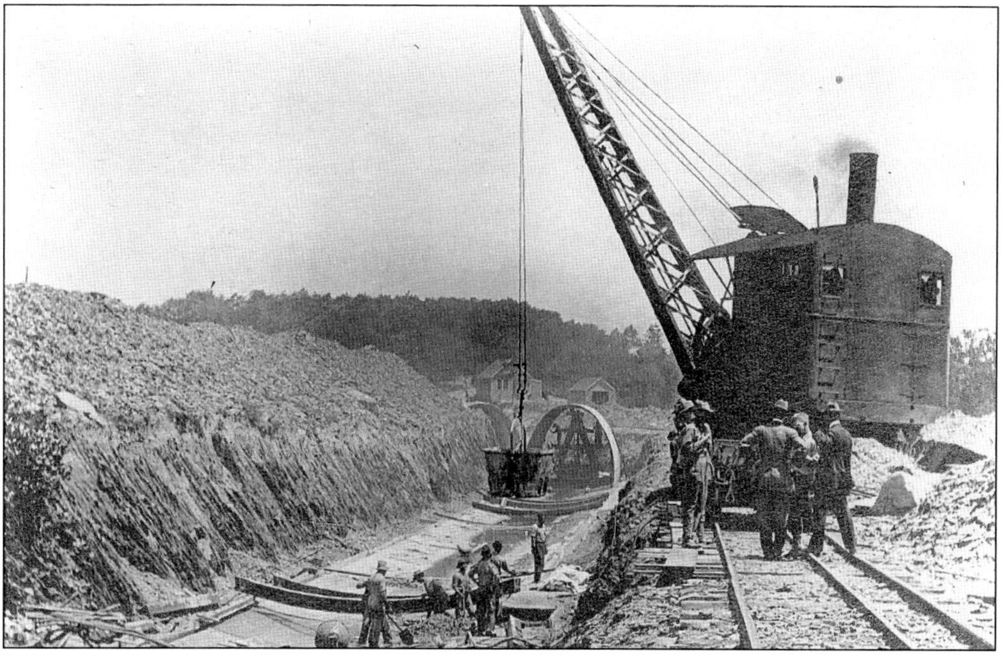

While near the Wallkill River the Catskill Aqueduct was a concrete conduit placed deep underground, in the sections of Gardiner near the Shawangunk Ridge and south of Ireland Corners, it was placed in a shallow trench, as illustrated here, and then covered with a thin layer of fill. The temporary rails (right) were for dinky steam engines to haul in supplies and for the traveling steam crane (shown) to place such supplies where they were needed. (Courtesy of Barbara Clinton.)

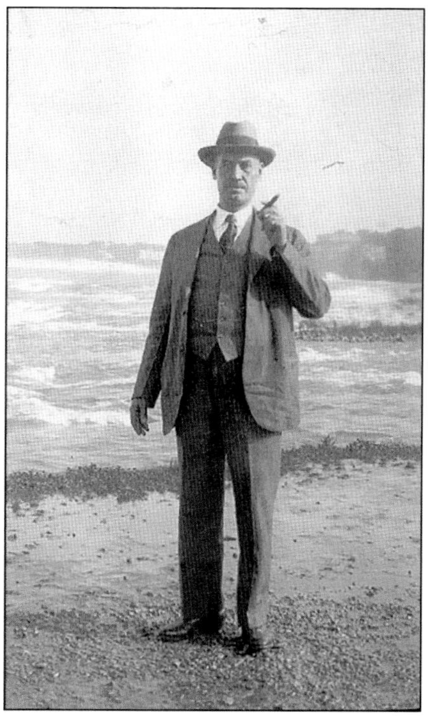

Construction engineer Ernest A. Herrick knew how to flourish a cigar. From 1901 to 1912, he was supervisor for Degnon Construction Company, the principal contractor building the Catskill Aqueduct in the New Paltz–Gardiner area. Herrick usually lived in Brooklyn. During aqueduct construction, however, he learned to know Gardiner, and from about 1939 to 1950, he lived in Gardiner on Bruynswick Road near McKinstry Road in a house later occupied by Ivan Klapper. Herrick's stepdaughter Helen married Richard Clinton Sr., who owned the Gardiner Hotel. (Courtesy of Barbara Clinton.)

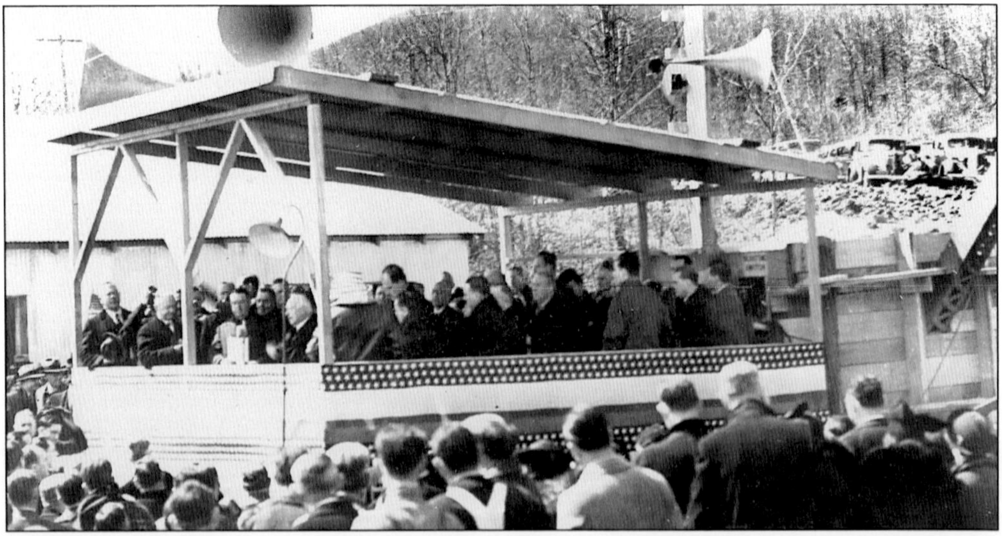

Construction of the Delaware Aqueduct, the second New York City aqueduct to pass through Gardiner, opens with a ceremony in Gardiner. The March 24, 1937 ceremony was held at a spot off Shaft Road, a road named for aqueduct Shaft No. 3, which was being built there. Mayor Fiorello LaGuardia of New York spoke. With his customary vigor, he explained his city's desperate need for water and praised the science that made it possible for this gigantic project to deliver water from distant mountains as needed. In the crowd of more than 1,000 who braved cold and mud to attend were the children of two of Gardiner's one-room schools, at Benton's Corners and Rutsonville. (Courtesy of New York City's Department of Environmental Protection.)

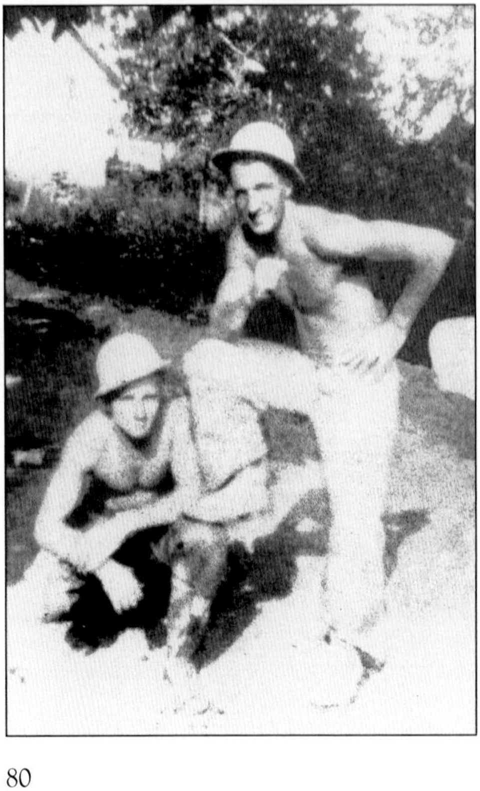

The Majestic brothers, Frank (left), age 18, and George, age 20, had been at work on the Delaware Aqueduct only a few months when this photograph was taken in the summer of 1937, in their backyard in Gardiner. They were wearing the aluminum helmets that had at first been provided to protect them at their work. Later they were provided with fiber helmets for better protection. (Courtesy of Frank Majestic.)

Three Aqueduct workmen prepare to drill near Shaft No. 17, between Armonk and White Plains. From left to right in this c. 1939 photograph are Frank Majestic, a driller, who recalls that while working at this site, he stayed during the week at a $10-a-week boardinghouse and went home to Gardiner weekends; an unidentified engineer, who decided where to drill; and an unidentified safety man, who used the bar he is holding to pry off any loose rocks so that they would not fall on the workers. (Courtesy of Frank Majestic.)

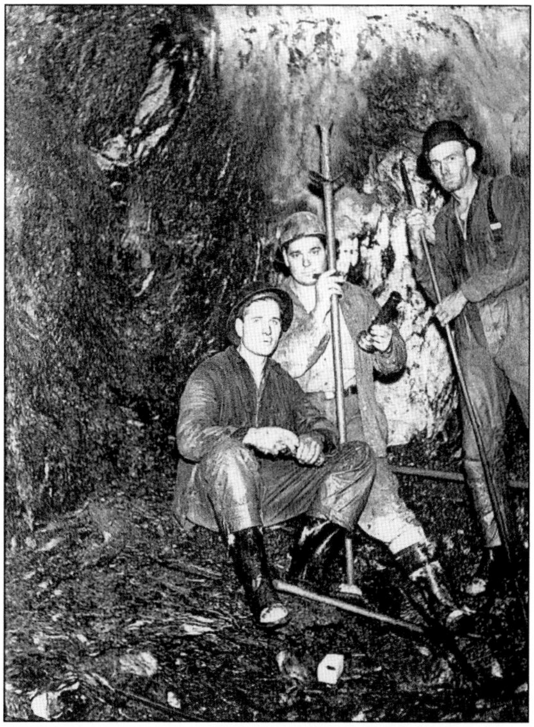

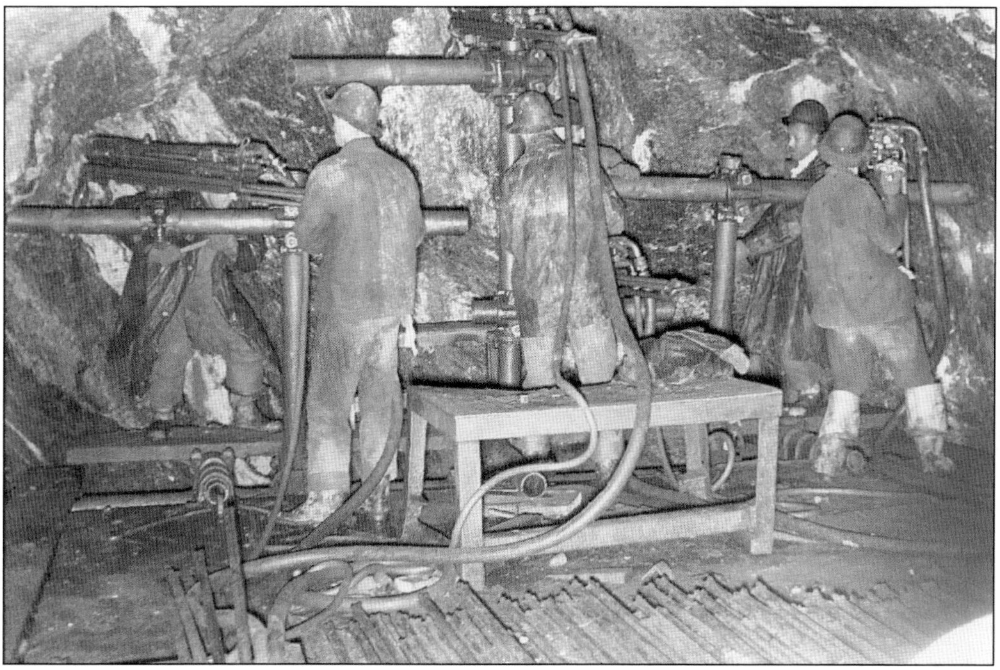

Frank Majestic (left) is occupied in drilling near Shaft No. 17. He stands on a jumbo, a carriage platform meant for drilling. The jumbo, moving on gantry rails, advanced into the tunnel as excavation progressed. Power for the drilling was supplied by compressed air hoses, fed by a compressor plant located near the shaft. Lined up in the foreground of this c. 1939 photograph are steel rods used in the drills. (Courtesy of Frank Majestic.)

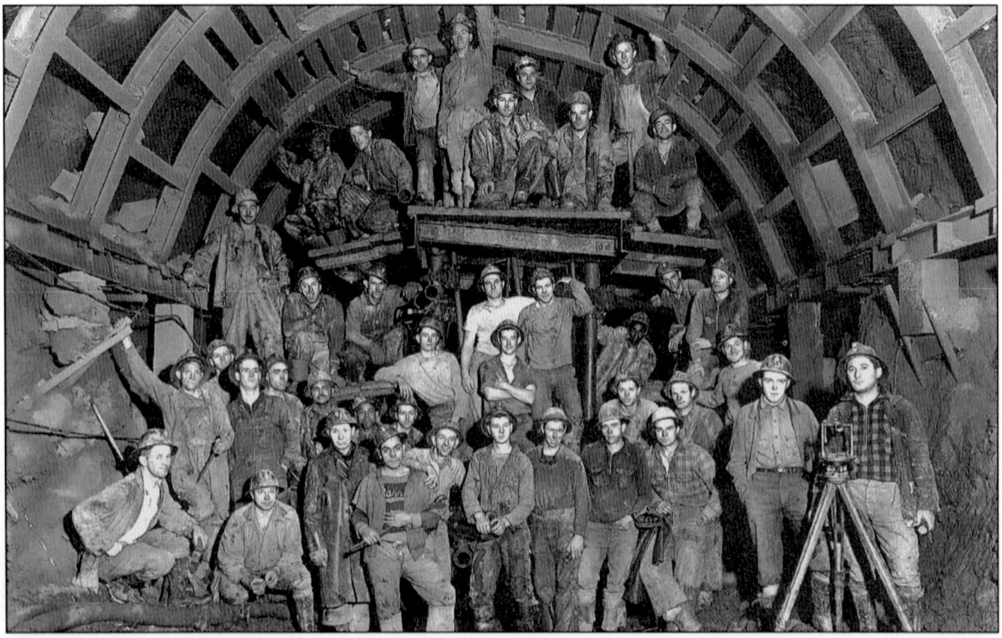

The Delaware Aqueduct tunnel was colossal—much larger than the Catskill Aqueduct tunnel. *Engineering News* called the Delaware Aqueduct "the greatest tunnel project ever attempted." This crew, working by Shaft No. 2 near Kerhonkson, consists of two gangs. The gang above the shelf, the smaller of the two, drilled holes in the rock where the tunnel was to be pushed forward, inserted dynamite in the holes, and wired the dynamite caps for blasting. This gang includes George Majestic (second from the left). The gang below the shelf maintained both the narrow-gage train tracks and the drainage ditches. (Courtesy of William and Carol Majestic Lohrman.)

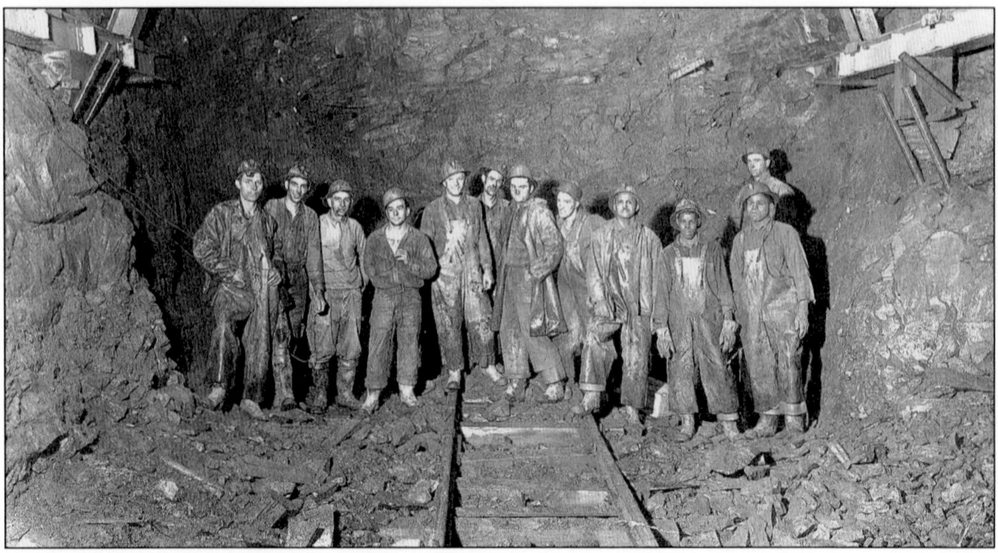

Workmen pose in the Delaware Aqueduct tunnel near Shaft No. 2. Among those in the *c.* 1940 view are the foreman (right rear) and George Majestic (eighth from the left), who later became a prominent Gardiner supervisor. The tunnel roof was braced with steel wherever the walls were soft enough to threaten to collapse. (Courtesy of William and Carol Majestic Lohrman.)

Six

Anniversary and Park Dedication

On October 7 and 8, 1978, Gardiner celebrated both the 125th anniversary of its founding as a town and the dedication of a new town park, George Majestic Park.

The major local sponsor for the creation of the town in 1853 was Joseph O. Hasbrouck, a Tuthilltown merchant. The new town was named, however, in honor of an earlier lieutenant governor of the state, Addison Gardiner. His home city of Rochester was in the western part of the state, and there is no known special tie between him and the new town. Except for possible political ties to him, there seems to be no obvious reason why he was chosen for the honor.

In the 1960s and 1970s, George Majestic, a longtime Gardiner supervisor, took the lead in creating and developing a new town park. After Majestic's death in 1975, the town board decided to name the park after him. His father, a cabinetmaker, was born in Austria, and his mother in Yugoslavia. Majestic himself, born in New York City, moved to Gardiner with his parents in the 1930s. After helping to dig the Delaware Aqueduct, he operated a hardware store on Main Street where the post office now stands. By 1967, he had relocated his store into what had been Moran's store. Majestic had vision, was tough, coped with endless contention, and was repeatedly reelected as Gardiner's supervisor.

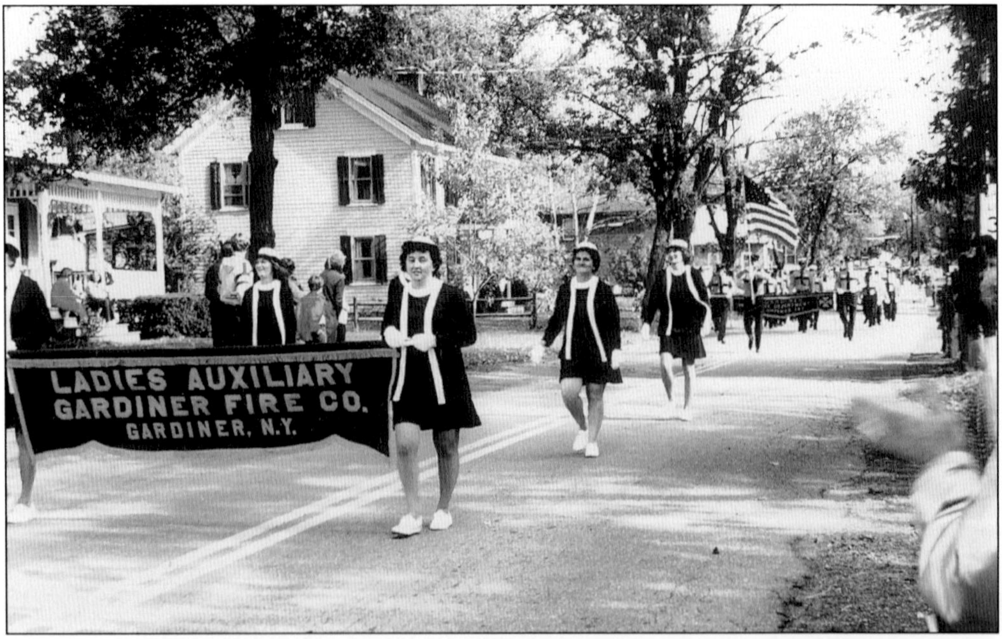

To celebrate the 125th anniversary of Gardiner's founding, the town held a parade on October 7, 1978. Among those marching are members of the Ladies Auxiliary of the Gardiner Fire Company. They include Gertrud Orlowski (far left, partially in view), Judy Sumnick (third from left), and Helen Roberts (fourth from left). (Courtesy of Minke Kwak.)

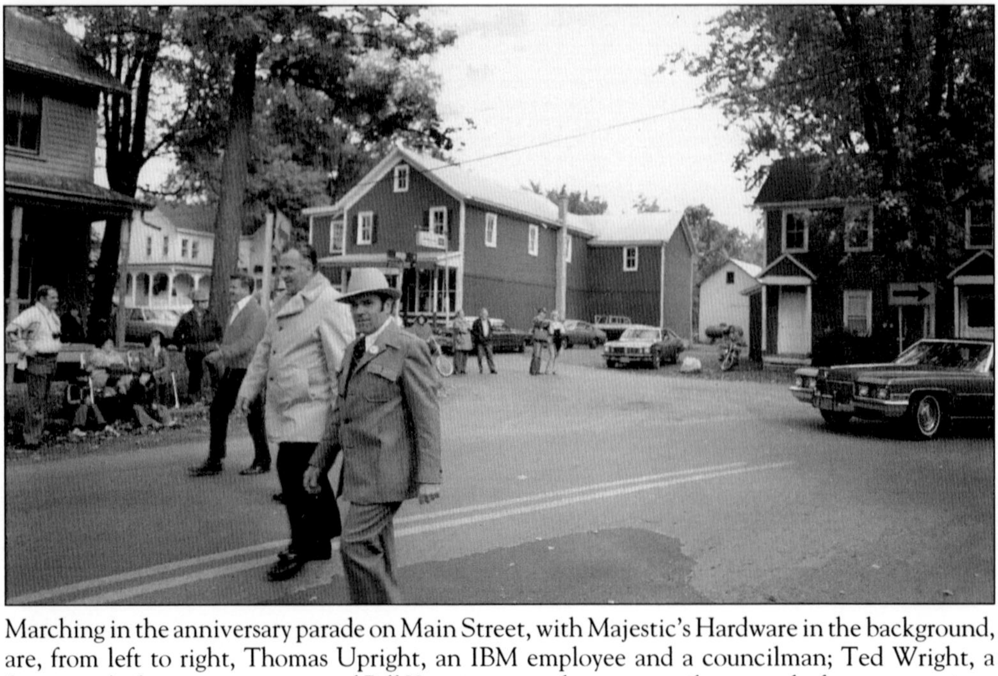

Marching in the anniversary parade on Main Street, with Majestic's Hardware in the background, are, from left to right, Thomas Upright, an IBM employee and a councilman; Ted Wright, a farmer and a former supervisor; and Bill Keeping, a teacher, a councilman, and a future supervisor. During the festivities, parachute jumpers who had flown up from the nearby Gardiner airport dropped down out of the sky. (Courtesy of William and Carol Majestic Lohrman.)

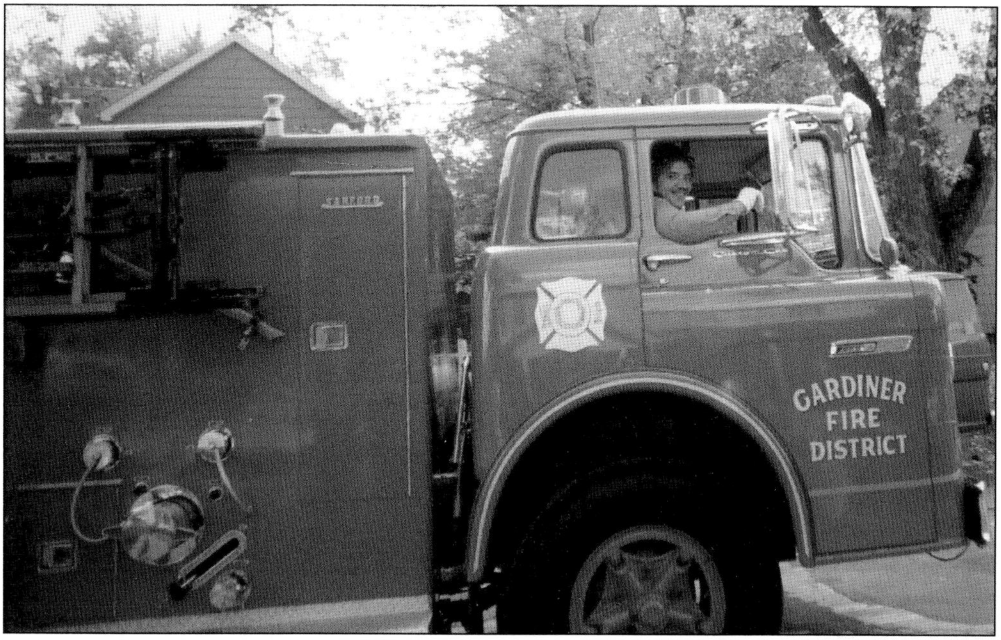

In the parade is a Gardiner fire truck, with Joe Romano at the window. Noisy though it was, the truck, a 1972 Ford, had long provided effective service pumping water for the fire department. It was still doing service when De Piero's barn burned in the summer of 2002. It is not likely to last much longer. (Courtesy of William and Carol Majestic Lohrman)

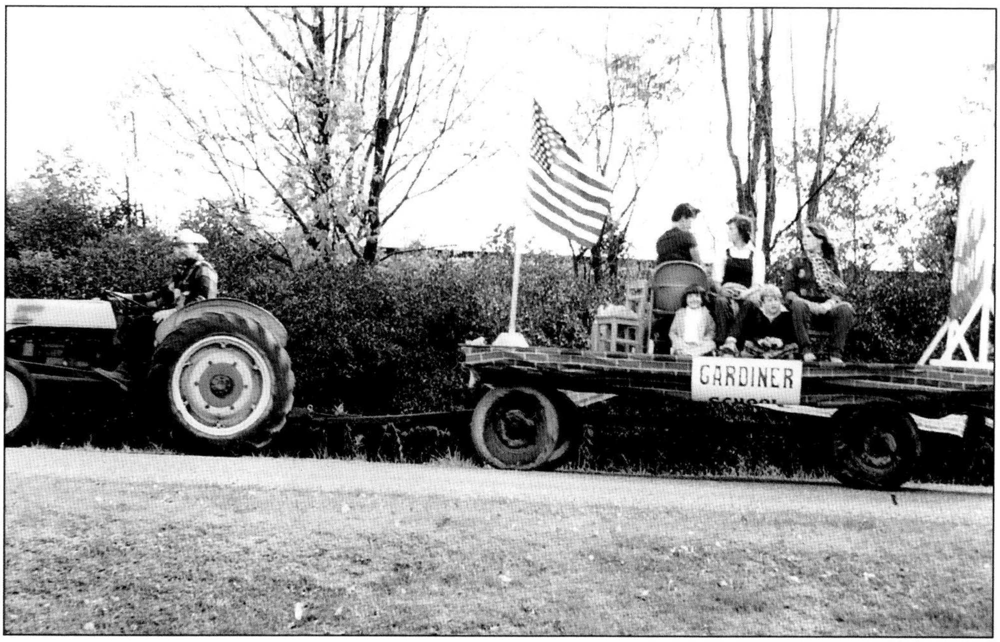

This Gardiner School float rolls down Sand Hill Road on its way to join the anniversary parade. At a time when the school was already threatened with being closed, the float offered a chance to affirm the school's value. John Kwak drove the tractor hauling the float. On the float were John Kwak's son David, along with Lynn Gorton and her children, Mandy, Isley, and April. (Courtesy of Minke Kwak.)

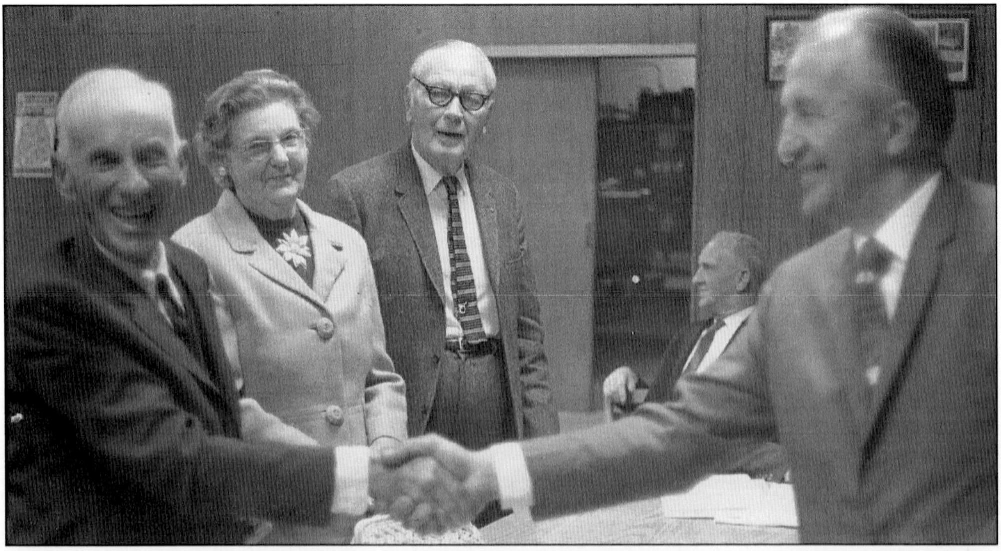

Supervisor George Majestic (right), who had long worked to create a town park, congratulates Thomas and Josephine Murphy (left) on the purchase of their property for inclusion in the park. Also pictured are Dr. Virgil DeWitt (standing) and John Grey (seated), both members of the town's recreation commission. This photograph was probably taken on January 24, 1972, when the deed was signed. The park was to consist of 26 acres, 16 from the Murphys and 10 from the DePuys. Much of the land had earlier been the dairy farm of Philip and Anna Donahue. (Courtesy of William and Carol Majestic Lohrman.)

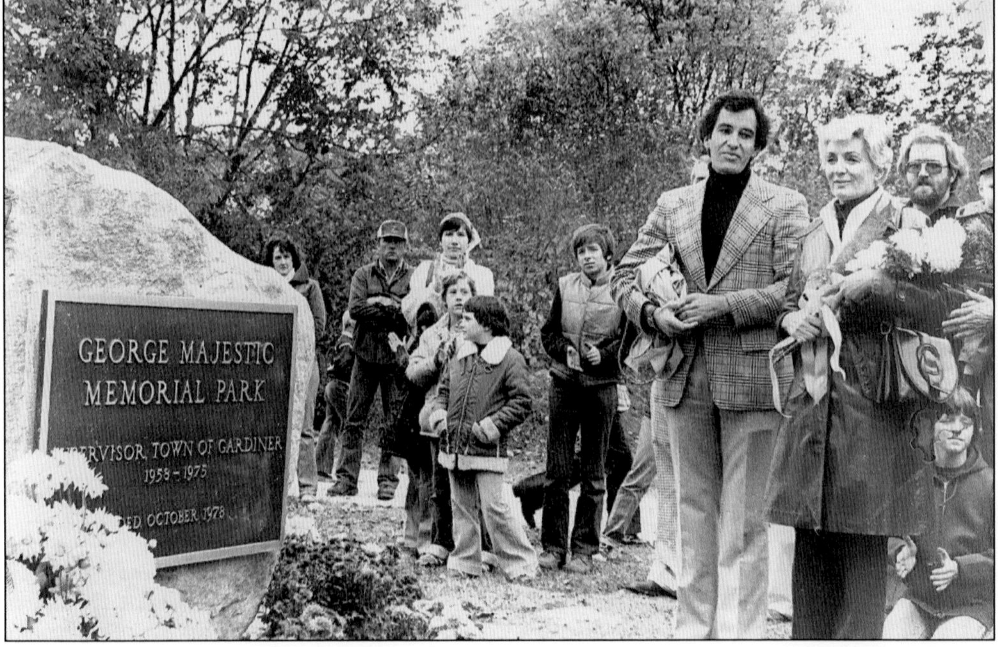

At the park dedication, George Majestic's widow, Irene Majestic (right foreground), stands in front of the plaque naming the park after her husband. Also in this October 8, 1978 photograph is her son George Majestic Jr. (left foreground). The park is on the edge of the Gardiner hamlet, south of Farmer's Turnpike. (Courtesy of the Gardiner Town Hall.)

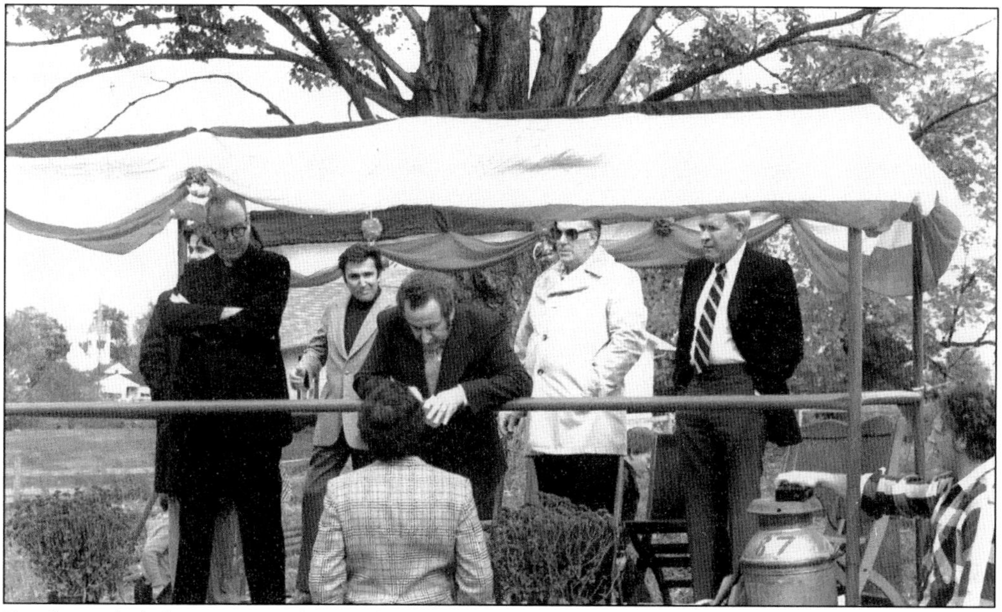

For the park dedication, speakers gather on a canopied platform provided by the Ladies Auxiliary of the Gardiner Fire Company. From left to right are Rev. Robert E. Moore of St. Charles Church; Maurice Hinchey, state assemblyman and later congressman; Dominick Formisano, postmaster and master of ceremonies; Bill Keeping, councilman; and an unidentified man. (Courtesy of William and Carol Majestic Lohrman.)

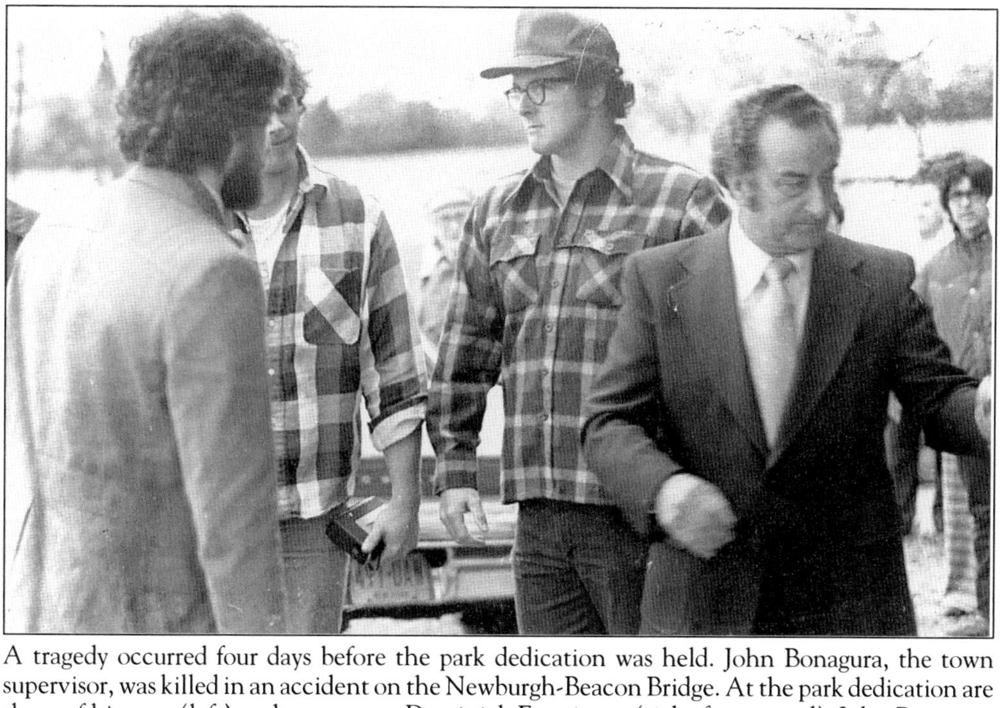

A tragedy occurred four days before the park dedication was held. John Bonagura, the town supervisor, was killed in an accident on the Newburgh-Beacon Bridge. At the park dedication are three of his sons (left) and postmaster Dominick Formisano (right foreground). John Bonagura was born in Chicago. He came to Gardiner in 1942 to work on his grandfather's farm on Phillies Bridge Road and stayed. (Courtesy of the Gardiner Library.)

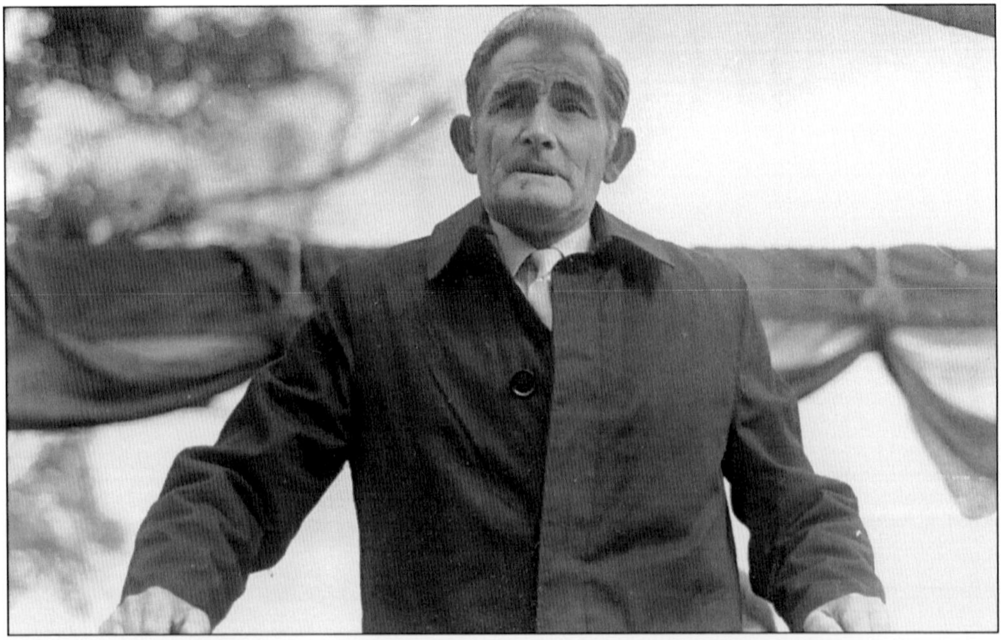

Samuel Stokes, town justice, was among the park dedication speakers. Although he was a Republican, Stokes had worked well with George Majestic, a Democrat. Stokes and his brother Fred, both born in Ireland, lived on adjoining farms on Albany Post Road near McKinstry Road. Of the two, Fred Stokes was devoted to farming, while Samuel Stokes, with his wife, Jane "Dolly" Stokes, was more devoted to community activism. (Courtesy of the Gardiner Library.)

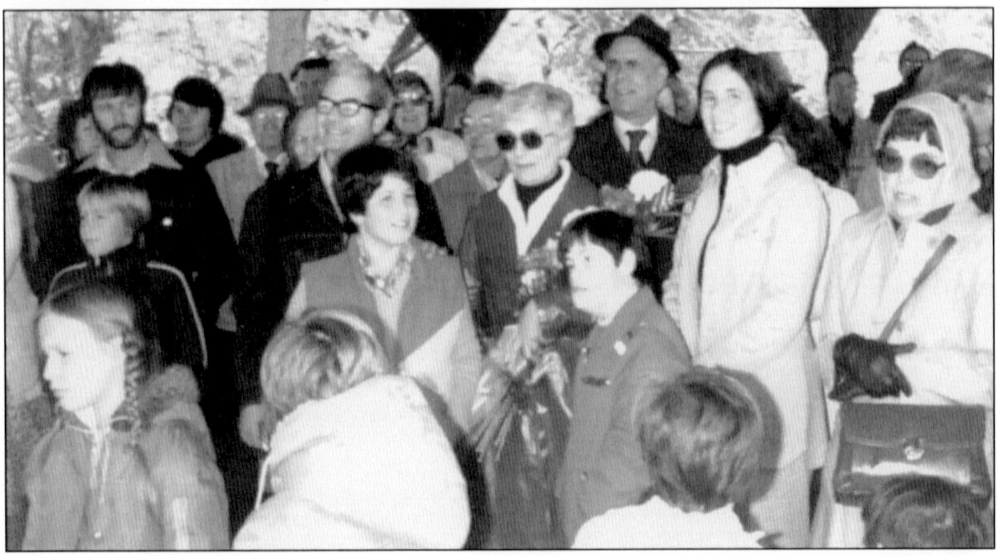

During the dedication in the park's just completed pavilion, George Majestic's widow, Irene Majestic (center, wearing dark glasses), stands with her right hand on the shoulder of her son Bobby Majestic and next to her daughter, town bookkeeper Carol Majestic Sobon (second from right). Behind the son is Frank Ogno (wearing glasses), a hamlet grocer who was chairman of the anniversary celebration. Behind the mother and daughter is Herman Walker (wearing a hat), a State University of New York, New Paltz, professor who served on many local boards. (Courtesy of William and Carol Majestic Lohrman.)

Seven

MINNEWASKA HOTELS

Quaker Alfred H. Smiley bought land around Lake Minnewaska in 1875, soon after his twin brother, Albert, had bought land around the nearby Lake Mohonk. By 1879, Alfred Smiley had built his first hotel on Lake Minnewaska, and by 1887, his second. Both hotels consisted of several stories and were romantically irregular in shape, with wings, porches, gables, and towers. As the Smileys expressed it, their purposes included fostering "restraint in human relationships in keeping with the Quaker faith" and preserving "this wonderful spot as an unspoiled sanctuary of nature."

In its early years, the resort consisted of 3,000 acres; by 1915, some 7,000 acres; by 1953, some 10,000 acres. The decorum that prevailed at the resort is suggested by the expectation as late as the 1950s that gentlemen wear coats in the dining rooms, that swimmers wear robes when walking to docks, and that guests not arrive on Sundays. At first, the hotels were lit by candles and kerosene lamps. By 1906, they were lit by gas, and by 1929, by electricity supplied by Minnewaska's own hydroelectric plant on the Peterskill.

In 1955, the Smileys sold their Minnewaska resort to its general manager, Kenneth B. Phillips, who had worked his way up from being a garage mechanic at the resort. The Phillipses at first pledged to keep the resort's Quakerly traditions. Gradually, however, they introduced changes, attempting to adapt to altered times. By 1969, in financial distress, they began to sell portions of their resort to the state, which used them by 1972 to create Minnewaska State Park. After a fierce struggle over proposals to build condominiums near the lake, which environmentalists opposed as unsuited to such a fragile site, the state bought the remaining Phillips property by 1987, adding it to the park.

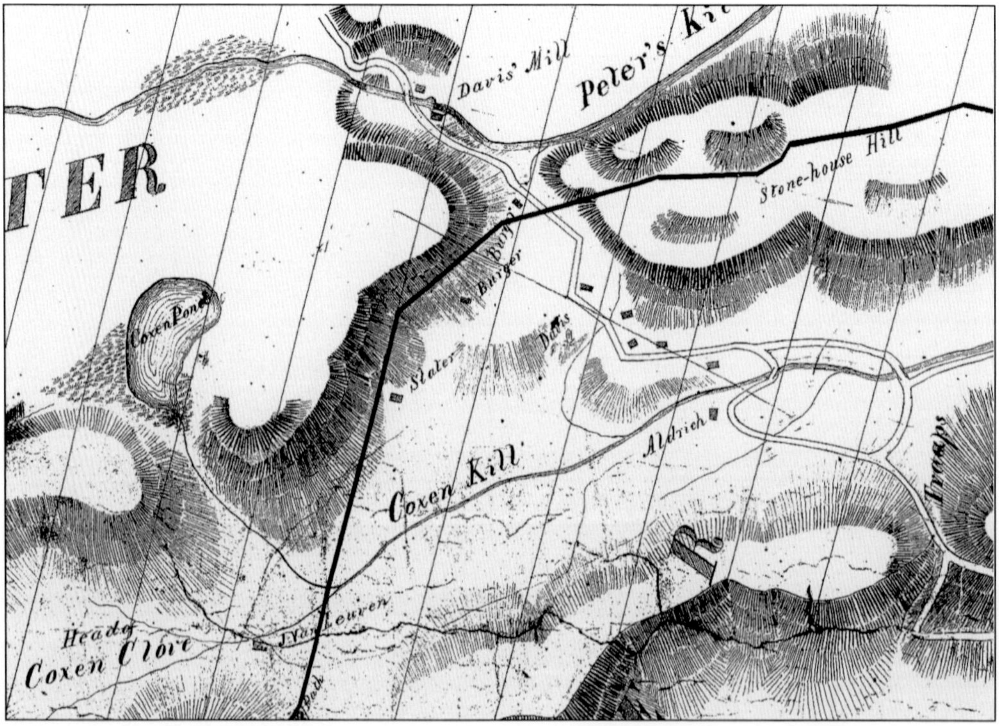

This map detail shows the Lake Minnewaska-Trapps area in 1860. On the Peter's Kill (top center) in the town of Rochester is the mill of George Davis, from whom Alfred Smiley later purchased much of the property. Coxen Pond (left center), also in Rochester, is the pond that Smiley later renamed Lake Minnewaska. The roads on the right half of the map were in the town of Gardiner, including the one (far right) passing through the mountain gap labeled "Traaps." (Courtesy of Haviland-Heidgard Historical Collection.)

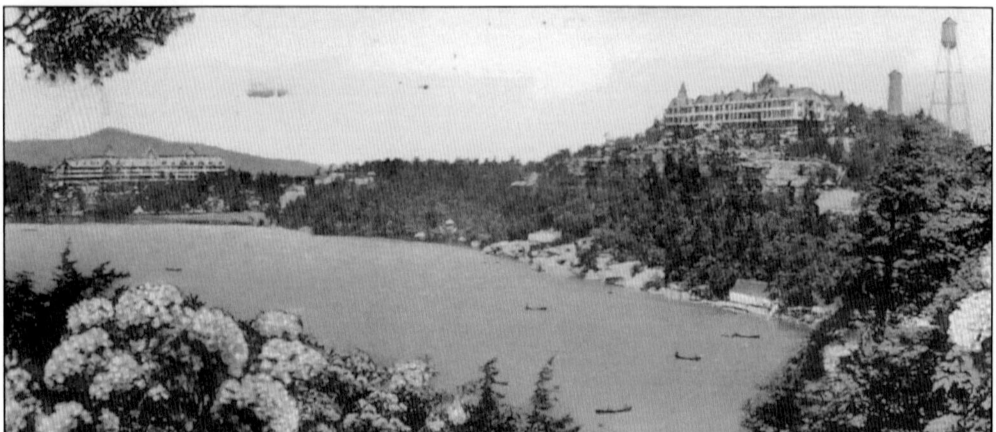

Laurel blooms along Lake Minnewaska, as shown in this 1935 postcard. Wildmere House is at the left, with the Catskill Mountains behind it, and Cliff House is at the right. Both hotels attracted guests who appreciated their Quakerly quiet, rustic simplicity, and commitment to temperance. Among the early eminent guests were editors E.L. Godkin of the *New York Evening Post* and Charles Dudley Warner of *Harper's Magazine*, and college presidents Thomas Chase of Haverford and James McCosh of Princeton. (Courtesy of Shirley Anson.)

In this illustration from a 1938 Minnewaska hotel brochure, skiffs show on Lake Minnewaska. Cliff House shows above, accompanied at the right by a water tower, a landmark that could be seen over much of Gardiner. Also visible are the railings of a long stairway leading down the cliff to the shore, where there were a boathouse, dock, and swim site. (Courtesy of Mohonk Mountain House Archives.)

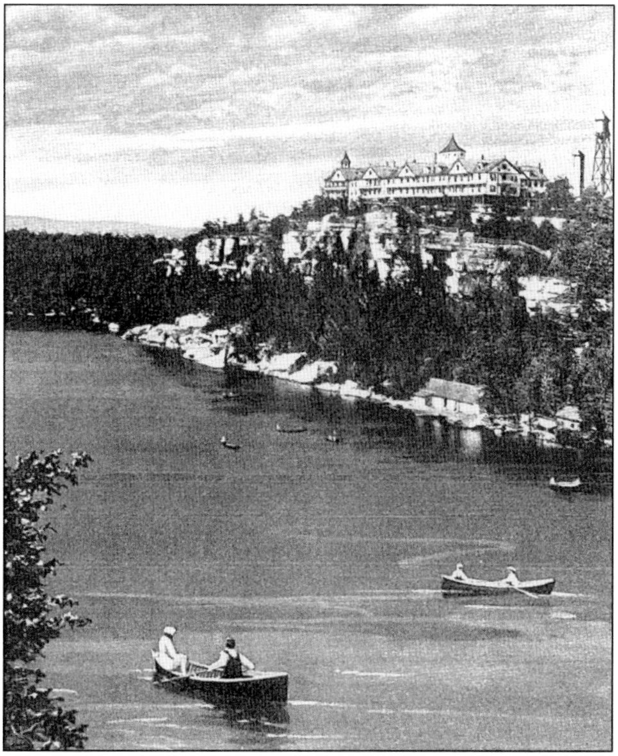

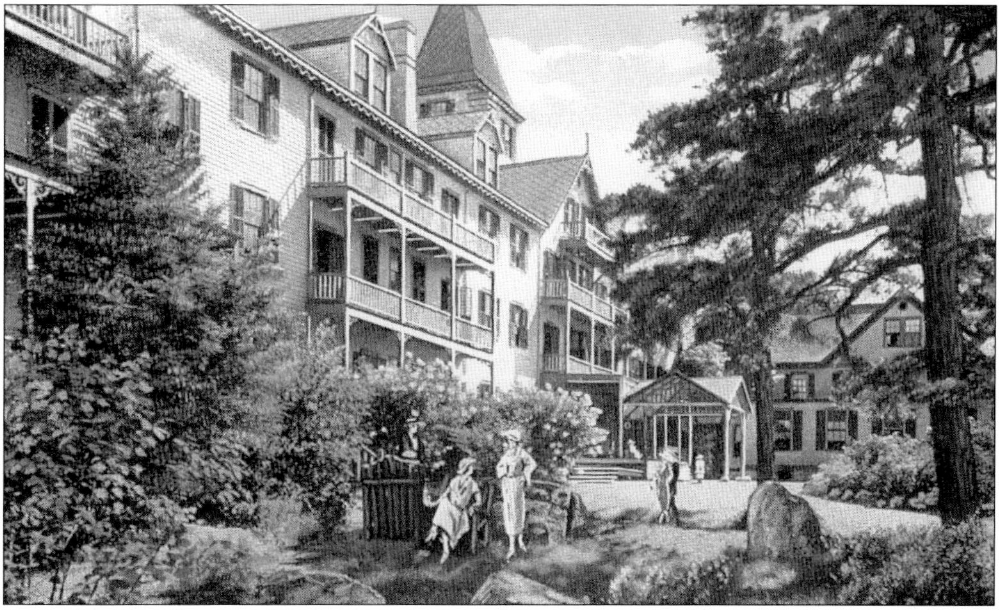

From the main entrance of Wildmere, guests were encouraged to explore the surrounding Shawangunk Mountains, including the extensive carriage roads, hiking trails, panoramic views, soaring cliffs, pine barrens, caves, and crevices. Guests could also explore other lakes, such as Lake Awosting, which was four miles to the southwest and four times larger than Lake Minnewaska but still within the Minnewaska resort's boundaries. This postcard view is perhaps from the 1920s. (Courtesy of Shirley Anson.)

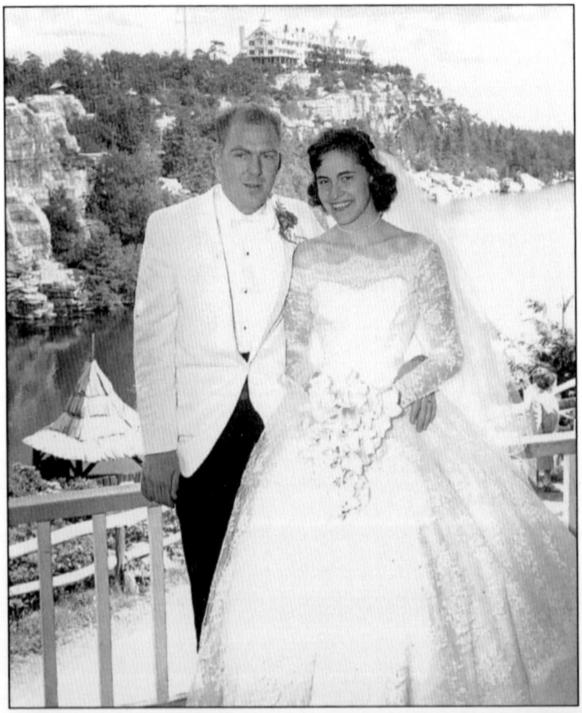

After they were married in the New Paltz Reformed Church in June 1958, Shirley Morse of Clintondale and Robert Anson of Poughkeepsie held their wedding reception at Wildmere House, where they were photographed on a porch overlooking Lake Minnewaska. They remember that the hotel served strawberry shortcake, which was delicious. They still keep Minnewaska photographs hanging in their home. (Courtesy of Shirley Anson.)

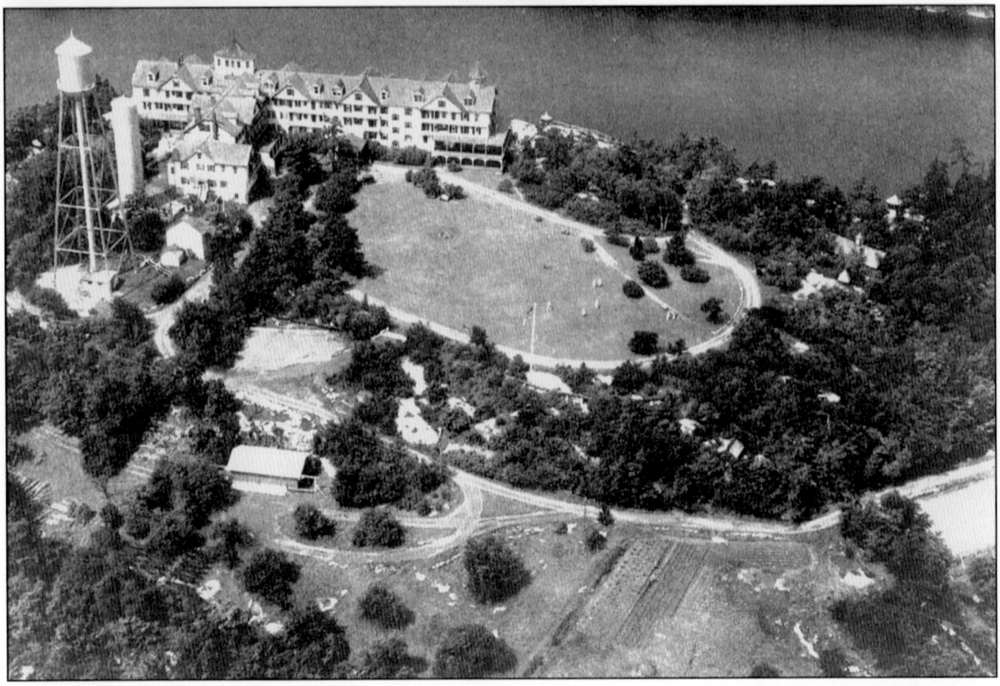

This 1938 aerial view of Cliff House shows Lake Minnewaska in the background. The lawn in the center was used for croquet, golf putting, and such hilarity as baseball games in which men dressed as women. Gardens are visible in the center foreground and tennis courts at the lower right. Cliff House ceased regular operation as a hotel in 1972, as it was too expensive to maintain. It burned in 1978. (Courtesy of Minnewaska State Park Preserve.)

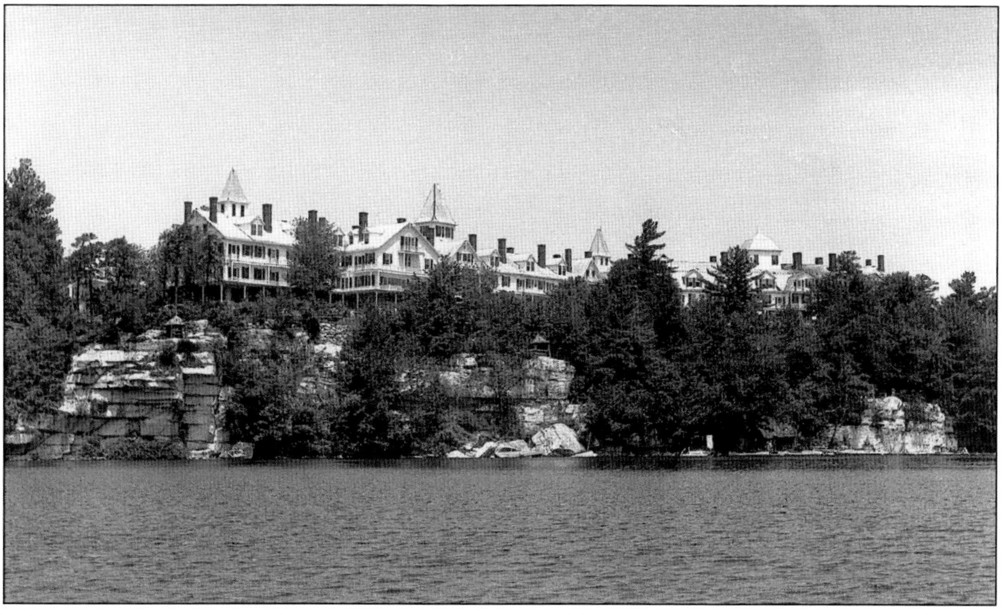

The romantic towers, chimneys, and dormers of Wildmere House are evident in this view from Lake Minnewaska, photographed by Eddie Bell in 1981. The lake's shore is rocky. The lake's area is 34 acres, and its maximum depth is 78 feet. (Courtesy of Minnewaska State Park Preserve.)

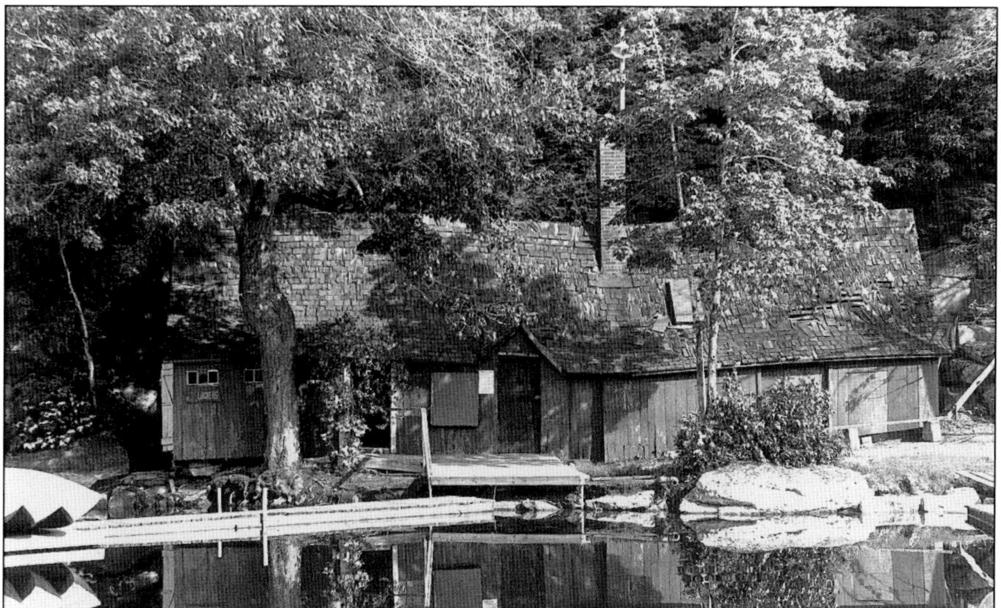

The rustic boathouse in front of Wildmere House was photographed in June 1981, with a boat and canoes showing on its dock (far left). The Minnewaska resort was financially distressed and had allowed the boathouse to deteriorate. Soon afterward, when the boathouse was dismantled, the Phillipses used some of its weathered boards to construct a porch ceiling for their new residence, Windsong, that they were building on a nearby cliff. (Photograph by Eddie Bell, courtesy of Minnewaska State Park Preserve.)

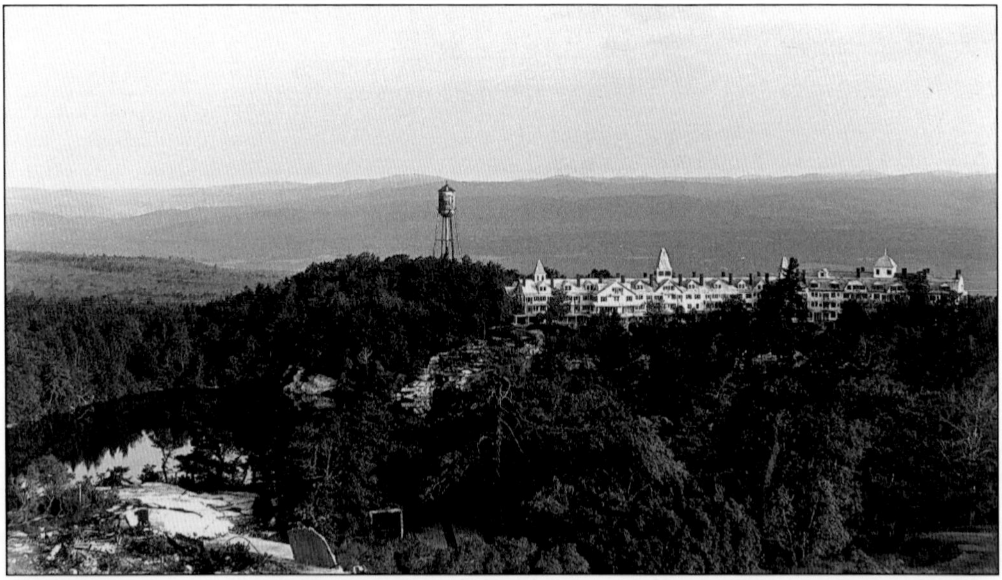

This photograph shows Wildmere House to the right, Lake Minnewaska to the left, and the Catskill Mountains in the background. It was taken by Eddie Bell from the site of the former Cliff House in June 1981. By that time, the Marriott Corporation had made a controversial proposal not only to replace Wildmere with a new hotel but also to construct 300 condominiums to be located east of the hotel between the lake and Beacon Hill. (Courtesy of Minnewaska State Park Preserve.)

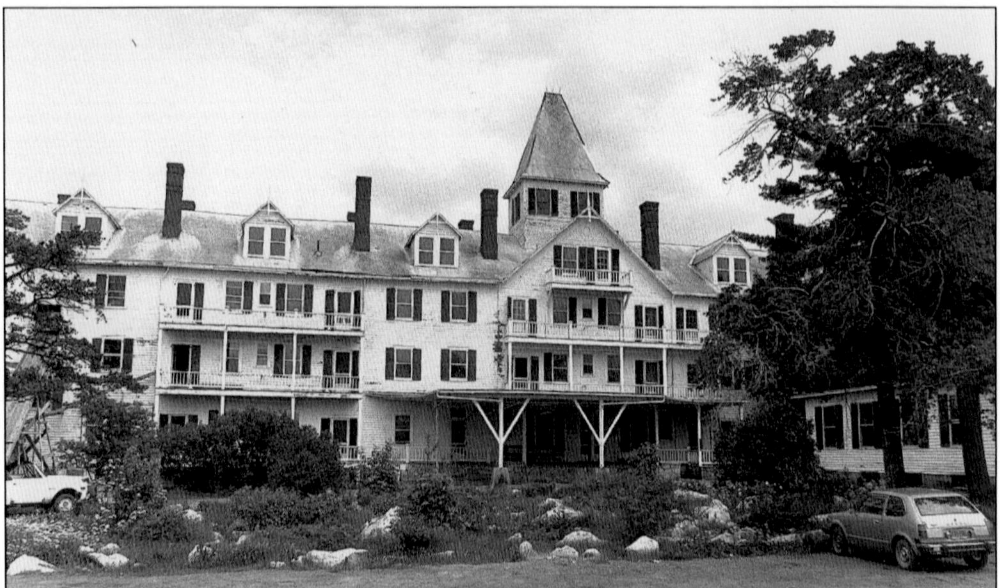

After Wildmere House had been condemned by the Ulster County Board of Health, the Phillips family closed it in the fall of 1979. They auctioned off some of its contents at once, more in 1981, with the help of the chute shown at the far left. At the time, environmental groups were challenging Marriott's condominium proposal as too large for the ecologically fragile mountain site. (Photograph by Eddie Bell, courtesy of Minnewaska State Park Preserve.)

Wildmere's east end fire escape was photographed in June 1981, when the Minnewaska resort seemed to be disintegrating. The state had already taken over much of the resort acreage as early as 1971–1972, when it acquired the Lake Awosting area. (Photograph by Eddie Bell, courtesy of Minnewaska State Park Preserve.)

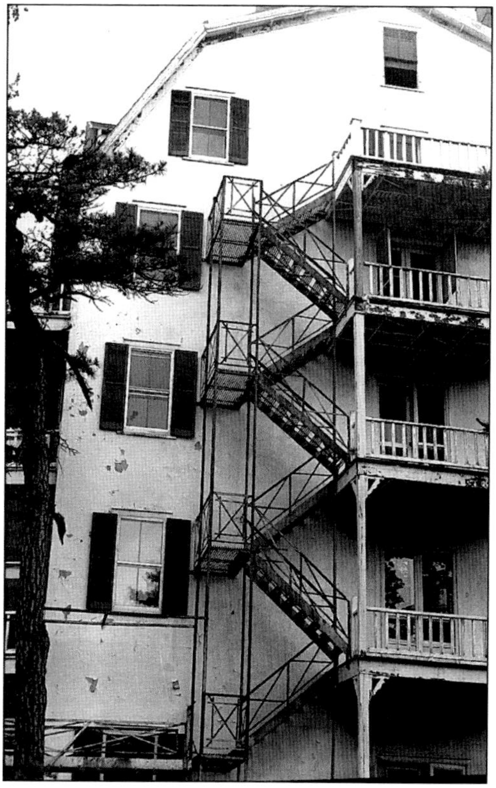

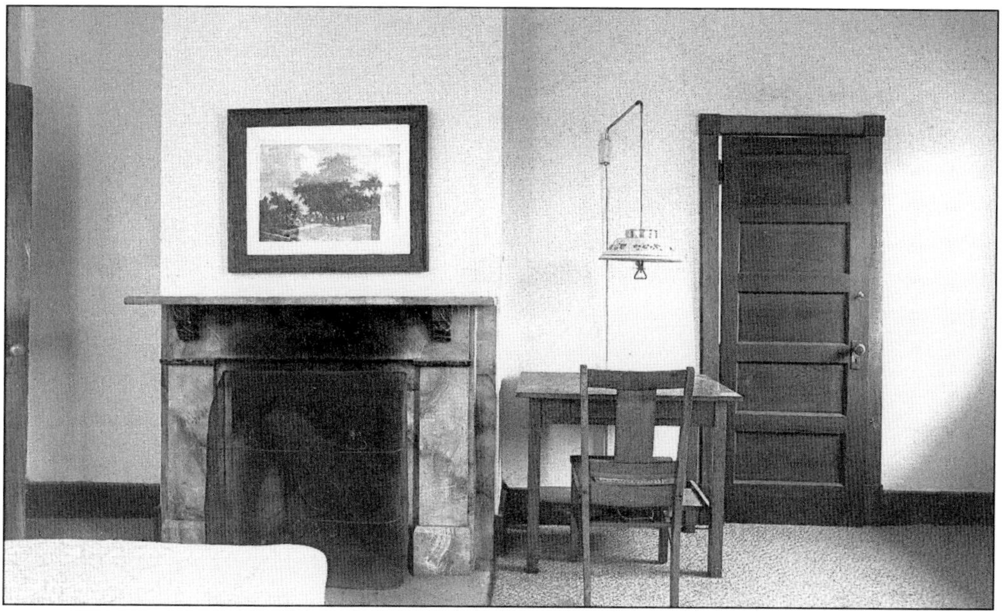

Although Wildmere House was no longer receiving guests, one of its guest rooms was photographed in June 1981. One of the proprietor's family, Mrs. Ken Phillips Jr., still hoping to find a way to rejuvenate the resort, had arranged to dress up this room for photographing, as if the hotel were still open. (Photograph by Eddie Bell, courtesy of Minnewaska State Park Preserve.)

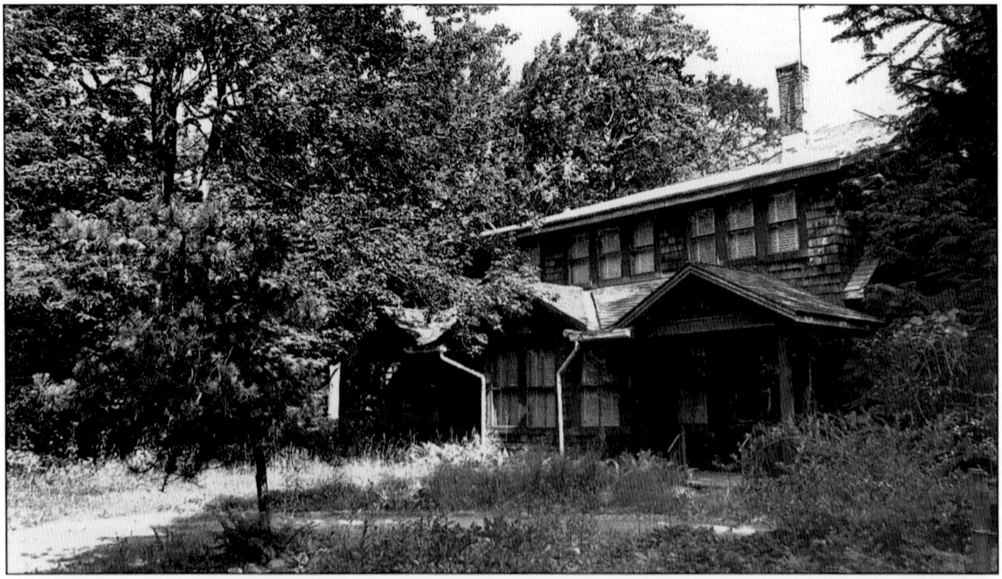

The residence of Ken Phillips Jr., to the west of Wildmere House, seems abandoned in this June 1981 view, showing its front from Sunset Carriageway. The building is easily visible today from the west end of the Lake Minnewaska parking area. Although the land surrounding it is part of Minnewaska State Park, the house is claimed to be owned by Smiley heirs. It is caught in legal tangles, however, and not occupied. (Photograph by Eddie Bell, courtesy of Minnewaska State Park Preserve.)

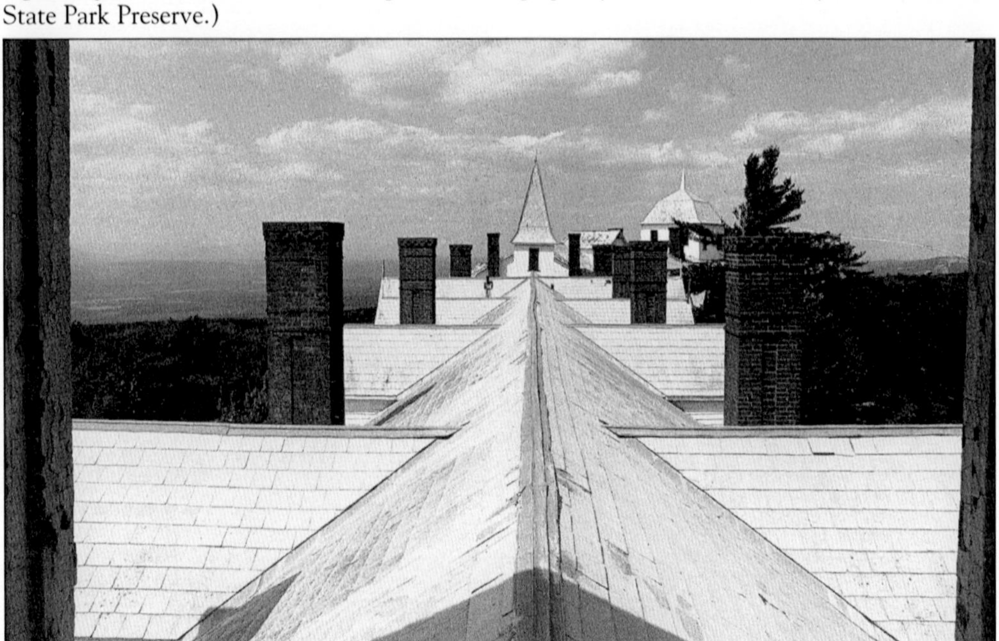

The Wildmere House roof, as photographed from a cupola, provided a poignant view in June 1981, when the Minnewaska resort, already over 100 years old, was sliding toward its demise as a private hotel resort. After Wildmere burned down in 1986, the state acquired almost all the rest of the resort, preparing the way for its transformation into a wilder, less man-made nature preserve. (Photograph by Eddie Bell, courtesy of Minnewaska State Park Preserve.)

Eight

Minnewaska Activities

Under the Smileys, the Minnewaska resort encouraged such restrained activities as corn roasts, nature walks, Sunday evening hymn sings, breakfast cookouts at Lake Awosting, and barbecues on Beacon Hill. The resort also encouraged more strenuous activities such as horseback riding, swimming, canoeing, tennis tournaments, baseball (including men competing against. women), long-distance hiking, and exploring caves or crevices. In addition, the resort provided entertainment "almost nightly at each house," without alcohol or dancing, including home talent theatricals, lectures (on topics such as travel or wildlife), and concerts (including, in the 1920s, singing by the Hampton Institute Quartet).

After they took over ownership of the resort in 1955, the Phillipses at first attempted to preserve its quiet Quakerly tradition. However, as they felt the pressure of new circumstances, by 1964, they permitted dancing, and by 1966, drinking in a wine cellar. As the Phillipses' hold on their resort loosened, swimmers dove from high rocks into Lake Minnewaska and swam along the Peterskill in its secluded pools, with or without swimsuits.

After a long process in which the state gradually took over Minnewaska, including taking over Lake Minnewaska in 1987, state officials decided to treat the resort less as a recreational park and more as an ecologically fragile nature preserve. Regulations, including swimming restrictions, increased. Ironically, this disturbed some of the very people who had worked to keep out private Marriott development and to bring in the state as a public agent to protect the site.

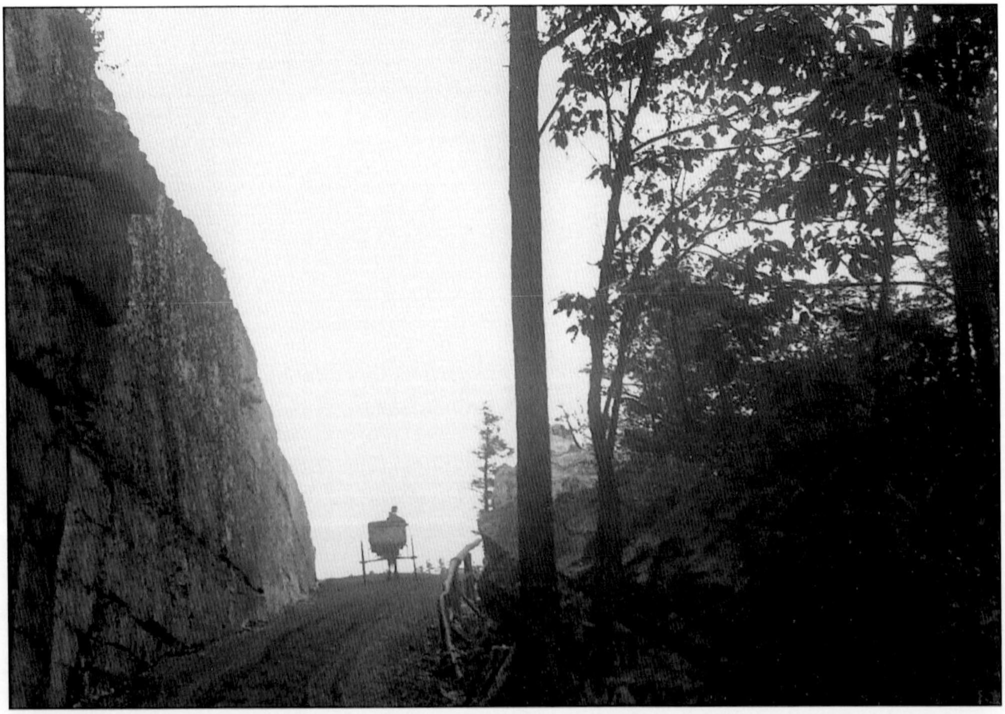

In the late 1890s, when this photograph was taken, the Minnewaska resort was constructing carriage roads on its approximately 5,000 acres. It was blasting, hauling gravel by wagon, and building retaining walls as needed. It was also encouraging guests to drive out on these new roads to explore lakes, experience wilderness, and discover awesome panoramic views. (Courtesy of Carol B. LeFevre.)

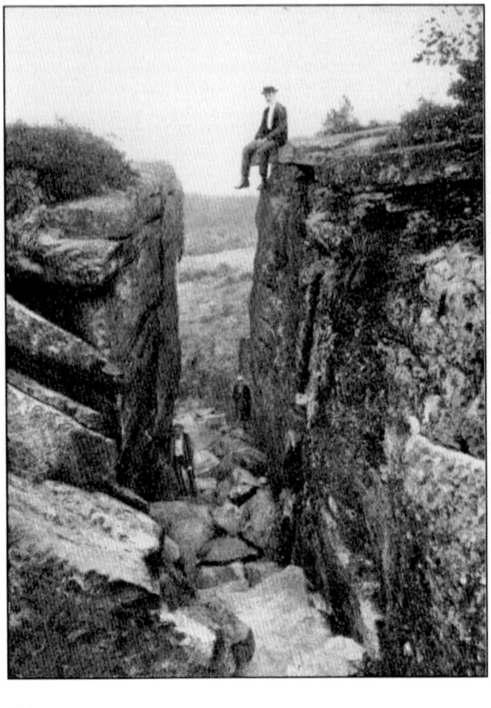

In this 1906 postcard view, a man sits above a crevice at Sam's Point, 2,255 feet high. An appealing destination for adventurers from Minnewaska or elsewhere, this point is on the Shawangunk Ridge outside of the Minnewaska resort boundaries, 3.5 miles southwest of Lake Awosting. Visible from much of Gardiner, it is on the boundary between the towns of Shawangunk and Wawarsing. (Courtesy of Daryl P. Carr.)

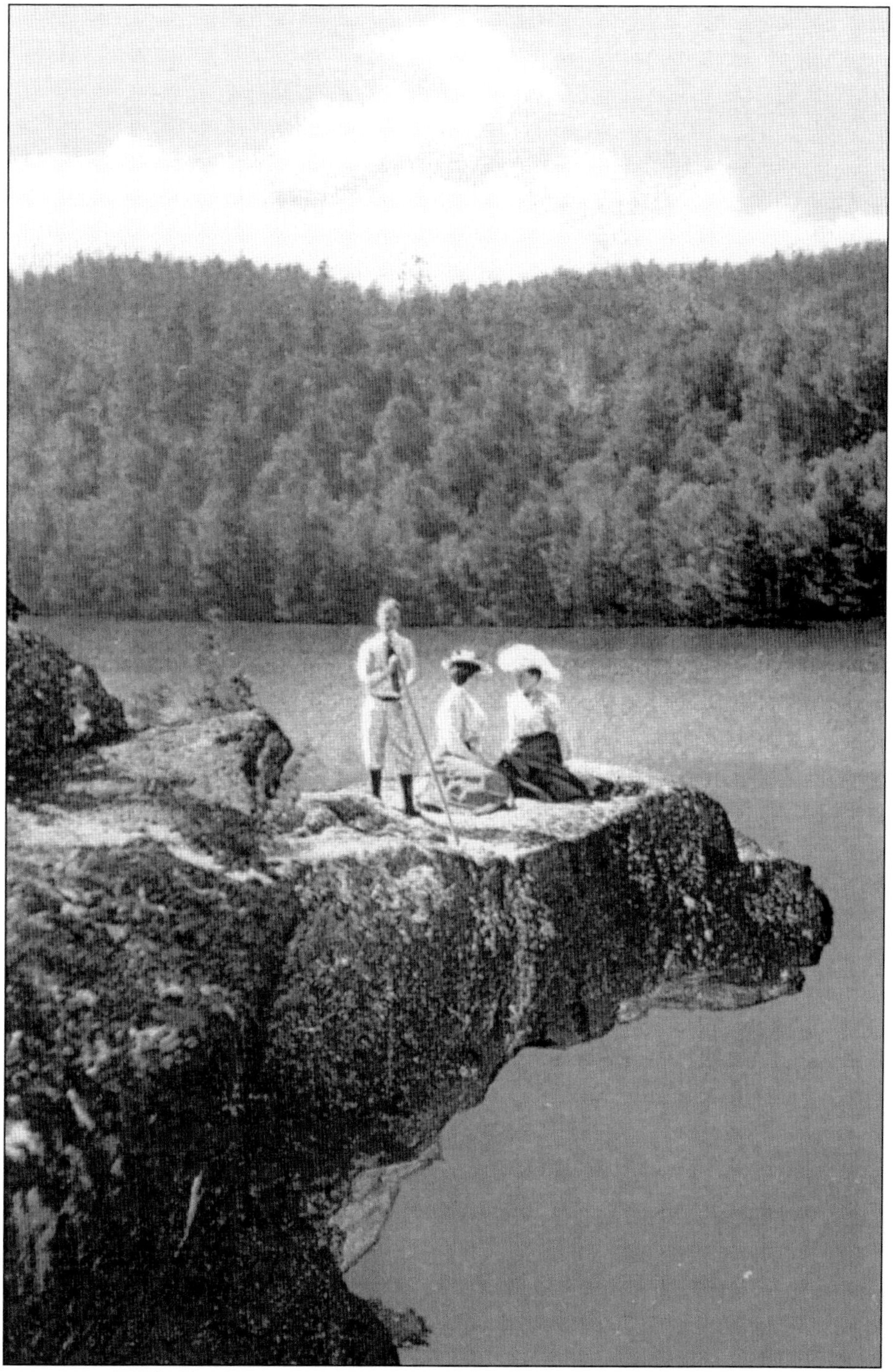

Hikers rest on Table Rock, a conspicuous shelf of rock overhanging Lake Minnewaska. The man among them seems pleased to be able to brace himself with his walking stick. The women appear to be finding themselves more comfortable focusing on each other than on their hazardous position. In the century since this postcard appeared, the rock has not yet fallen into the lake. (Courtesy of Mary Ann Osgood.)

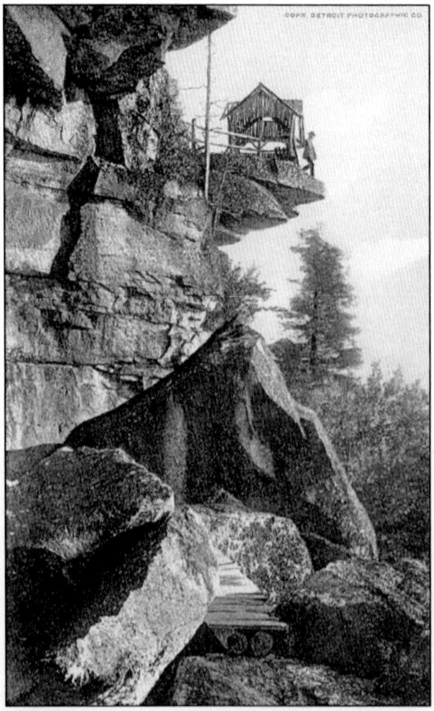

Summerhouses (gazebos) were prevalent at Minnewaska, both near the lake, like this one, and for miles out from it at overlooks along the carriage roads, enhancing the scenery. At one time Minnewaska had so many summerhouses that it kept two men busy full time repairing them. The houses were constructed of perishable materials, including in the early years thatch and in later years wooden shingles or boards. They were clamped to the rocks on which they stood by iron rods that were inserted into holes drilled into the rock. Where the summerhouses are now gone, the stubs of iron rods are often still visible in holes in the rocks. (Courtesy of Shirley Anson.)

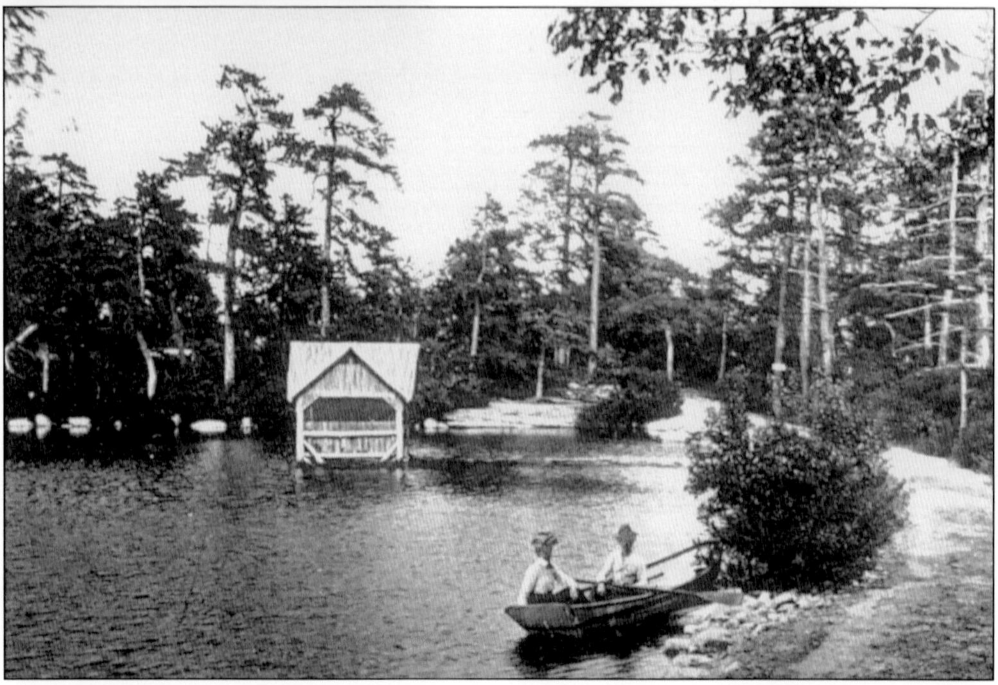

This summerhouse, called Stepping Stone, was at the southern end of Lake Minnewaska. It was reached by a stone walkway leading out into the water. Although the summerhouse is now gone, the walkway to it is still visible in the water. Summerhouses were provided, according to the Smileys, to encourage guests to "enjoy the beauty of the scene" or to take time out for "quiet meditation." (Courtesy of Shirley Anson.)

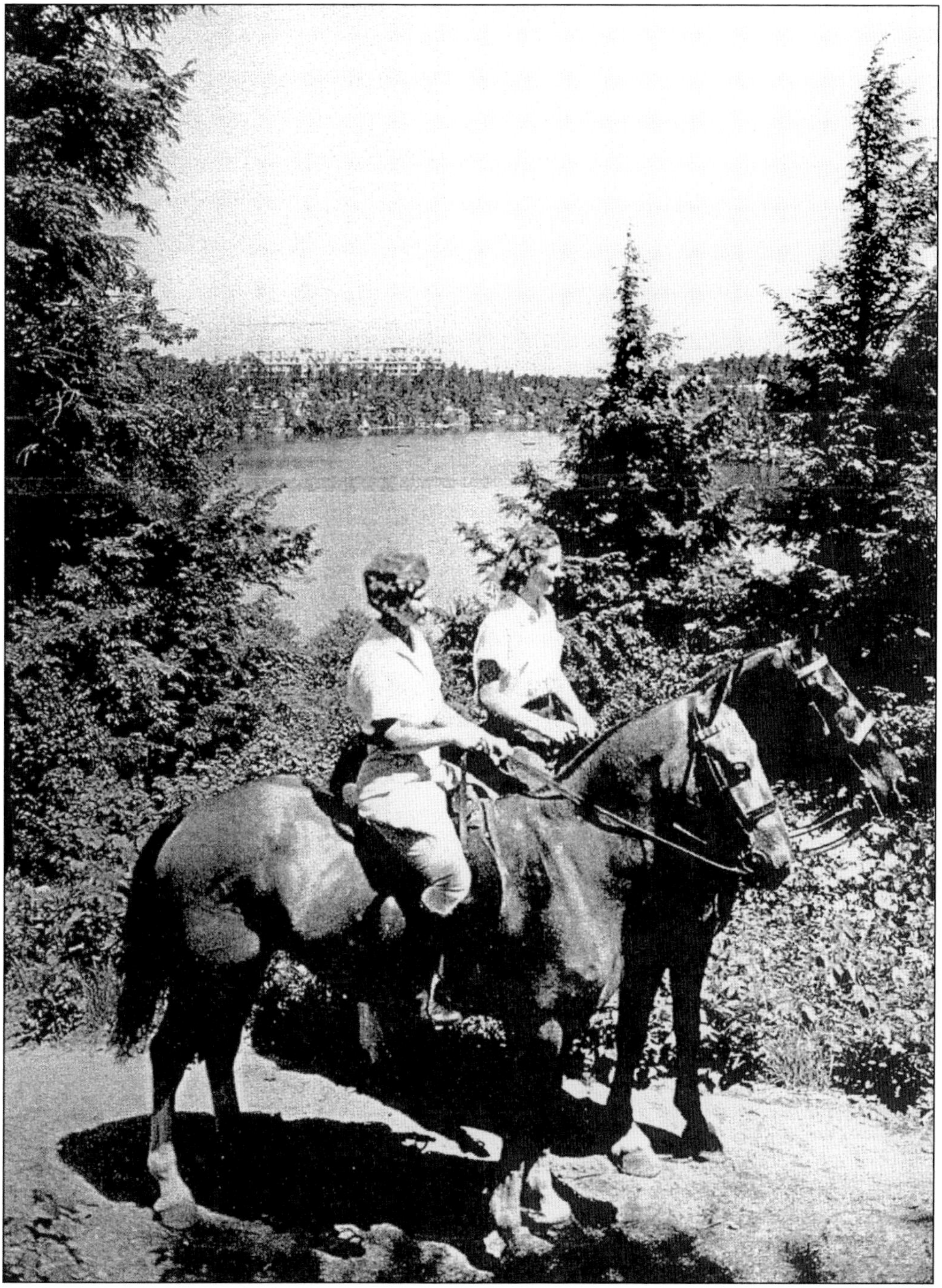

By the 1920s, Minnewaska had built 50 miles of roads reserved for horseback or carriage riding, with automobiles excluded. Carriage roads were traditionally 8 to 12 feet wide and covered with crushed shale, a stone readily available in the Shawangunks. Guests could rent horses at the resort or bring their own, stabling them at the resort. This view is from a Minnewaska brochure of 1938. (Courtesy of Mohonk Mountain House Archives.)

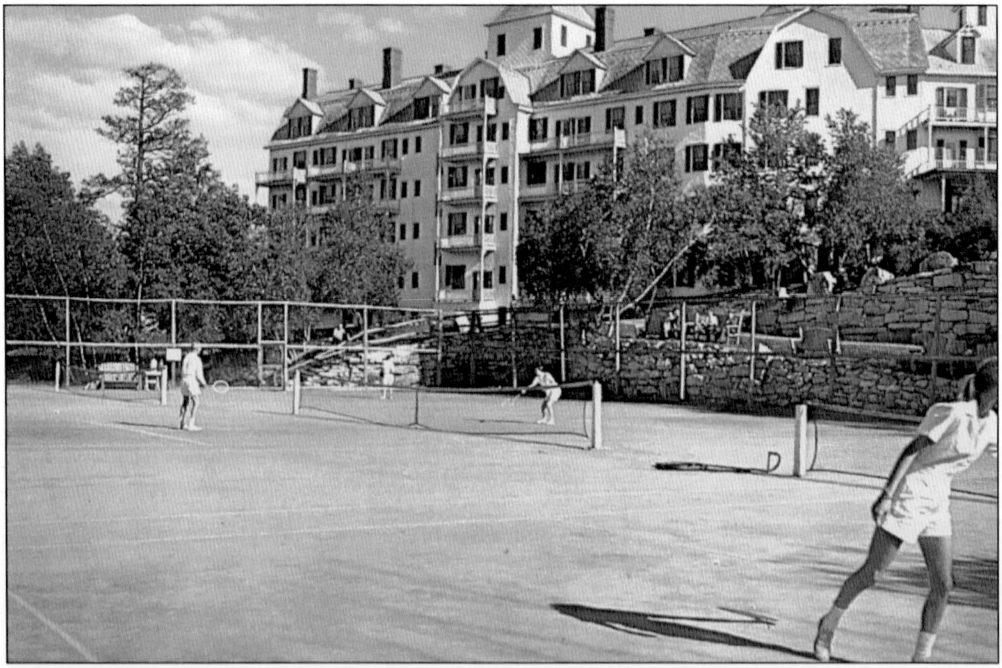

By 1932, there were five tennis courts at Minnewaska, all available for guests to use without charge. Three were near Wildmere, including this one, and two were near Cliff House. (Courtesy of Haviland-Heidgard Historical Collection.)

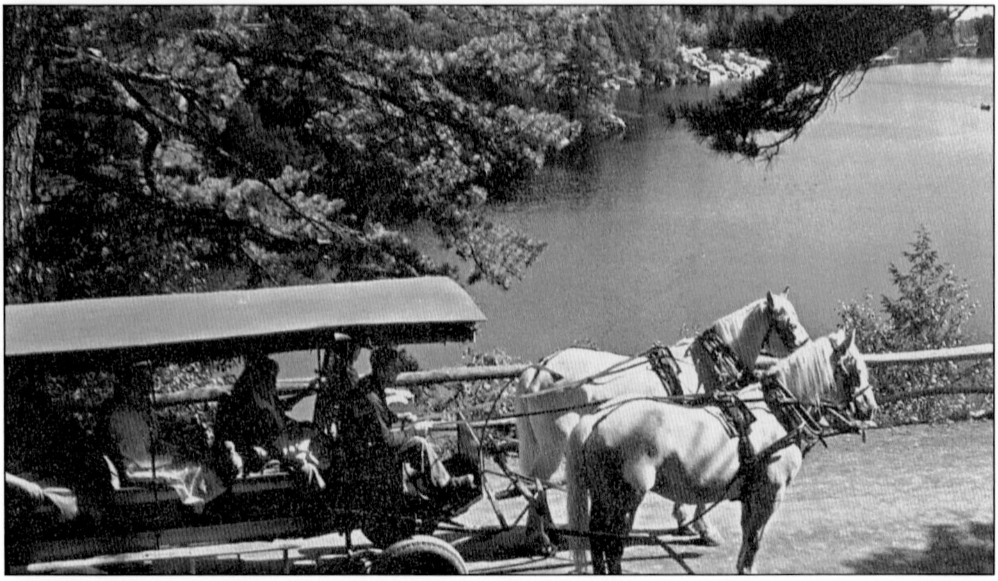

Carriage rides were still traditional at Minnewaska when this photograph appeared in 1955 in a Minnewaska advertisement. Such rides were popular, both for hotel guests and day visitors. It was at about this time that Anna Heany Donahue, who had once taught at Gardiner's Guilford School, joined friends to visit Minnewaska for a day of carriage riding. (Courtesy of Haviland-Heidgard Historical Collection.)

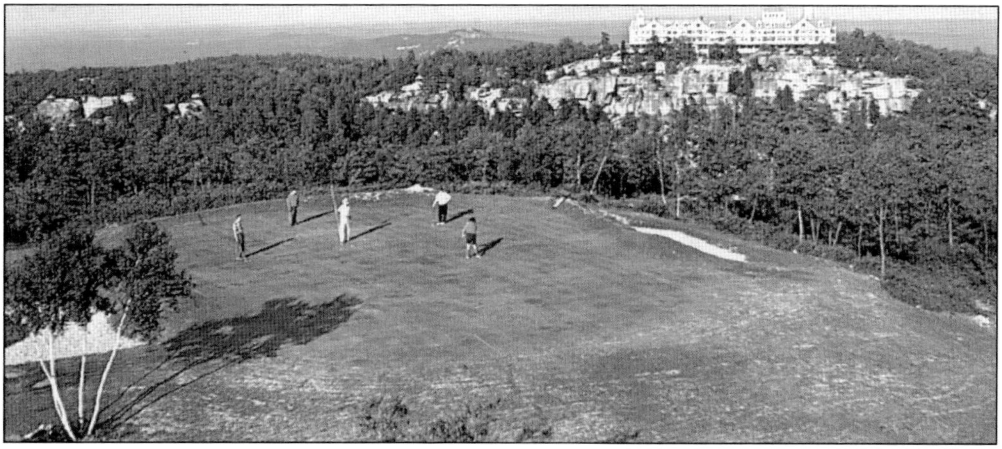

In its early years, Minnewaska provided golfers with putting greens at Cliff House. After the Phillips family took control of Minnewaska, a new full-scale golf course was created and opened in 1957 across the lake from Cliff House. It was constructed by cutting trees, burying the stumps in the woods, filling in with shale dug out of nearby shale banks, and adding topsoil trucked in from Kerhonkson. Now abandoned, the course site is known as the Meadows and is growing up to brush. (Courtesy of Haviland-Heidgard Historical Collection.)

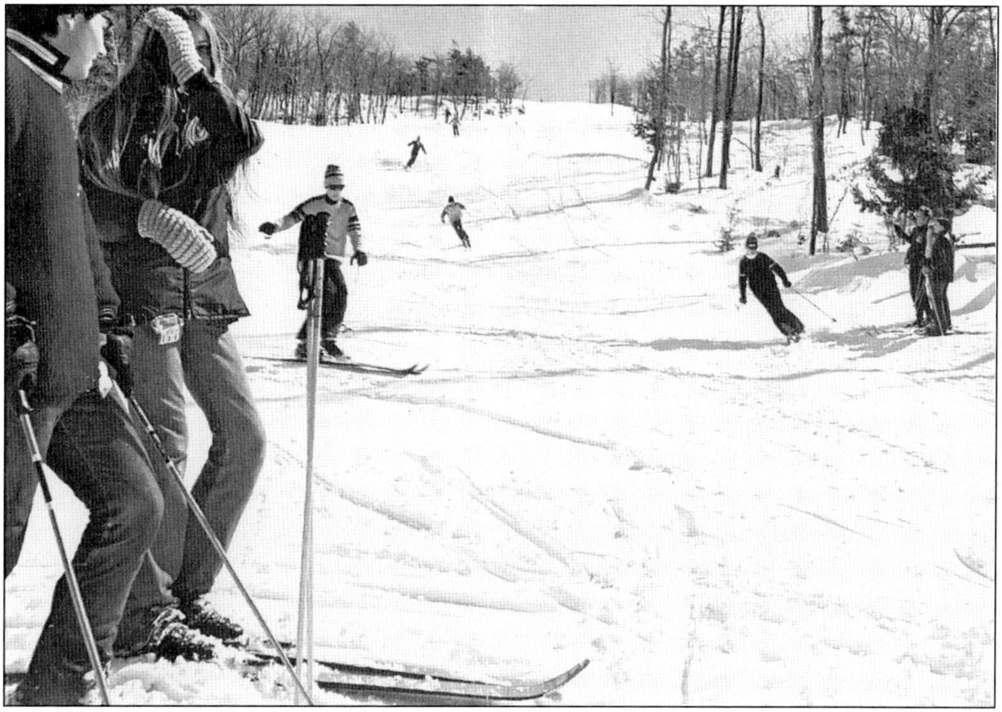

Minnewaska opened its ski slopes, Ski-Minne, in 1964 to revive its finances. Located below Beacon Hill, north of the Minnewaska Trail (Route 44-55), the slopes ran downhill toward the Peterskill. Open day and night, they included routes for beginners, intermediates, and advanced. Ski-Minne had lifts, warming rooms, instructors, a restaurant, a bar, and dancing. How the drinking and dancing would have gone over with Minnewaska's founders, the Quaker Smileys, can only be imagined. This view appeared on a Minnewaska brochure c. 1974. (Courtesy of Marybeth Majestic.)

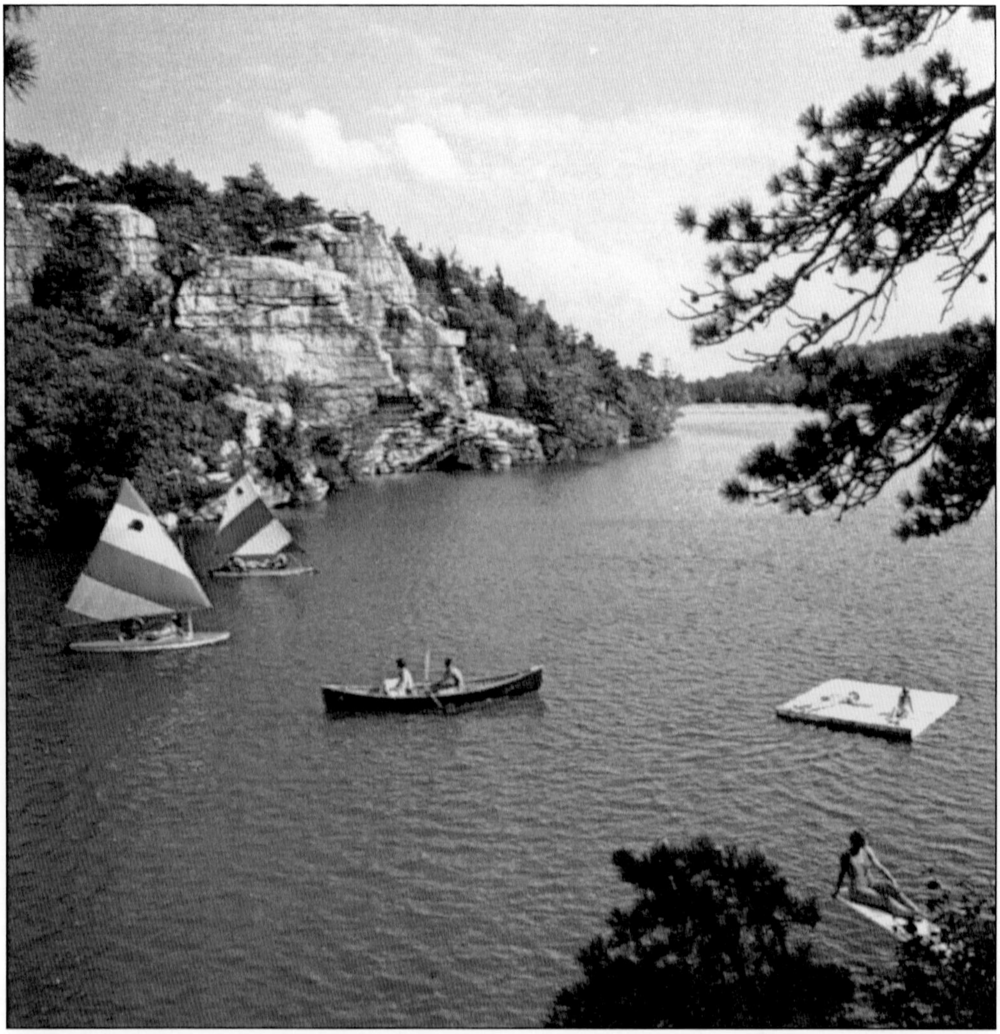

Under the Smileys, sailing became a traditional sport at Lake Minnewaska, and many children learning to sail there. By the mid-1970s, under the Phillips management, sailing was still encouraged, as this *c.* 1974 advertising photograph illustrates. By this time swimming restrictions had been relaxed, allowing guests to swim out into the lake to a raft or even, as became the custom for numbers of guests, to swim the whole length of the lake before breakfast. (Courtesy of Marybeth Majestic.)

In the 1970s, at the time of this postcard view, the Phillipses still controlled Awosting Falls as part of their Minnewaska resort. They allowed guests to swim in the pond at the bottom of the falls, surrounded by cliffs, tall trees, and the thunder of the falling water. However, to the regret of many, the public has not been able to swim at the falls since they became part of Minnewaska State Park. (Courtesy of Haviland-Heidgard Historical Collection.)

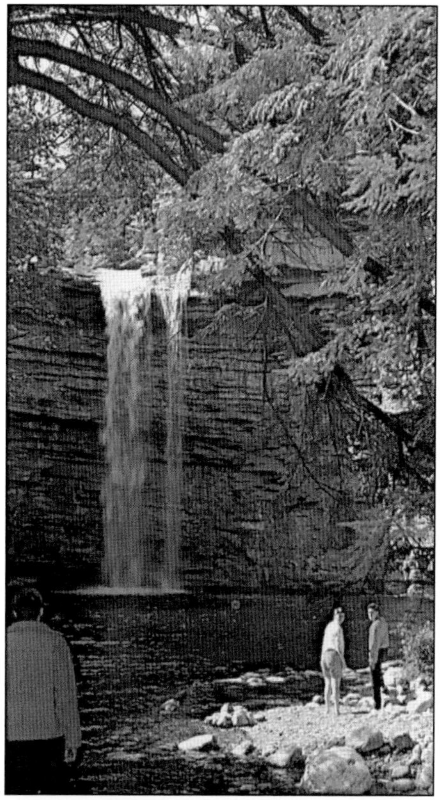

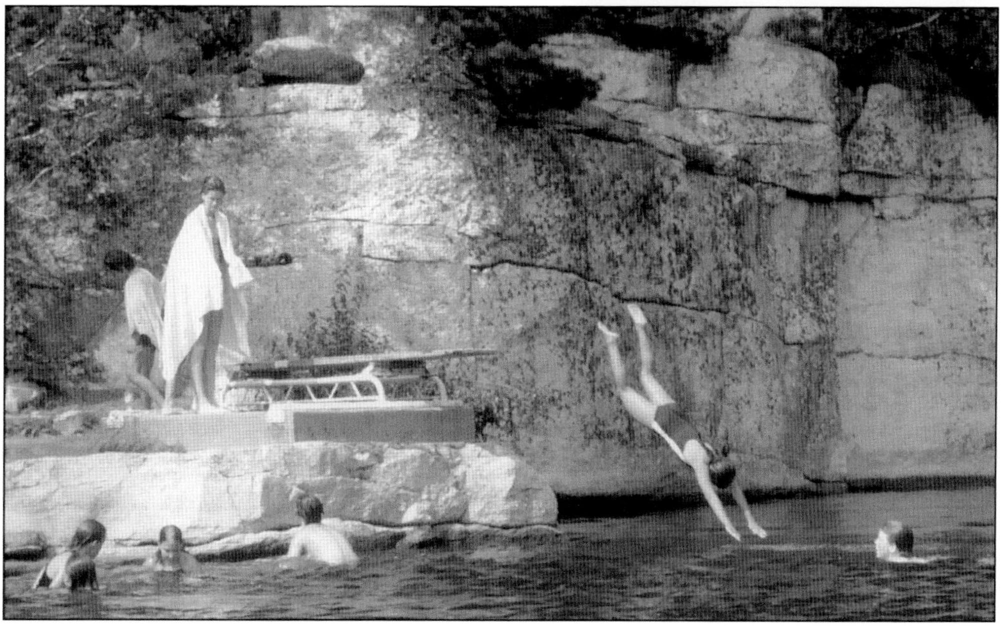

By the summer of 1980, the Minnewaska hotels were closed. However, the Phillipses kept the resort open for day use and allowed swimming anywhere in Lake Minnewaska. Three of these swimmers, all of Gardiner, are identified: Kim Ryan (tall, wrapped in a towel), Judy Lehrer (diving), Kris Ryan (far right). (Photograph by Marion W. Ryan.)

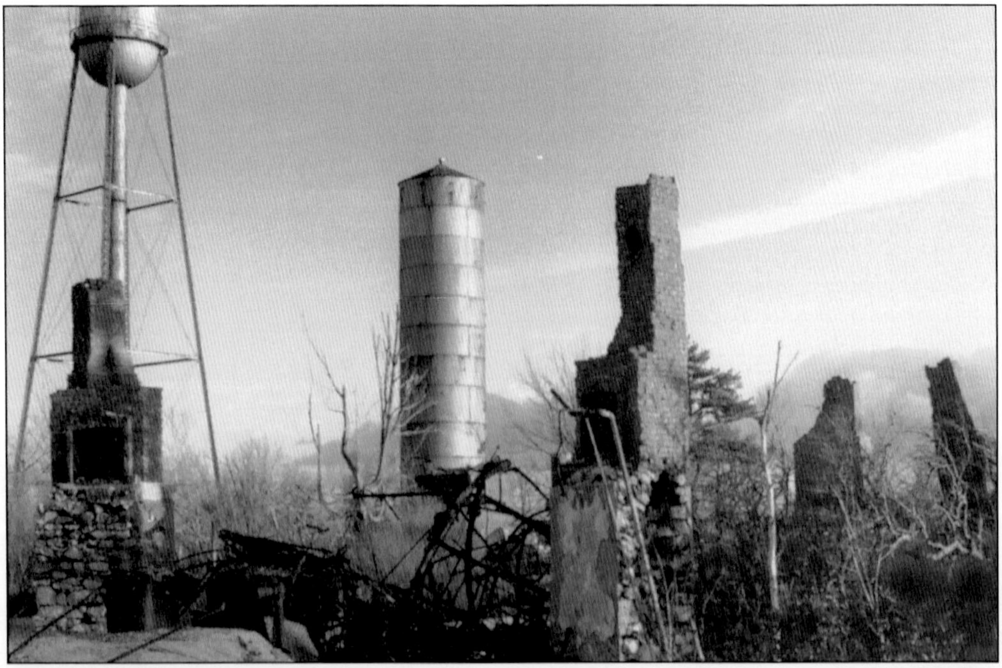

As mountain hotels went out of fashion, Cliff House became unprofitable. In 1972 the Phillips family abandoned it for regular hotel use. In 1978, it burned, uninsured. In 1980, when this photograph was taken, its water tower and standpipe were still upright among the ruins. After the site became a part of Minnewaska State Park in 1987, the state bulldozed the ruins away, leaving scarcely a hint that a hotel had once been there. (Photograph by John Giralico.)

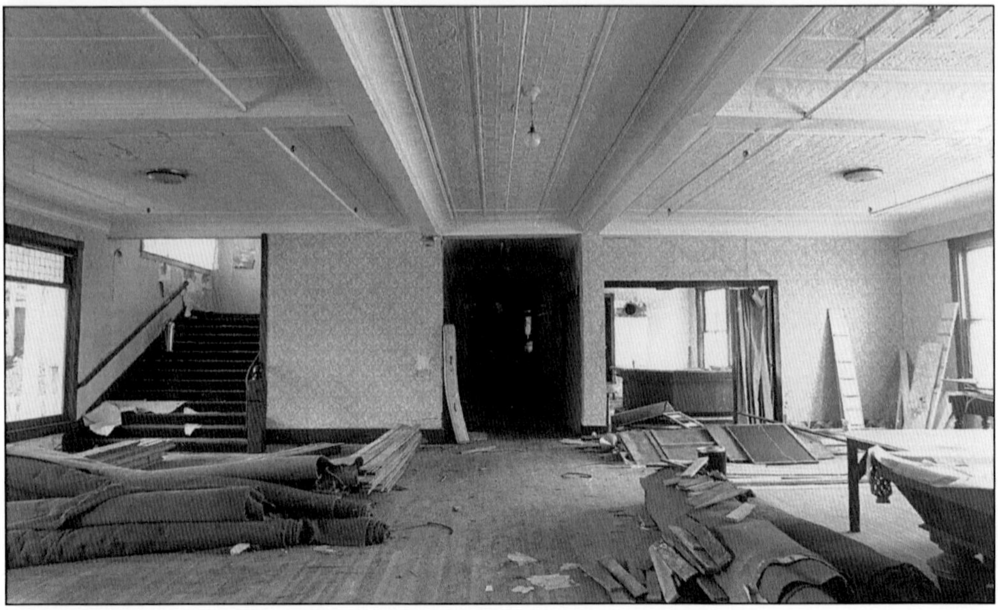

Wildmere Hotel closed in 1979. This photograph shows the dismantling of its game room in 1981. Visible are some rugs rolled up (left) and a pool table (right). The room was below the main floor, as the stairs coming down into it suggest. (Photograph by Eddie Bell, courtesy of Minnewaska State Park Preserve.)

Wildmere House, already abandoned, burned in June 1986 in a fire that officials termed suspicious. The fire occurred when the owners were trying to ward off the state's plan to seize by eminent domain what remained of the Minnewaska resort for inclusion in the new Minnewaska State Park. Despite the efforts of about 450 firefighters, the 99-year-old hotel was destroyed, leaving a pathetic fire escape reaching up to nowhere. (Photograph by Jon Margolis, courtesy of the *Huguenot Herald.*)

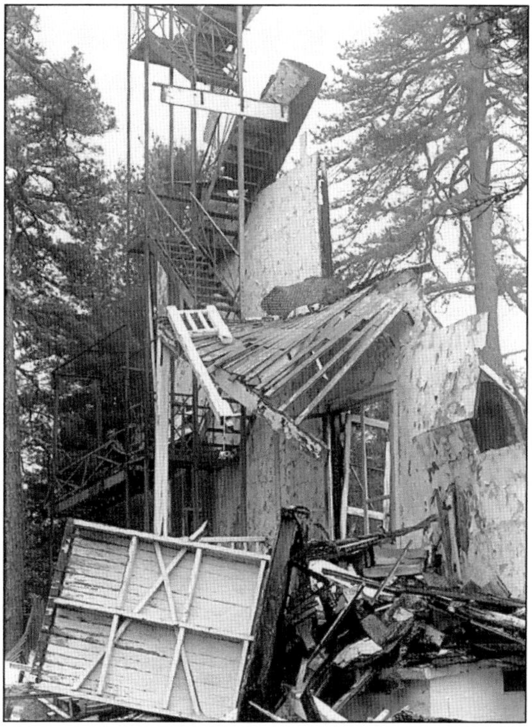

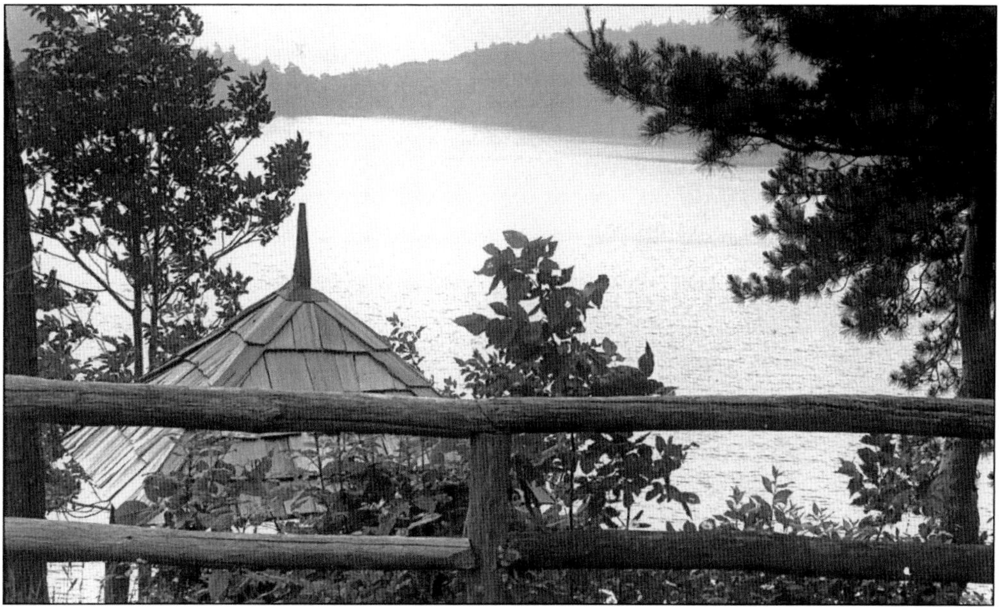

As seen from in front of the ruins of Wildmere House just after it burned, a summerhouse, railings, and nearby trees were untouched by the fire. The next year, 1987, they all became part of the new Minnewaska State Park, when the state, to the cheers of environmental groups, bought all the remaining Phillips land. A little-heard question was Would the state preserve the memory of the hotels by keeping available such historic remnants as summerhouses, railings, and hotel foundations? (Photograph by Jon Margolis, courtesy of the *Huguenot Herald.*)

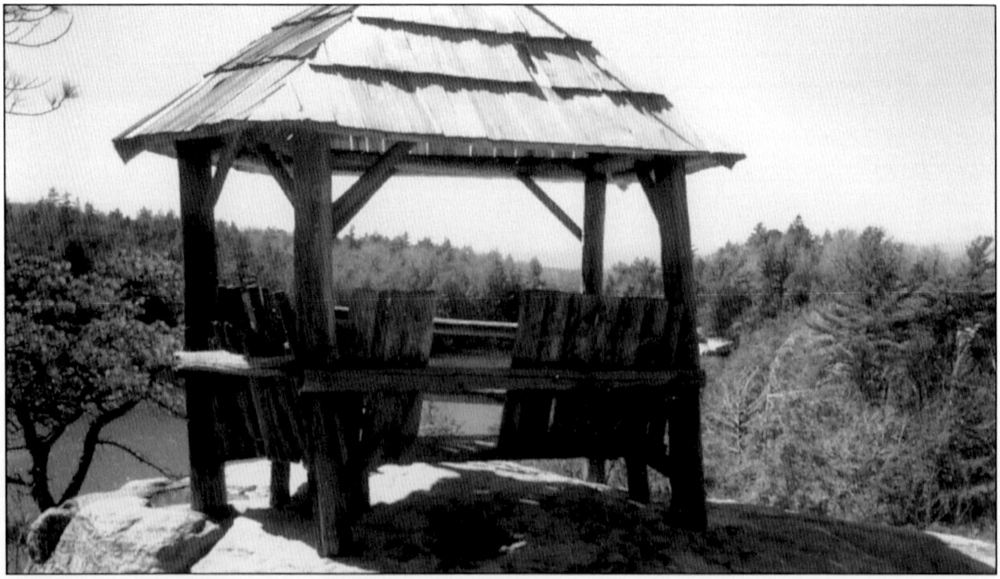

As the only summerhouse still existing at Minnewaska, this one, on the east side of Lake Minnewaska, attracts the curious. Its roof, posts, and inside benches are made of wood and are now deteriorating, as seen in this photograph taken in May 2002. In 1993, when several summerhouses still existed, a Minnewaska State Park master plan called for the park to restore or construct replicas of selected summerhouses, but the park administration has not yet done so. (Photograph by Bob Tucker.)

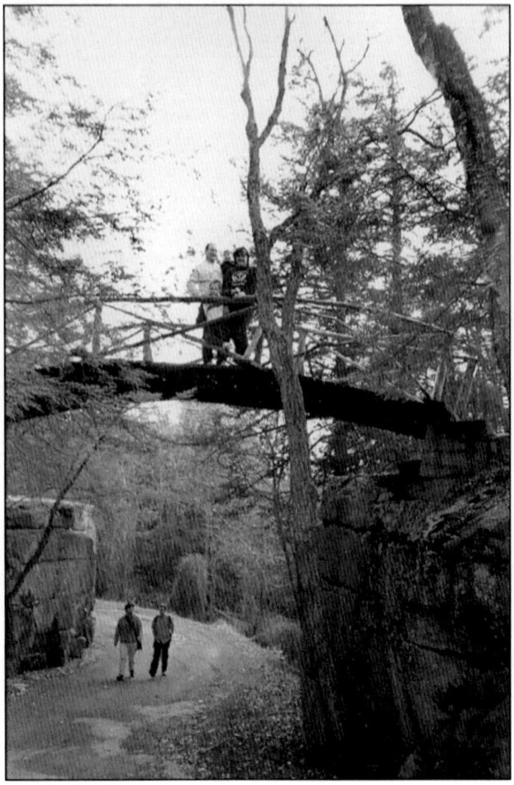

On the east side of Lake Minnewaska, a hiking trail crosses over a carriage road on Dry Bridge, a long-cherished structure. In 1932, the bridge was straight; by the 1980s, after having been rebuilt, it was curved. The bridge has been preserved and, as can be seen in this photograph taken in 2000, hikers continue to pass both over and under it. The hikers passing over the bridge are a family from Colorado. (Photograph by Bob Fisher.)

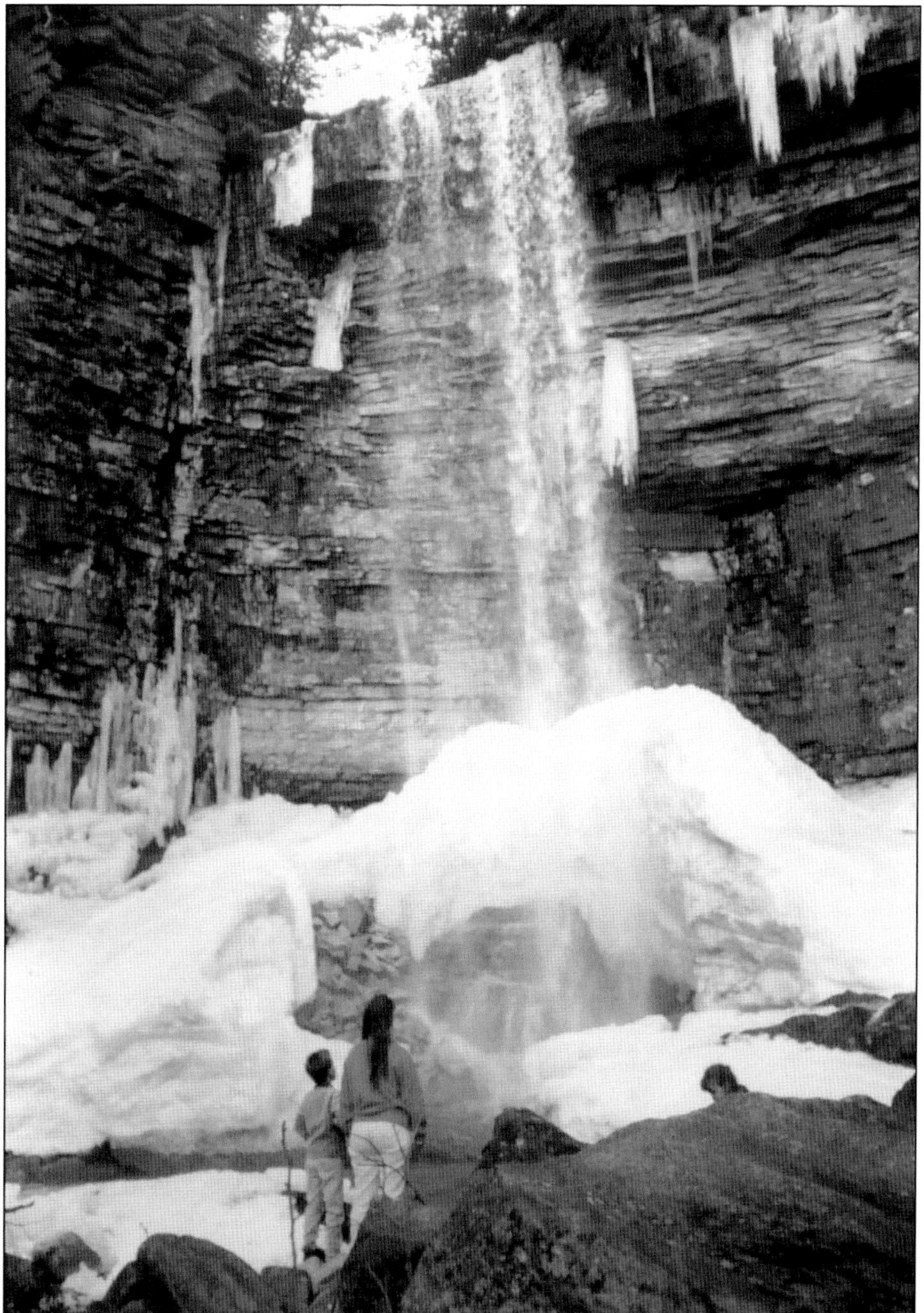

Stony Kill Falls, 87 feet high, was part of the Minnewaska resort, and is now part of Minnewaska State Park. Minnewaska guests traditionally reached it by the carriage road from Lake Awosting. It is still possible to hike to the falls along that route, about two miles from the lake. The falls also can be reached by driving south on Shaft Road, in the town of Wawarsing, to its end and then hiking in about half a mile on an unmarked trail, through an abandoned gravel pit. In this February 1999 photograph, Cindy Nadjzion of Cragsmoor was visiting the falls with her children. (Photograph by Bob Fisher.)

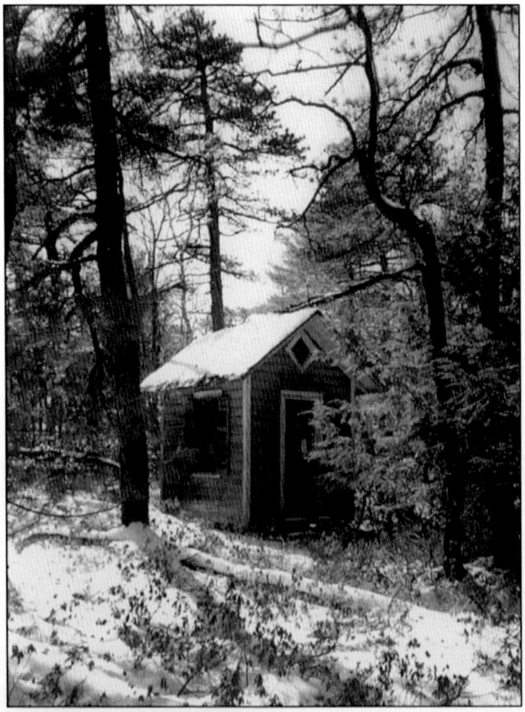

With a piano inside, the Music Box once served as a hut for music practice. It is one of at least two such huts placed in the Minnewaska woods, where the sounds coming from it were not likely to bother hotel guests. It is the only such music hut remaining. Located on the east side of Lake Minnewaska between the park police office and Dry Bridge, it has a wood shingle roof, a diamond-shaped window over its door, and shutters for the windows. Now neglected, it is deteriorating, as can be seen in this photograph taken in March 2002. (Photograph by Bob Fisher.)

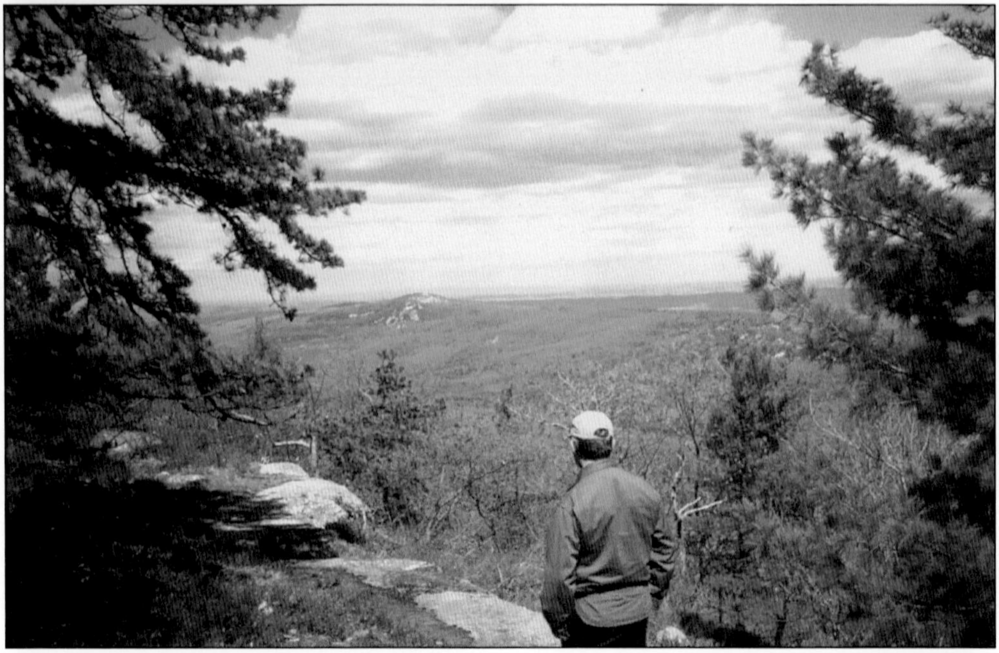

Hiker Rene F. Ramos of Queens has reached a lookout near the site of the former Cliff House, on the Beacon Hill Trail. He looks northeast over the Coxing Kill Valley, toward Mohonk Mountain (center left) and Trapps Mountain (center right). In this May 2002 photograph, the main part of Gardiner is visible (far right) in the Wallkill River Valley. From the Lake Minnewaska parking lot, the loop trail to Beacon Hill and back is approximately 2.25 miles and rough going in places. (Photograph by Carleton Mabee.)

Hikers at Minnewaska in March may find ice slowing their walk but enhancing the evergreens. In this March 2002 photograph, Dan Smith and his mother, Eleanor Smith, of the family who long operated the Tuthilltown Grist Mill, are hiking from the top of Awosting Falls down the twisting carriage road toward the pool at the bottom of the falls. (Photograph by Bob Fisher.)

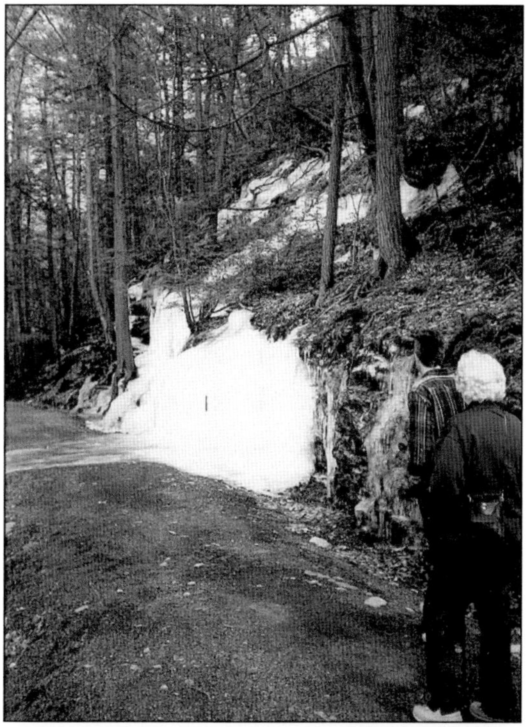

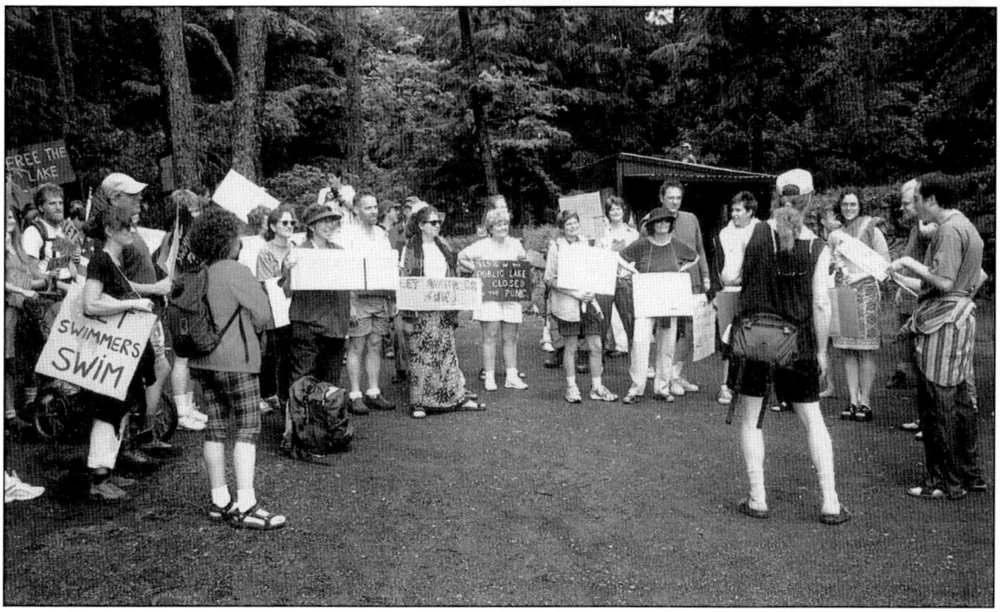

Protesters march around Lake Minnewaska chanting slogans calling for Minnewaska State Park to relax its swimming restrictions. Written on the signs they carry are "Let Swimmers Swim," "Free the Lake," and "It's Our Tax Money . . . Our Lake." Shown in this June 2001 photograph are two of the leaders in the demonstration and in the accompanying campaign of letter-writing, petitioning, and negotiating with park officials: Ray Greenberg of Gardiner (right foreground, with his back to the camera) and Judy Mage of New Paltz, (left center, wearing a black hat and carrying a horizontal sign). (Courtesy of Judith Mage.)

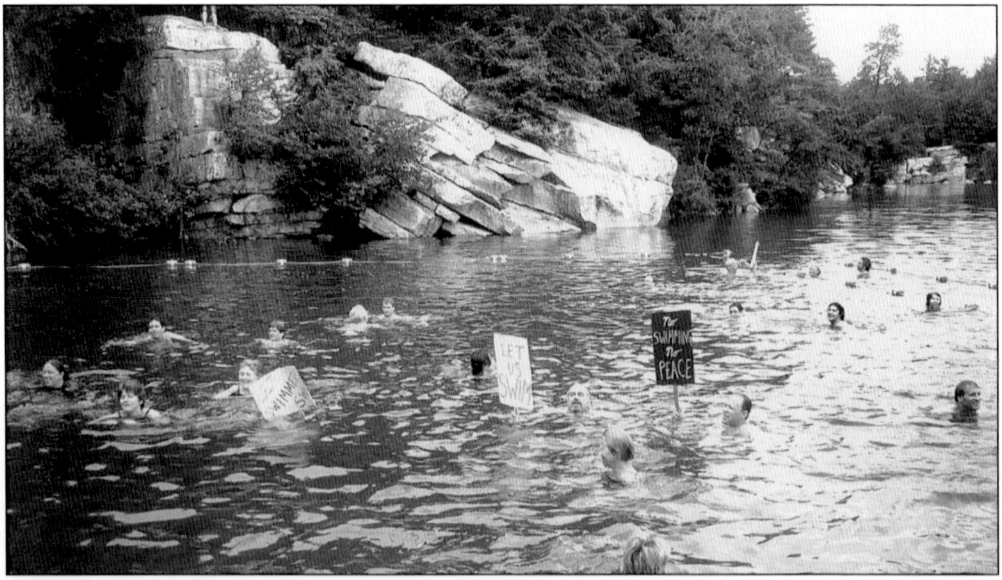

Demonstrators conduct a "swim-in" at the restricted site at Lake Minnewaska, appealing for greater freedom to swim there. Shown in June 2002, the group reached an unusual agreement with state park officials that year. The group agreed to create a nonprofit organization to test swimmers, insure them, and take responsibility for them, in return for the privilege of long-distance swimming, without lifeguards, from a site on the lake's eastern side where Cliff House guests used to swim. (Courtesy of Judith Mage.)

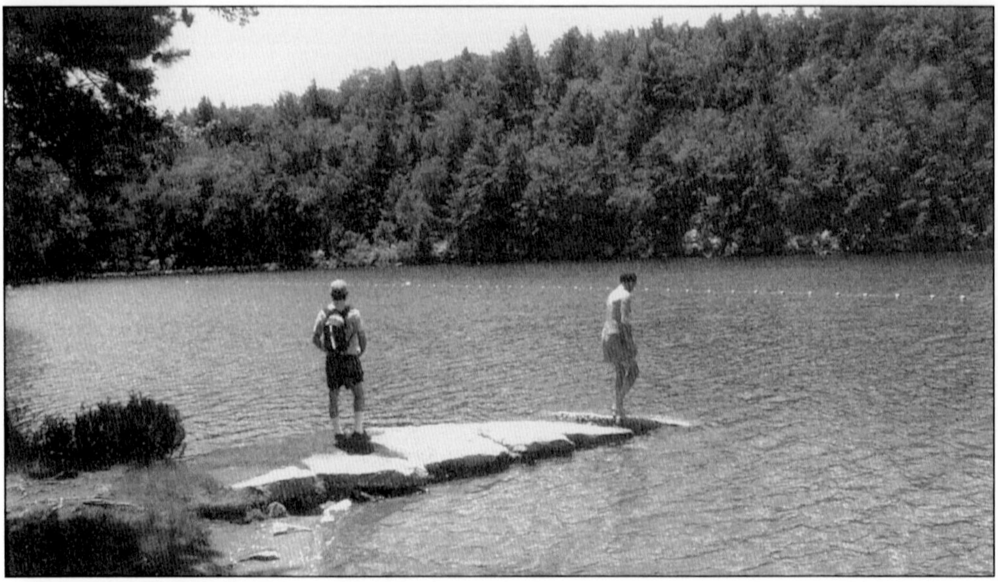

By 2002, the Minnewaska State Park had loosened its swimming restrictions and bathers were allowed to swim without the presence of a lifeguard at this site on Lake Minnewaska's east side––if they followed certain rules. The row of stones on which the boys are standing once led to a summerhouse. The line of baubles visible in the lake marks a route suitable for swimming laps. The group that won the the relaxation of the rules is asking for further reduction in the park's swimming restrictions, as at Lake Awosting and the pond below Awosting Falls. (Photograph by Carleton Mabee.)

Nine

Adventuring: Climbing and Diving

While traditional sports continue to thrive in Gardiner, in recent decades two new extreme sports have developed there as well: rock climbing and skydiving. These new sports have become so prominent that they mark Gardiner as distinctive.

The mountain hotels, Mohonk and Minnewaska, encouraged hiking on difficult paths and even exploring caves and crevices, but they did not encourage vertical rock climbing. Such a sport was hardly known in the Shawangunks until 1935, when chemist Fritz Wiessner, an immigrant from Germany, began climbing here. Gradually, rock climbers learned to concentrate on Gardiner, on its easily accessible Trapps Mountain cliffs, on land at first environmentally protected by Mohonk Hotel, and then later by an agency spun off from it, Mohonk Preserve. Rock climbers have made Gardiner the most prominent site for rock climbing in the Northeast.

In the 1930s, Ted Wright and Bill Everts, both sons of Gardiner farmers, created an airport for their own sport. It was on Everts family farmland, on Sand Hill Road. In the 1940s, Wright developed it into a commercial airport. In the 1970s, it was sometimes used for parachute jumping, with small planes and patrons who were little skilled. From the early 1980s, however, brothers Bill and Joe Richards, both pilots, concentrated on developing the airport for parachute jumping. Patrons became more skilled and came from greater distances. The airport enlarged. Today, sky divers provide frequent spectacles for Gardiner, as they drop out of the sky, one by one or two by two, dangling under their colorful parachutes.

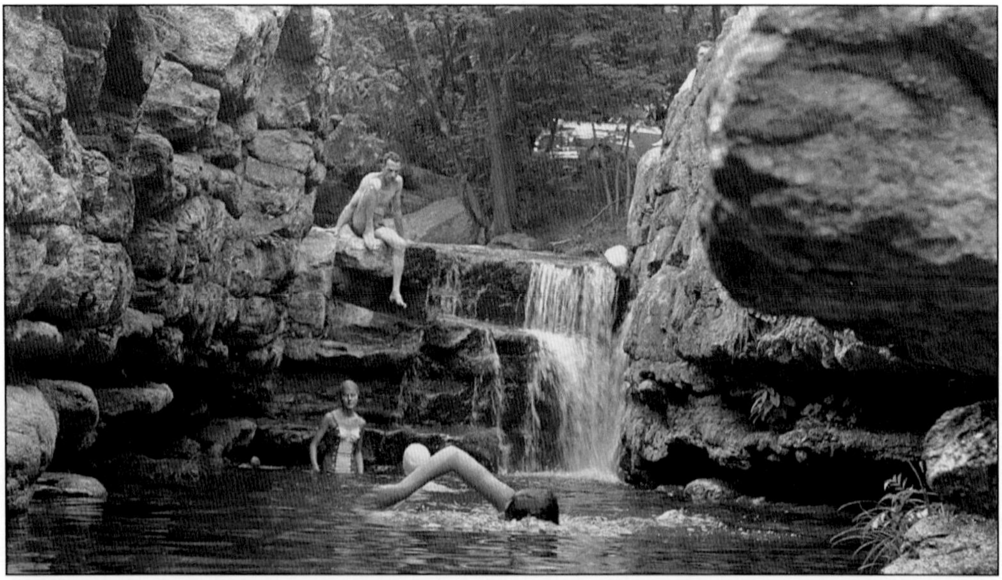

These swimmers enjoy their traditional sport at Split Rock, in the Trapps neighborhood of Gardiner, c. 1945. Although the water is hardly extensive or deep enough for significant swimming, for generations the Coxing Kill, off Clove Road, including Spit Rock, has been a favorite site to picnic and at least splash, with or without a swimsuit. Split Rock is the historic site where the Enderly family operated a sawmill for over a 100 years. (Courtesy of Haviland-Heidgard Historical Collection.)

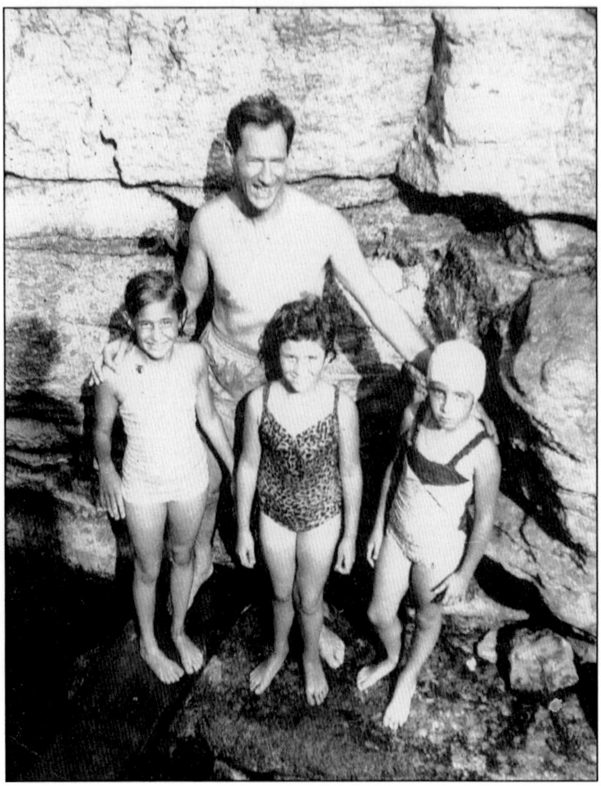

At Split Rock for a swim are father Seon Felshin, daughter Annie (left), daughter Nina (right), and a friend. The picture was taken in 1952, at a time when the Felshins, who lived in New York City, regularly sent their children to a small summer camp on Shaft Road in Gardiner. The parents would then come to Gardiner to visit the children at at camp. Now on Mohonk Preserve land, Split Rock is still open to the public. (Courtesy of Annie Felshin O'Neill.)

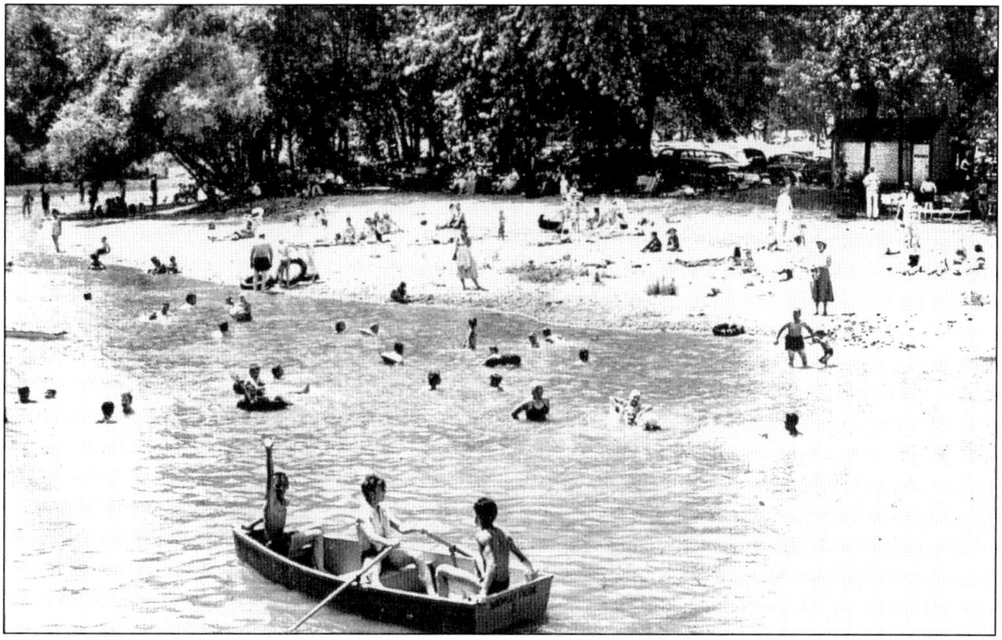

Midway Park was a popular swimming site on the Shawangunk Kill in the 1950s and 1960s. Located near Benton's Corners, it was run by the MacEntee family, who lived nearby. It had picnic tables, a pavilion, and a baseball field. In this postcard photograph taken in the mid-1950s, the boaters are, from left to right, Tom Conner, Ted McIntosh, and Bill Hanson. (Courtesy of Kathleen R. Conner.)

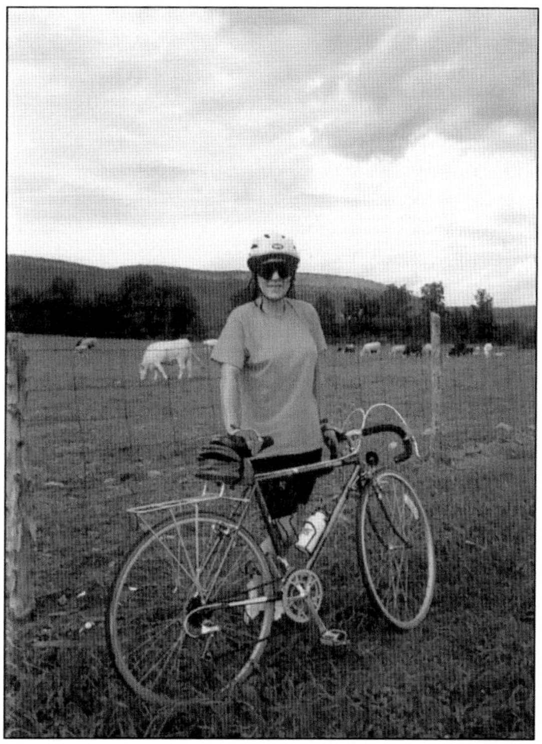

A cyclist on Bruynswick Road rests by the Jehovah Witnesses' Watchtower Farm No. 2 in 1989. Cattle and the Shawangunk Ridge are visible behind the cyclist, Nina Felshin, who had often vacationed in Gardiner since the 1950s. (Courtesy of Annie Felshin O'Neill.)

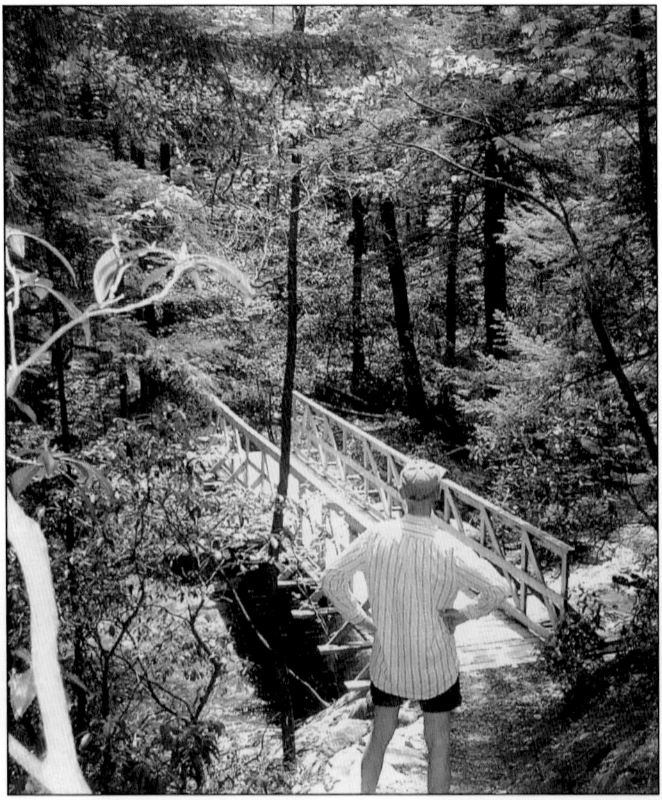

A hiker approaches a bridge over the Peterskill about a mile south of the Awosting parking lot, in Minnewaska State Park. Generations of hikers crossed over the Peterskill near here by jumping from rock to rock. This was easy in a dry summer but sometimes impossible in a wet spring. The bridge was built in 1998 by the New York–New Jersey Trail Conference, whose volunteers maintain all the trails in the park. (Photograph by Rene F. Ramos.)

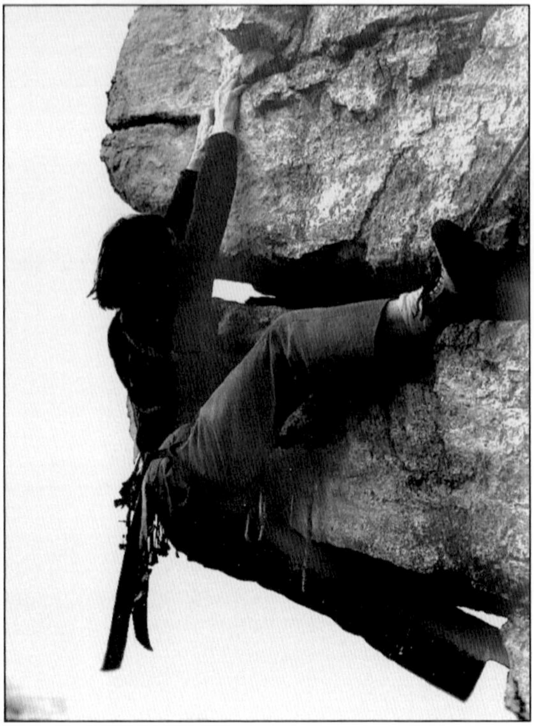

Ivan Rezucha of Gardiner dangles high in the air on the Near Trapps Mountain, on Mohonk Preserve land in the town of Gardiner. According to the rock-climbing custom of the time, 1981, he is wearing clunky, above-the-ankle shoes, which climbers no longer wear. By the 1980s, rock climbing had become popular in the "Gunks," as rock climbers call the Shawangunk Mountains. Rock climbing was already drawing enthusiasts to Gardiner from long distances. (Courtesy of Annie Felshin O'Neill.)

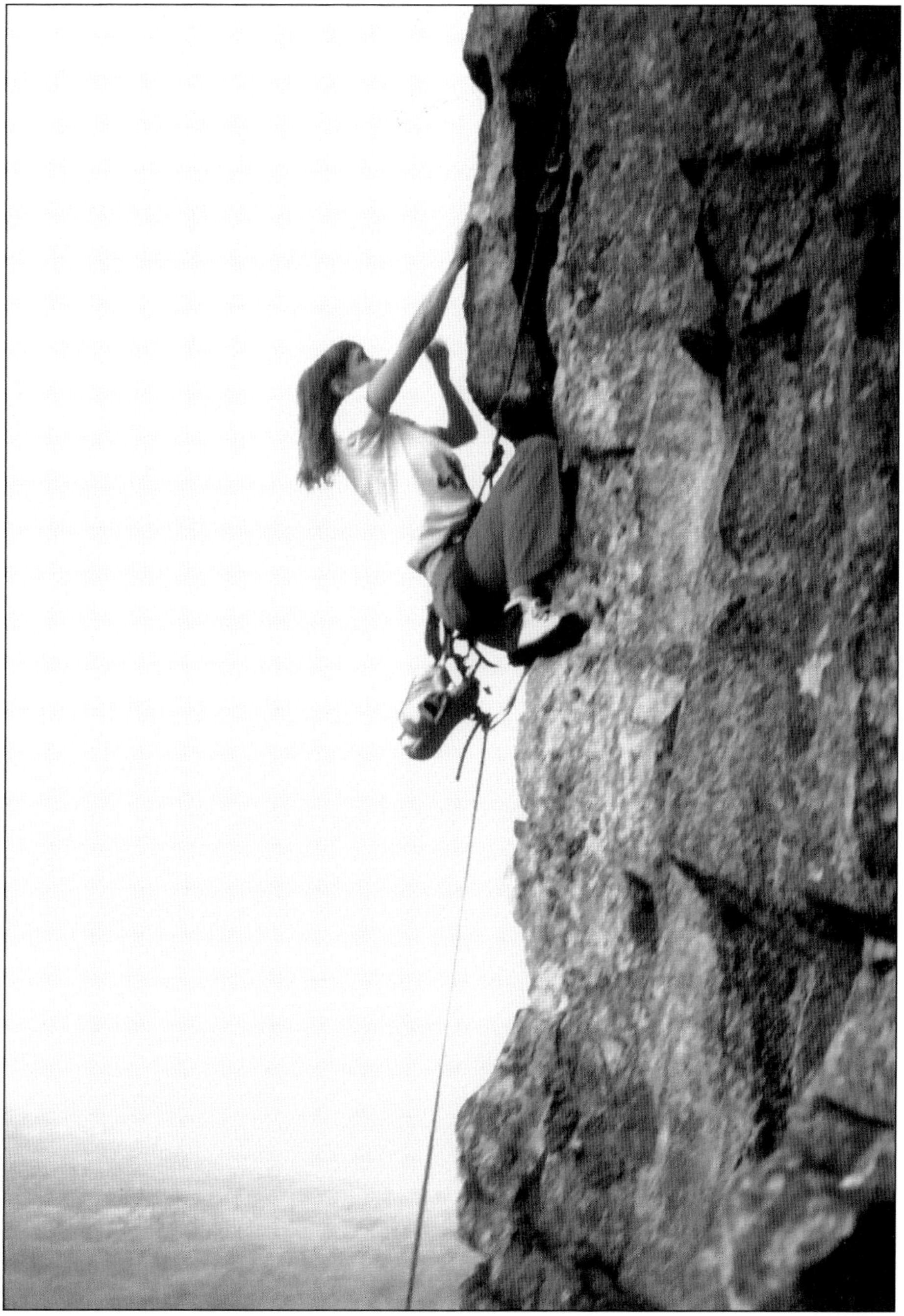

Annie Felshin O'Neill climbs Trapps Mountain, on Mohonk Preserve Land in the town of Gardiner. She is climbing the route called 'Los Tres Cabrones," which at the time this photograph was taken in 1983, she was helping to set out, along with Ivan Rezucha. She was to become known for setting out other routes as well. She first came to Gardiner as a child for vacations. By the 1970s, she lived in Gardiner, had become a sculptor, and had begun to climb. Today, she is the editor of the newsletter of the Friends of the Shawangunks, which advocates preserving open space in the Gunks. (Courtesy of Annie Felshin O'Neill.)

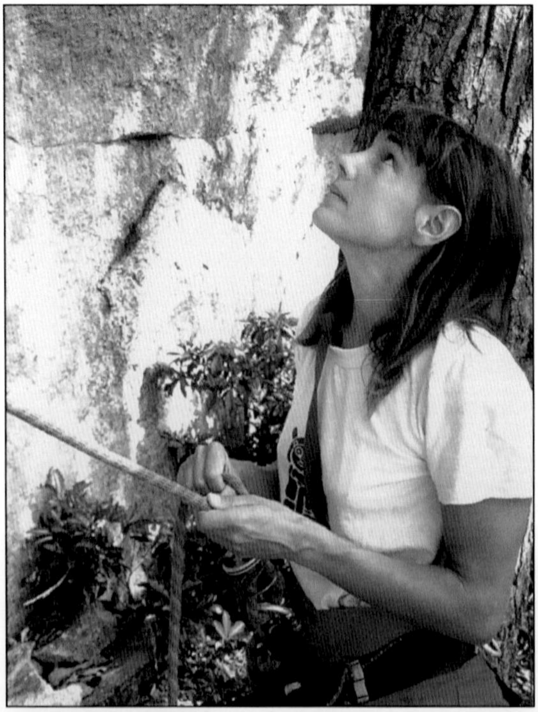

In this 1983 photograph, Annie O'Neill is belaying—that is, she is holding a rope, ready in case of a mishap to break the fall of the climber by pulling the rope taut in the belaying plate. While most rock climbers in the Gunks are the adventurous young, ages vary, and while most are men, a substantial number are women. (Courtesy of Annie Felshin O'Neill.)

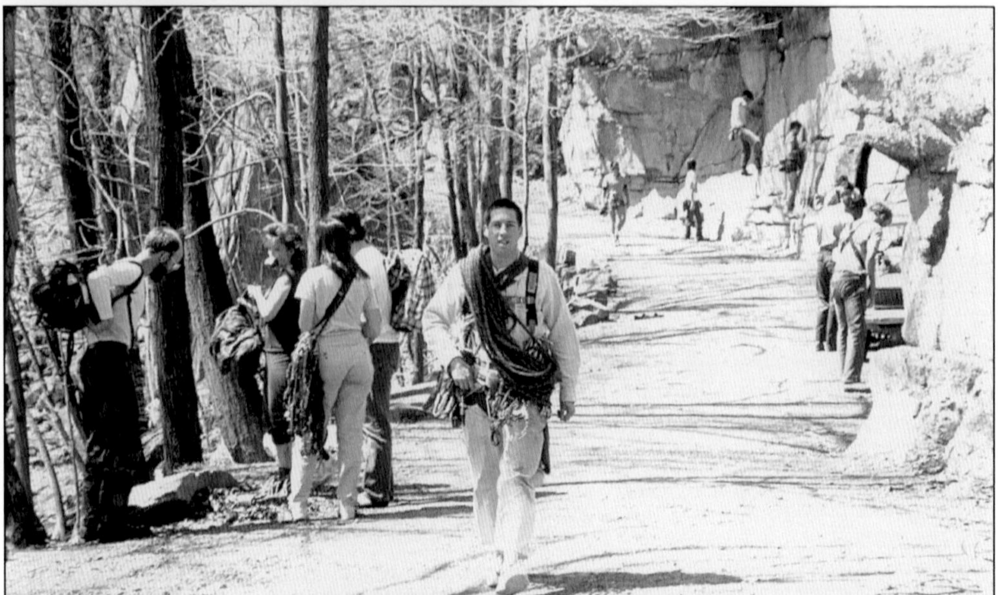

Undercliff Road on the Trapps, pictured on a weekend in April 1986, was already known nationwide as a rock climbing site and was crowded. Since then the site has become still more crowded, leading 50,000 climbers to Gardiner annually. Other nearby sites accessible from Mohonk Preserve include routes of varying degrees of difficulty, such as Near Trapps, Millbrook, and Lost City. In 1996, Minnewaska State Park opened a new site to rock climbing: the former Ski Minne site, the first New York state park to open any such climbing site. (Photograph by Jon Margolis, courtesy of the *Huguenot Herald*.)

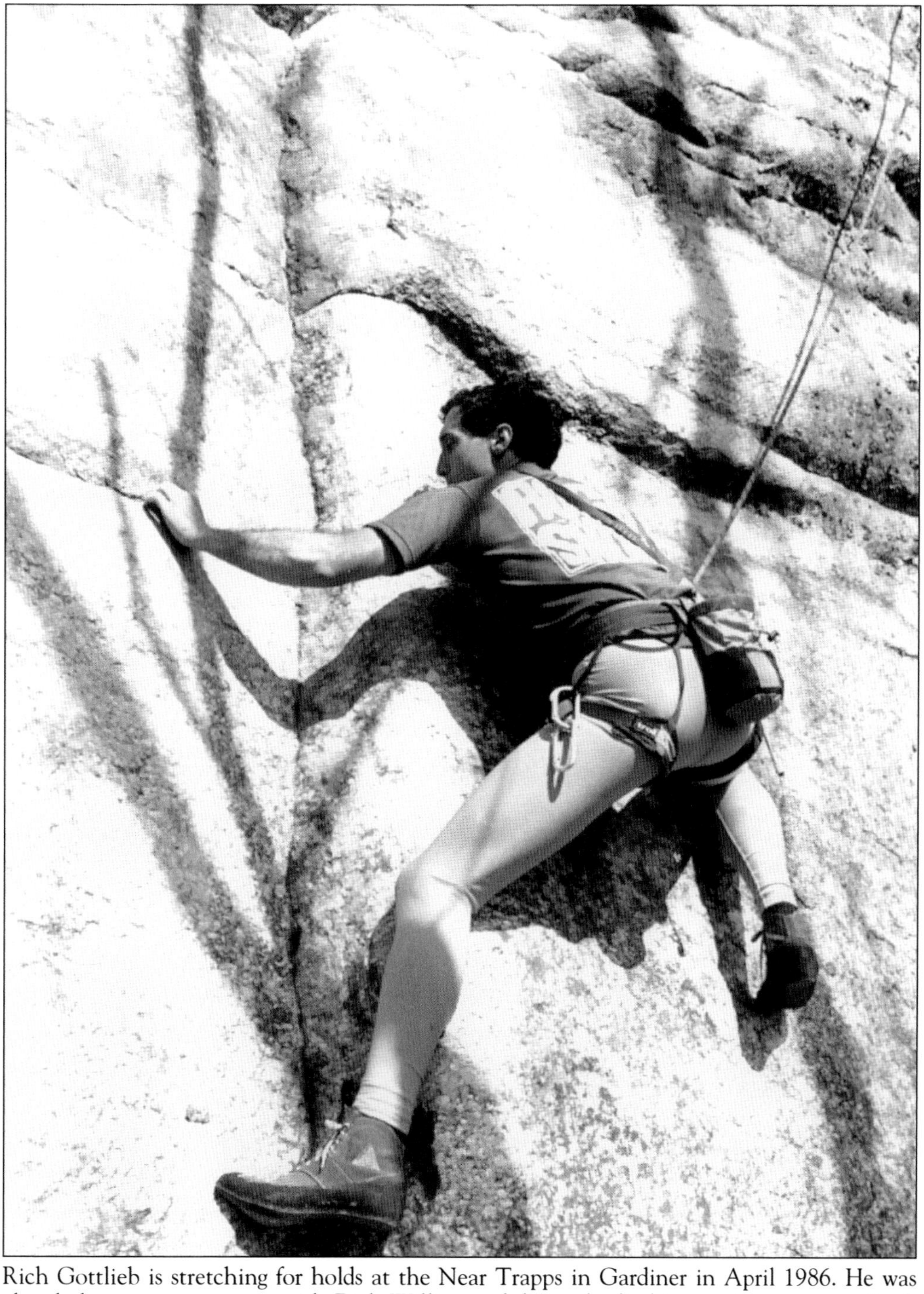

Rich Gottlieb is stretching for holds at the Near Trapps in Gardiner in April 1986. He was already known as co-owner with Dick Williams of the rock climbing equipment store Rock and Snow, in New Paltz, which is named on his shirt. This closeup view of the rock shows not only its cracks but also its rough, conglomerate texture, with pebbles embedded in it—all appealing to rock climbers as offering possible holds. (Photograph by Jon Margolis, courtesy of the *Huguenot Herald*.)

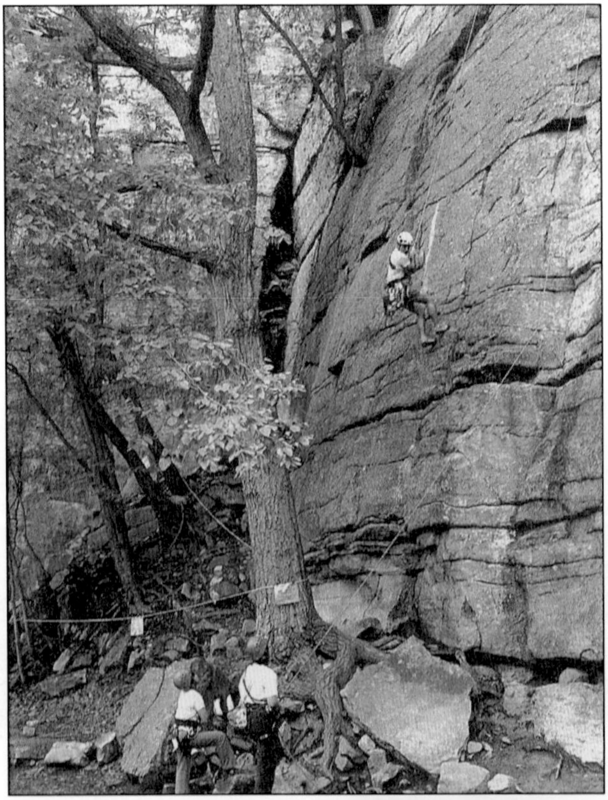

Mohonk Preserve has placed a rope (left), with signs attached, to block off an area of cliff that climbing has eroded, marking it for rehabilitation. As a result of such erosion, Mohonk Preserve since 1986 has prohibited climbers from placing pitons (metal spikes) in the rock, because they chip the rock away. However, Mohonk Preserve does permit climbers to use wedges (nuts), as they are less damaging. (Photograph by Rene F. Ramos.)

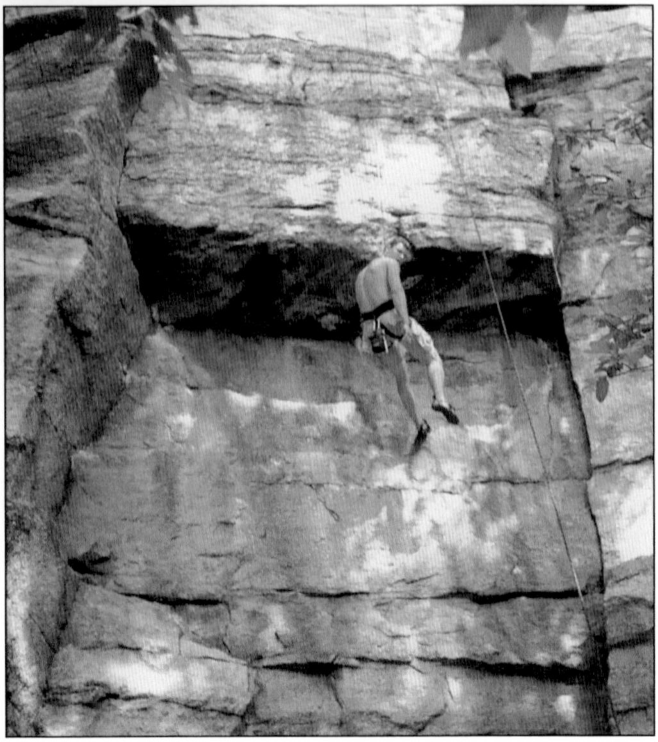

For safety, some climbers wear a helmet, shirt, and trousers, but the climber shown in this 2002 photograph does not. In the 1960s, rock climbers such as Dick Williams resisted efforts to regulate rock climbing in the interests of safety; they became known for climbing naked, regardless of the increased risk, pitting unadorned man directly against nature. Occasionally a climber falls and is injured or dies. (Photograph by Carleton Mabee.)

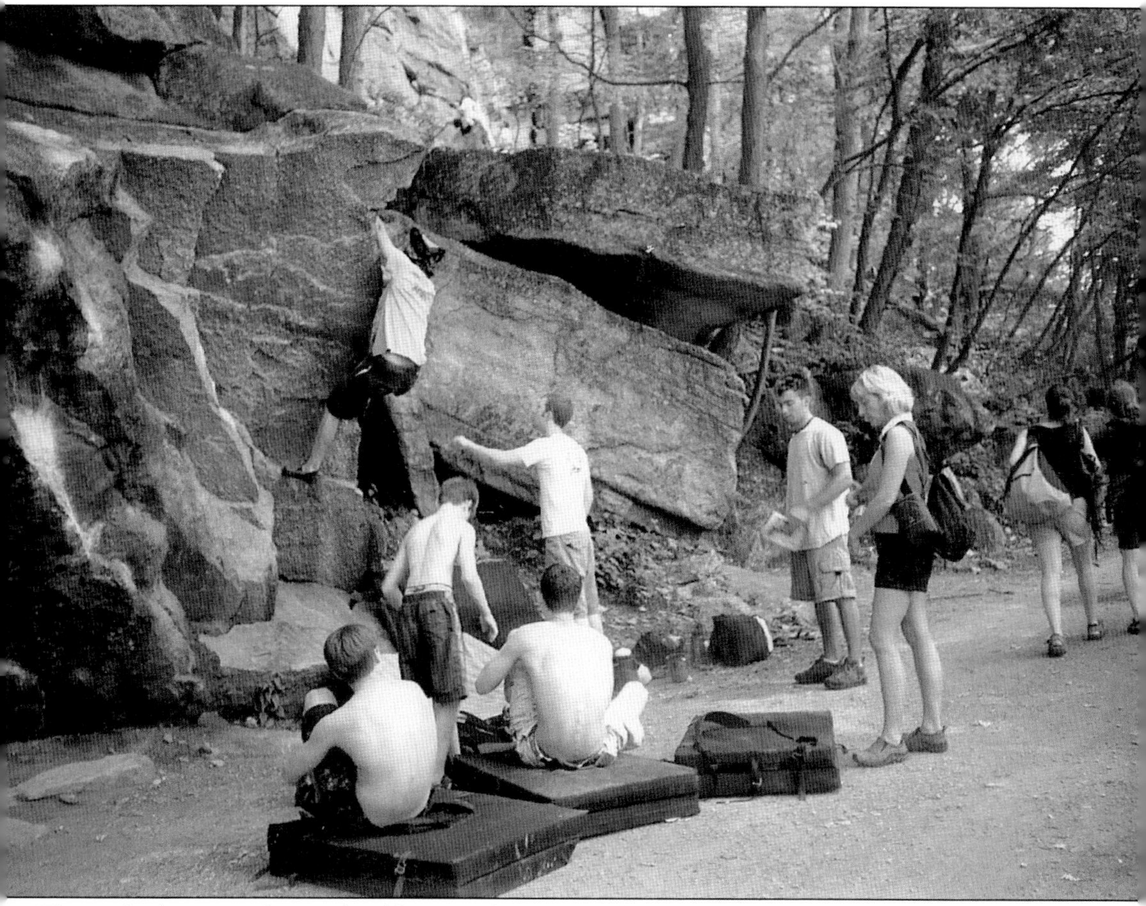

These climbers are shown "bouldering," that is, climbing boulders near ground level. This picture was taken in June 2002. Boulderers climb without rope support, in extremely awkward positions, making their sport potentially as difficult as the more common type of rock climbing. They sometimes place pads on the ground for safety, in case of a fall, and climb with friends who stay on the ground to hold out their hands to break any fall. (Photograph by Carleton Mabee.)

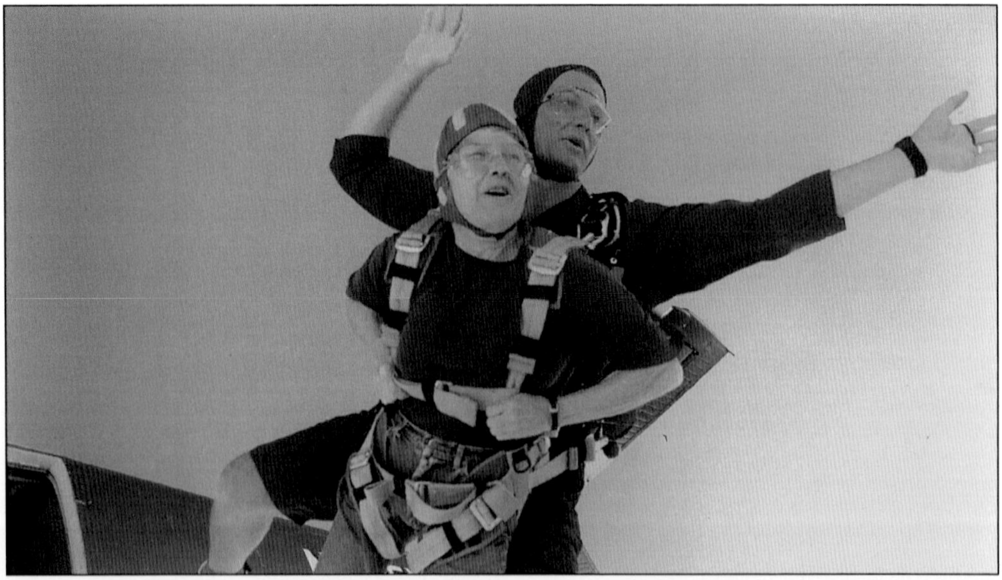

Two sky divers jump out of a plane, harnessed together: Maggie MacDowell (left), a Gardiner real estate broker on her first jump, and Geoffrey Park, an Englishman who is a regular instructor at Skydive the Ranch airport. This August 2001 picture was taken just after they jumped; before they jumped, MacDowell was instructed to extend her arms soon after becoming airborne. However, preoccupied with the intensity of jumping into space, she forgot. (Photograph by Carol Sternberg, courtesy of Margaret MacDowell.)

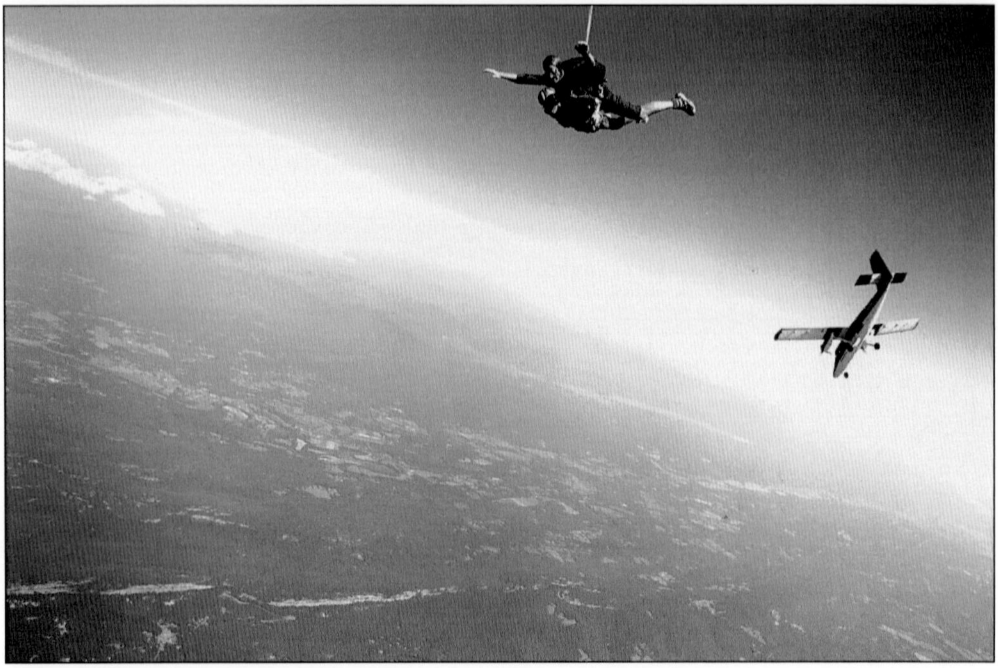

Maggie MacDowell and Geoffrey Park are in a free fall. The plane out of which they jumped shows at the right. It is doubtful that MacDowell has yet extended her arms. About 13, 000 feet below them, the Shawangunk Mountain Ridge shows (especially lower left) as a line of white-faced cliffs. (Photograph by Carol Sternberg, courtesy of Margaret MacDowell.)

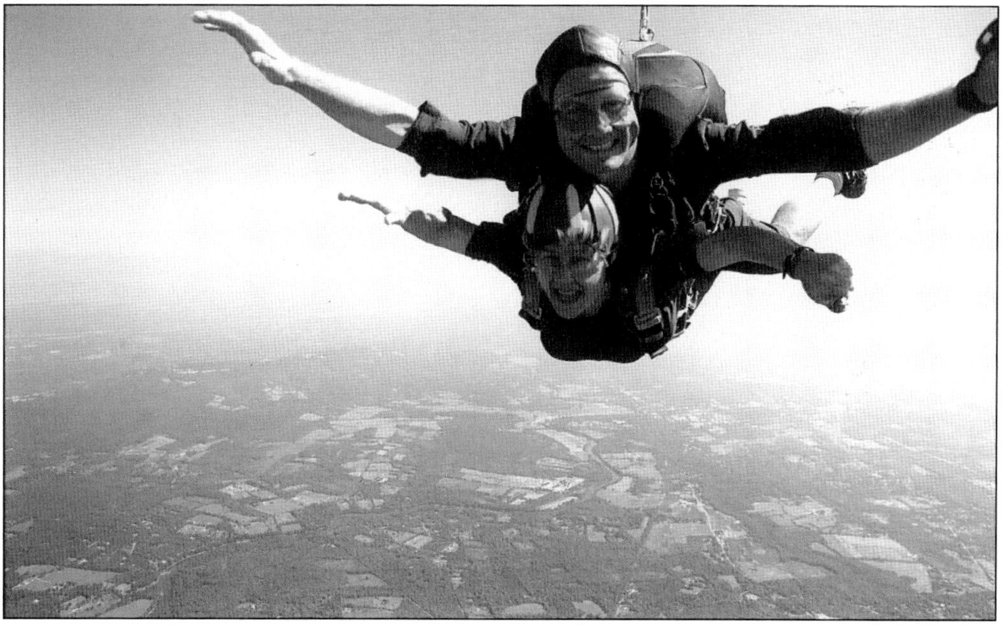

As Maggie MacDowell and Geoffrey Park continue to fall, they both have their arms out. (Since MacDowell did not raise her arms, Park lifted them up for her.) Photographer Carol Sternberg, who was diving alongside them in order to capture these images, came so close to them that as they fell, they talked and laughed with each other. Gardiner is spread out below them. (Photograph by Carol Sternberg, courtesy of Margaret MacDowell.)

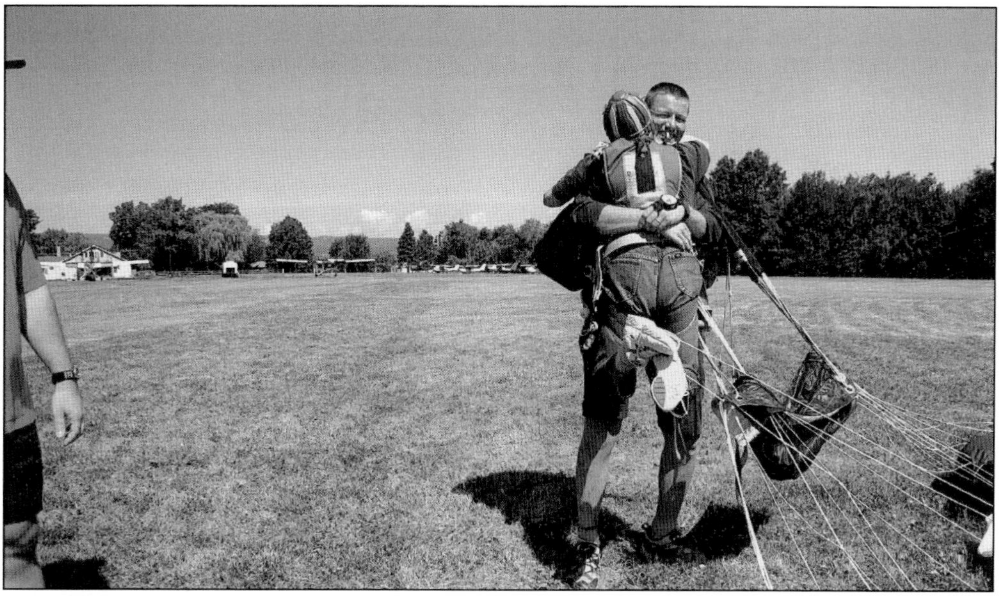

Maggie MacDowell and Geoffrey Park are shown just after landing at the Gardiner airport, They landed as those jumping in tandem do, not by both trying to land on their feet, because as closely harnessed together as they were, they might tangle their feet. They landed with Park sliding in on his heels and seat, taking the weight of both of them. Safely on the ground again, MacDowell hugs Park in thanks, while he, tall as he is, lifts her off her feet. (Photograph by Carol Sternberg, courtesy of Margaret MacDowell.)

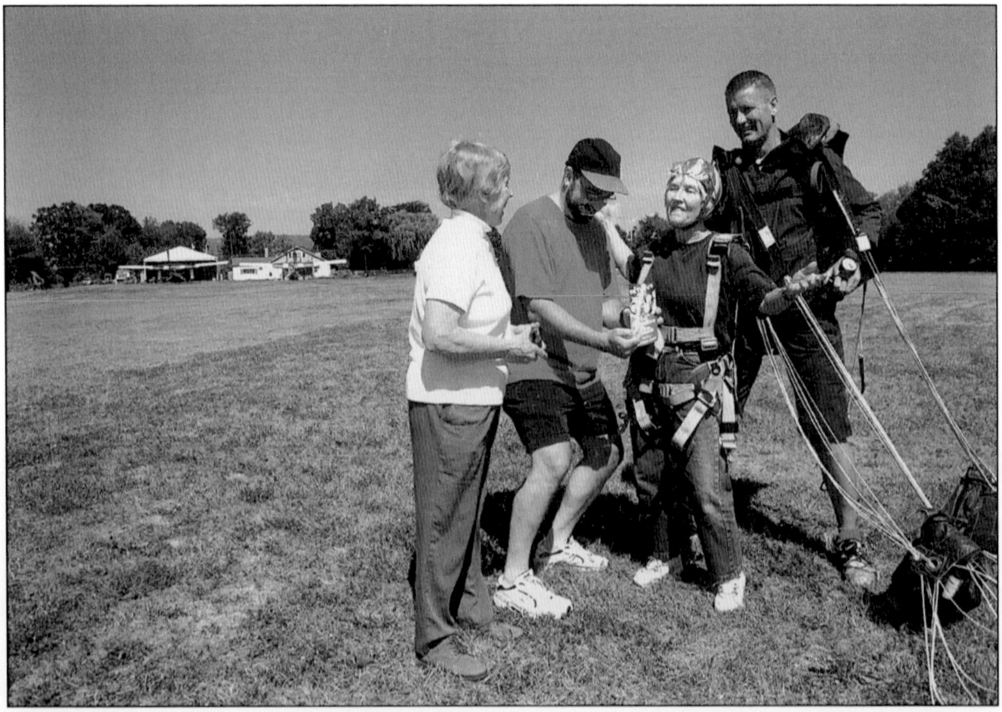

Two friends of Maggie MacDowell crowd around, congratulating her. The friends are Gardinerites Mary Lou Schnell and Jim Davies, a commercial airline steward. They are congratulating MacDowell on having successfully jumped out of the Gardiner sky to celebrate her 75th birthday. (Photograph by Carol Sternberg, courtesy of Margaret MacDowell.)

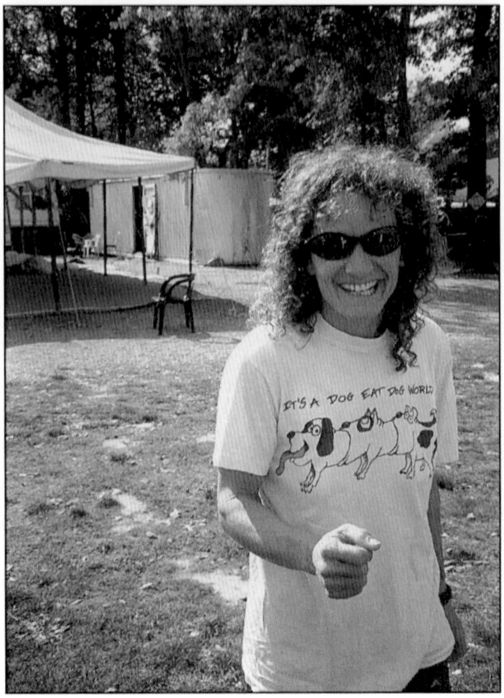

Carol Sternberg is the photographer who dove alongside Maggie MacDowell and Geoffrey Park to photograph their August 2001 dive. Shown by Gardiner's Sky Dive the Ranch airport office, she is the airport's regular diving photographer. (Courtesy of Margaret MacDowell.)

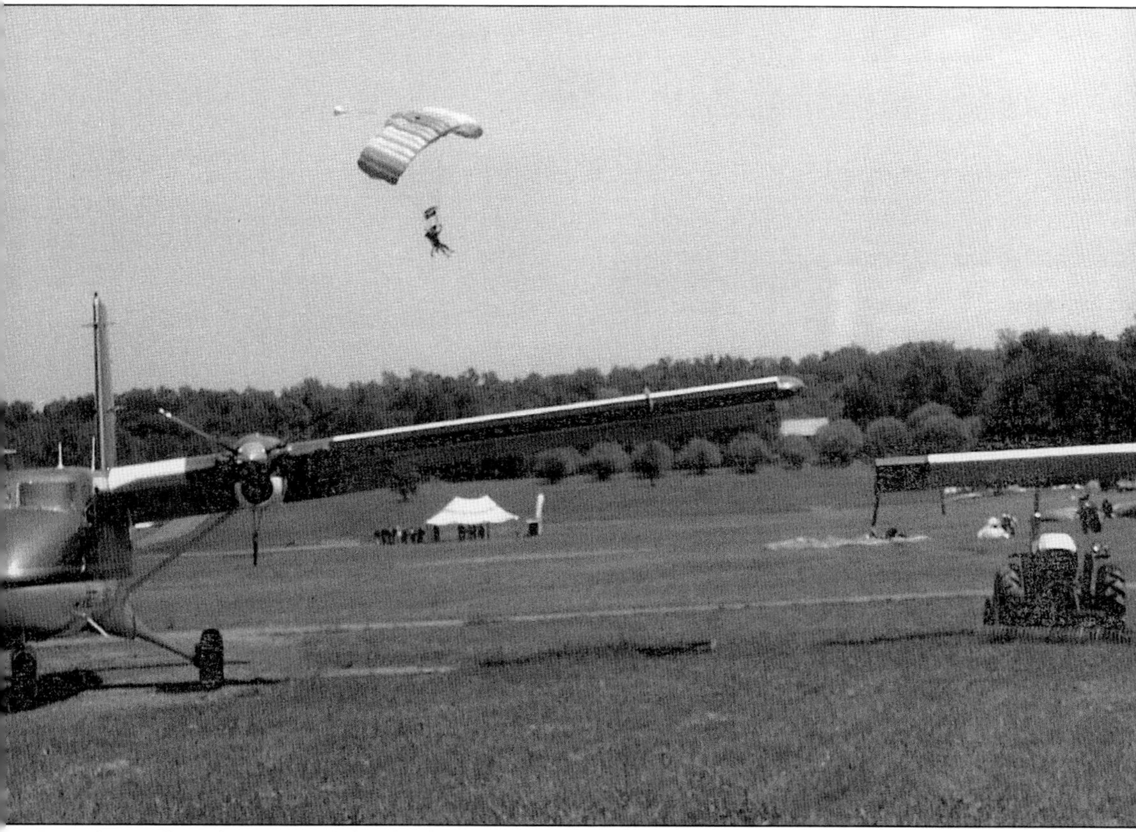

Two divers float down out of the sky, harnessed together in tandem under one parachute. They are ready to land at Gardiner's airport, Skydive the Ranch. The tent visible in the center of this 2002 photograph is the airport's holding area, where would-be divers line up to wait for a turn to climb into the next available plane. As many as 20 divers at a time pile into a plane, ready to jump out, one by one or two by two. (Photograph by Rene F. Ramos.)

ACKNOWLEDGMENTS

The author gratefully acknowledges that the following were among those providing images for this book.

Shirley Anson, Clintondale
Eddie Bell, Gardiner
F.W. Beers, *County Atlas of Ulster, New York*, 1875
Matthew Bialecki, Gardiner
Ralph Buchanan, New Paltz
Mike Carey, Middletown
Daryl P. Carr, Gardiner
Children's Aid Society of New York City
Barbara Clinton, Gardiner
Kathleen R. Conner, Gardiner
Joan Wells Decker, Gardiner
Mary Tubbs Decker, Gardiner
Erma DeWitt, Gardiner
Paul Donahue, New Paltz
Gladys P. Dubois, Gardiner
Robert W. Fisher, Wallkill
Gardiner Library
Gardiner Town Hall
John Giralico, New Paltz
Doris Van Leuven Hall, Napanoch
Alice Hasbrouck, New Paltz
Kenneth E. Hasbrouck, *History of the Township of Gardiner*, 1953
Haviland-Heidgard Historical Collection, Elting Memorial Library, New Paltz
Jay Honold, Gardiner
Huguenot Herald, New Paltz
John K. Jacobs, Clintondale
Joseph L. Katz, Gardiner
Minke Kwak, Gardiner
Carol B. LeFevre, Gardiner
William Lohrman and Carol Majestic Lohrman, Gardiner
Margaret S. MacDowell, Gardiner
Judith Mage, New Paltz
Frank Majestic, Gardiner
Marybeth Majestic, Gardiner
Jon Margolis, New Paltz
Harold Marks, Gardiner
Vivian R. McCord, Gardiner
Minnewaska State Park Preserve, Rochester

Mohonk Mountain House Archives, New Paltz
Mohonk Preserve, Gardiner
Betty Moran, Gardiner
New Paltz News, Highland
New York City's Department of Environmental Protection, Flushing, Queens
Office of Plattekill Town Historian, Modena
Annie O'Neill, Gardiner
Mary Ann Osgood, Gardiner
Donald Otis, New Paltz
Rene F. Ramos, Forest Hills, Queens
William B. Rhoads, New Paltz
Marion W. Ryan, Gardiner
Ken Shuker, Cornwall
Gail Slotwinski, Bearsville
Daniel Smith, Gardiner
Diane P. Smith, Gardiner
Carol Sternberg, Gardiner
Times-Herald-Record, Middletown
Enrico Togna, Randolph, New Jersey
Robert S. Tucker, Los Angeles, California
Richard Tuman, High Falls
Harold Van Leuven, New Paltz
VirTis Company, Gardiner
Laura F. Walls, Gardiner
E.J. Whitney
Joan Wustrau, Stormville

The author gratefully acknowledges that the following were among the printed works providing background information for this book.

Fagan, Jack. *Scenes and Walks in the Northern Shawangunks*. New York: New York-New Jersey Trail Conference, 1999.

Fried, Marc. *The Huckleberry Pickers: A Raucous History of the Shawangunk Mountains*. Hensonville, New York: Black Dome Press, 1995.

Galusha, Diane. *Liquid Assets, A History of New York City's Water System*. Fleischmanns, New York: Purple Mountain Press, 1999.

Hasbrouck, Kenneth E. *History of the Township of Gardiner*. Gardiner, New York: Gardiner Town Board, 1953, revised, 1978.

Knickerbocker, Nan L. *Minnewaska . . . Story of the Origin and Growth of the Lake Minnewaska Mountain Houses*. New York: 1937.

Larsen, Robert A. *Trapps Mountain Hamlet, An Interpretive Walk Through a Vanished Shawangunk Community*. New Paltz, New York: Mohonk Preserve, 1999.

Mabee, Carleton. *Listen to the Whistle: An Anecdotal History of the Wallkill Valley Railroad in Ulster and Orange Counties, New York*. Fleischmanns, New York: Purple Mountain Press, 1995.

Thompson, Ed. *Road to Gardiner*. 2001.

Togna, Enrico. *Every Day It Got Better*. New York: Vantage Press, 2002.

INDEX